POLITICS AND THE POET

Wordsworth in 1805 (*aet.* 35) from a tinted drawing by
H. Edridge, A.R.A.

POLITICS
AND THE POET

A Study of Wordsworth

by

F. M. TODD

LONDON

METHUEN & CO LTD

36 ESSEX STREET · STRAND

821.71
W9262t0p
81660

CATALOGUE NO. 5883/U

PRINTED IN GREAT BRITAIN BY
THE CAMELOT PRESS LTD
LONDON AND SOUTHAMPTON

Contents

Illustrations

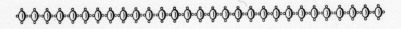

Acknowledgments

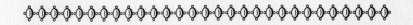

This book is based on a thesis presented to the University of London in 1948 and accepted as satisfying the requirements for the Ph.D. degree.

My work in London was made possible by the Shirtcliffe Research Fellowship awarded to me in 1945 by the University of New Zealand, and the year which I spent in Cambridge from 1954 to 1955 on a Nuffield Foundation Fellowship gave me time to complete the preparation of the MS. for publication.

I am also indebted to Professor Bruce Pattison, Dr Edith Batho and to Miss Helen Darbishire for the help and encouragement which they have given me during my work on Wordsworth.

I am grateful to Mrs Raunsley and the National Portrait Gallery for permission to reproduce the portraits by Edridge and Haydon respectively.

Finally, I should like to thank the Council of the Canberra University College which has given financial assistance towards the cost of publication.

F. M. T.

University College, Canberra

Where is the favoured being who hath held
That course unchecked, unerring and untired,
In one perpetual progress smooth and bright?—
A humbler destiny have we retraced,
And told of lapse and hesitating choice,
And backward wanderings along thorny ways.

Prel., XIV, 133-8

... if men will impartially, and not asquint, look toward the offices and function of a poet, they will easily conclude to themselves the impossibility of any man's being a good poet, without first being a good man.

BEN JONSON, Dedication of *Volpone*

In such a confused medley of right and wrong, it was hardly possible for any statesman to act in a way that will now be wholly approved. Men alive must choose their parts, and posterity be wiser if it can.

G. M. TREVELYAN, *British History in the Nineteenth Century and After* (1937), 72-3

Introduction

This book is the result of an attempt to investigate and document Wordsworth's notorious change of political heart. It is not a biography of the poet, but a study of certain events in his life and time, and of their effect on the development of his ideas on man and society.

The aim has not been to divert attention from Wordsworth's poetry, but to fill in some of the background essential to an appreciation of that poetry and to an understanding of the poet. The extent to which this background *is* essential is suggested by his own view of himself as one who 'united some of the faculties which belong to the statesman with those which belong to the poet'.[1] In 1833 he told an American visitor, Orville Dewey, that 'although he was known to the world only as a poet, he had given twelve hours thought to the conditions and prospects of society, for one to poetry'.[2]

There is then some point in devoting our reasonably exclusive attention to this rather vexed question of his political development. Not that this is a 'defence', nor an attempted refutation of the so-called 'apostasy'. There can be no question that in his age Wordsworth was opposed to most of the political opinions which he had held in his youth. He for one had no doubt of the fact. 'I should think that I had lived to little purpose', he wrote to his friend James Losh in 1821, 'if my notions on the subject of government had undergone no modification—my youth must, in that case, have been without enthusiasm, and my manhood endued with small capability of profiting by reflexion.'

If this is apostasy, then an apostate he was, and, it is to be hoped,

[1] A. de Vere, 'Recollections of Wordsworth' in *Essays chiefly on Poetry* (1887), II, 281.

[2] Dewey, *The Old World and the New* (1836), 90.

apostates we all are. It is only when we look into the circumstances of the change in Wordsworth's case that we begin to discover things worth discovering. For in trying to establish why and how he changed his opinions we come up against qualities in him, flattering or not, which do add to our knowledge of him, and to our appreciation and understanding of his work.

This study is then an explanation and not a defence of Wordsworth's political development. The explanation can be found largely in two rather obvious but hitherto neglected sources: in the poetical works of William Wordsworth, and in the political events of his age. Briefly, he changed his political outlook because of his experience of English and French politics between 1790 and 1830, and because during that same period, or at least from 1795, he paid an increasingly deferential attention to his own poetry and to the ideals it embodied. He was slowly driven to a political position which was inherent in the interpretation of human life expressed by his poetry. He did not lose faith in man, but in the power of political action to effect an increase in real human happiness; the move was from a faith in 'external' action to one in that 'internal' regeneration which he had been preaching in every poem he wrote after 1795.

This is not to deny that his poetry and its ideals were initially the product of a liberal, a politically radical fervour, related to that fervour emotionally if not logically. It was only later that the poet himself realized that the superficial liberalism of the *Lyrical Ballads* concealed all the elements of an outlook essentially conservative, essentially at variance with the philosophy and practice of political liberalism as the nineteenth century was to develop it.

Yet while, with this reservation, we accept the connection between republicanism and Wordsworth's early inspiration, there is no justification for linking causatively the later change in his political outlook with the equally notorious decline in his poetic powers. Indeed the effect of the later reconciliation between his political and poetic ideals should have been entirely beneficial.

The reasons for Wordsworth's poetic decline are outside the scope of this book. In the present state of ignorance about the whole question of poetic inspiration, one can only hazard explanations. Perhaps he lived too long,[1] perhaps his kind of poetry needed youth, 'animal spirits', novelty. He certainly changed his ideas on what poetry should be, and this might have been fatal, for him at least. He was, of course, for the last thirty years of his life, a religious poet to an extent not fully realized.

All these factors probably played their part, but we must be wary of basing any explanation on the somewhat quaint assumption that no Tory could be a true poet. The sincere conservative was no more debarred from inspiration than the sincere republican; in fact his later political opinions were much more closely related to his artistic creed, to his 'poetic' beliefs, than was his early radicalism.

There still exists of course the widespread opinion that he based his later attitudes on a culpable misinterpretation of the facts; that his development was too often influenced by thoughtless reaction; that, as a poet of wisdom and experience, he was false to the bases of his original inspiration and allowed himself in his later years to be swept along by a panic of timidity that we are ready to condone only in smaller men.

In considering this more delicate question, we must remember the disadvantages of the past when under the inquisition of posterity. If we are to be accurate and just, we must admit our superior wisdom; we must recognize that we see much more clearly the true significance of events, say in the period from 1810 to 1840, than did Wordsworth or any of his contemporaries. *We* know, for example, that the French revolutions of 1789 and 1830 were not likely to be duplicated in the England of 1831; we must remember that Wordsworth and most of his contemporaries, not all men of craven spirit, did not know this. With a century of democracy behind us we are generally of the opinion that such a system of government is ideal; with a less fortunate and less attractive example before his eyes, Wordsworth was not so convinced.

In short we must beware, in Wordsworth's own words, of

[1] The fact that he did grow old is something to which critics have never been completely resigned, ever since Sydney Smith admitted after a meeting in 1836: 'It surprised me—one always fancies a poet must be young.'

'unreasonable expectations'; we must not expect a man to be wiser than the facts of his experience will allow him to be. Wordsworth's opinions are not to be judged by comparison with things as they *were*, (or as *we* think they were) so much as by comparison with things as he *thought* they were; not by the outcome of the events going on about him, but by what, on the basis of his own experience, he was convinced *would be* their outcome.

From this point of view it is plain that we can condemn his initial naïve enthusiasm for the French Revolution as we condemn his opposition to the Reform Bill, without implying in either case that his erroneous judgment was indicative of any wilful self-deception. Naturally, we welcome the liberalism of his youth more than the conservatism of his age, and not only because we find it so difficult to sympathize with the conservatism of the early nineteenth century. His early ideas found expression in noble poetry, divorced from party animosity; his later opinions, or rather his expression of them, were too often under the domination of passing events, too often soured by personal bitterness, and too often the subject of electioneering prose and dull verse.

If he did lose faith in the power of political reform to increase human happiness, his own experience was the basis of that loss; he did come to suspect the validity of his youthful conclusions, but he found much to retain in his early expression of them, and little to hide. As the scholarship of the late Ernest De Selincourt and Miss Darbishire has shown, the emendations made by the Tory in his Jacobinical verse are rarely as significant as the passages he saw fit to leave uncorrected. Yet as a politician Wordsworth was rarely dispassionate, and at all times in his life the violence of his expression is misleading, making us see a more ferocious Jacobin and a more hide-bound Tory than other evidence proves him to have been. De Vere saw clearly[1] that beneath the seeming placidity of the Rydal laureate lay 'the precinct of the storm', for 'the more impassioned part of his nature connected itself especially with his political feelings'.

It is not in such a man that we look for changeless consistency.

[1] *Loc. cit.*

But we have a right to expect, and I believe we do find, as the consistent basis of his political thought, an honest sincerity and a sympathetic benevolence leading him to opinions serious and responsible. From a study of these principles, and from an investigation of the changes that his practical opinions underwent, there is much to be learned of the man and the poet.

CHAPTER I

The Undergraduate

Our knowledge of Wordsworth's three years at Cambridge from 1787 to 1790 is unencouragingly meagre, but it is possible to piece together a more complete picture of the poet during his years of adolescence than has yet been achieved.

He went up to the University in 1787, at the age of seventeen, with every reason to be thankful for the escape he was making from his guardians. After the death of their mother in 1778 and of their father five years later, William, his sister Dorothy, and their three brothers had been left in the care of their uncle, Christopher Crackanthorpe, and their maternal grandparents, the Cooksons. Apparently nothing was spared to make them realize their dependent situation in the Penrith household, and Dorothy's letters make pathetic reading. 'Many a time', she wrote to her friend, Jane Pollard, in the summer of 1787, 'have W[illia]m, J[oh]n, C[hristopher], and myself shed tears together, tears of the bitterest sorrow, we all of us, each day, feel more sensibly the loss we sustained when we were deprived of our parents, and each day do we receive fresh insults. You will wonder of what sort; believe me of the most mortifying kind, the insults of servants, but I will give you the particulars of our distresses as far as my paper will allow, but I cannot tell you half what I wish and I fear that when I have finished you will feel yourself almost as much in the dark as ever. . . . The servants are every one of them so insolent to us as makes the kitchen as well as the parlour quite insupportable. James has even gone so far as to tell us that we had nobody to depend upon but my Grandfr, for that our fortunes we[re] but v[ery] sma]ll, and my Brs cannot even get a pair of shoes cleaned without James's telling them they require as much waiting upon as any *gentlemen*, nor can I get anything done for myself without absolutely entreating it as a [fav]our. James happens to be a particular favourite [with] my Uncle Kit, who has taken a dislike to my Br [and] never takes any notice of any of us, so that he thinks [whi]le my Uncle behaves in this way to us he may do anything. We are found fault with every hour of the day both by the servants and my Grandfr and Grandmr, the former of whom never speaks to us but when he scolds, which is not seldom.'[1]

We have of course become inured to harrowing stories of the wretched childhood of our poets, but Wordsworth's treatment at the hands of his relatives, both at this and at later stages, is one of the facts worth keeping in mind in considering the growth of his republicanism. There can be no doubt, for example, that in 1793, when he returned from France to spread terror in the parlours and parsonages of his relatives with the news that he was the father of Annette Vallon's child, their hostility did much to exacerbate the bitterness of those revolutionary sympathies which had been stimulated in him by the 'heart-bracing colloquies' with Beaupuy. Certainly traces of that bitterness are to be detected in the 'Letter to the Bishop of Llandaff' which he wrote in the same year.

So it is worth noting that at an earlier stage the stubborn William was singled out for particularly spiteful treatment. The Crackanthorpes, with their appropriately Dickensian name, gave the poet his first taste of tyranny.

This domestic oppression no doubt affected him all the more deeply because it was in such marked contrast with the complete freedom which he enjoyed at his school at Hawkshead. It is this freedom which he most often remembers in *The Prelude*, for its memories never ceased to haunt him. This was the side of his childhood that he preferred to remember, schooldays peculiarly free from regimentation, spent in a unique society relatively untainted by distinctions of birth and wealth. That there was another side to the picture his sister's letters make clear, and we shall have later occasion to return to the misleadingly selective nature of Wordsworth's recollections of his youth as presented in *The Prelude*.

[1] Letter No. 1 in *Letters*, ed. de Selincourt, Oxford (1935-9).

The third conditioning factor of importance in this context
is the Lonsdale debt. When Wordsworth's father died, he was
owed about £5,000 by his employer, the Earl of Lonsdale. The
Earl's refusal to pay left the children of his former agent in actual
poverty, and so, of course, placed them in absolute dependence on
their guardians. The 'bad Earl', as he was tritely called, was
certainly no prepossessing example of the virtues of the nobility
to be put before the young poet at such an impressionable age.
We shall see how in later years Wordsworth's support of the
aristocracy and their privileges was coloured by his acquaintance
with the generosity of Lonsdale's successor and with the cultured
patronage of Sir George Beaumont; in his youth the ruthless
dishonesty of Lonsdale had, of course, the opposite effect. Legal
proceedings were hardly possible in the straitened circumstances
of the plaintiffs, and, in any case, as far as local action was concerned, the noble and notorious debtor successfully forestalled
them by the simple expedient of retaining for himself all the
available counsel. It was certainly with some feeling that Wordsworth could later write in his letter to the Bishop of Llandaff:
'I congratulate your Lordship upon your enthusiastic fondness for
the judicial proceedings of this country. I am happy to find you
have passed through life without having your fleece torn from
your back in the thorny labyrinth of litigation.'

It can have been then with no regrets that Wordsworth
escaped to the University, lamenting only that he must leave
Dorothy until that time when they could be reunited in their
own home, that 'sole bourn, sole wish, sole object of my
way' for which they were both to long during the next eight
years.

There is, of course, no reason to imagine that because Wordsworth had been made happy at school, miserable by his guardians
and poor by Lord Lonsdale, he therefore went up to Cambridge
ripe for republicanism. It is probable that his political opinions
in 1787 were of no greater consequence than those of most
seventeen-year-old undergraduates; nevertheless, these factors
in his environment did represent a predisposition that was to
make him at least receptive to opinions which seemed to acquire
some backing from his own experience.

He did, indeed, think it of some importance in explaining his later democratic sympathies, that,

> born in a poor district, and which yet
> Retaineth more of ancient homeliness,
> Than any other nook of English ground,
> It was my fortune scarcely to have seen,
> Through the whole tenour of my schoolday time,
> The face of one, who, whether boy or man,
> Was vested with attention or respect
> Through claims of wealth or blood.
>
> (*Prel.*, IX, 215-22.)

When he refers to Cambridge, he often tries to make out something of the same case. In one part of *The Prelude* for example, he says of the

> . . . academic institutes
> And rules, that they held something up to view
> Of a Republic, where all stood thus far
> Upon equal ground; that we were brothers all
> In honour, as in one community,
> Scholars and gentlemen; where, furthermore,
> Distinction open lay to all that came,
> And wealth and titles were in less esteem
> Than talents, worth, and prosperous industry.
>
> (IX, 224-32.)

His plain intention in this passage is to couple the egalitarian society of the Lakes and the republican society of Cambridge as two factors in his early life which predisposed him to a later enthusiasm for the French Revolution and its doctrines of political equality and republicanism. But just as we can see how misleadingly selective is his poetic recollection of his childhood, so too his memories of Cambridge deserve a closer examination.

Few of his contemporaries seem to have been so struck by the nobility and virtue of the University of the time. There was indeed some strictly comparative praise. Gibbon said that Cambridge was 'less deeply affected than her sister with the vices of the cloyster', and Clement Carlyon, an acquaintance of Coleridge's, admitted in his *Early Years and Late Reflections* (1836) that 'whilst it was said that, at Oxford, the candidate for a fellowship must be well-dressed, of gentle lineage, and moderately learned, the humble sizar at Cambridge was invited to enter the lists for academic honours and emoluments, without there being any question asked as to the tailor who made his coat, or the station in life of his parents'. Coleridge too rejoiced that he was at Cambridge and not at Oxford, 'a childish University', where his friend Southey found equally 'a waste of wigs and want of wisdom' that did not belie his expectation of 'pedantry, prejudice and aristocracy'.[1] But it is a letter which he wrote in 1800 to his friend Estlin which does more to make us suspect Wordsworth's picture of a republic of learning. At Cambridge, he declared, 'the Gentleman is the all-implying word of honour—a thing more blasting to real virtue, real liberty, real standing for the truth in Christ than all the whoredoms and impurities which this Gentlemanliness does most usually bring with it'. One of the sources of his admiration for Southey was his wonder that anyone could emerge unspotted from an eighteenth-century university: 'To those who remember the state of our public schools and universities some twenty years past', he wrote in *Biographia Literaria*, 'it will appear no ordinary praise in any man to have passed from innocence to virtue, not only free from all vicious habit, but unstained from one act of intemperance or the degradations akin to intemperance.'

Nor was Coleridge the only critic. The *Reminiscences of the University, Town, and County of Cambridge* (1854), by Henry Gunning, were written, so the author said, 'to attempt a description of the manners and habits prevalent in my early days, and which are so justly abhorrent to modern usages'. Although Gunning was a Whig who had suffered for his opinions in a Tory society, his picture of dissoluteness and corruption covers every aspect of university life. In his Preface he writes frankly and with italicized indignation: 'I believe the time I came to College (1784) to have been the worst part of our history. Drunkenness being the besetting sin of that period, I need scarcely add that

---

[1] He made a more enlightening comparison in describing to his wife the wild excesses of the Göttingen students in 1799 as 'such a scene of uproar [as] I never witnessed before, no, not even at Cambridge'.

many other vices followed in its train. But one vice then prevailed
—men of commanding talents and great acquirements scrupled
not, *as Examiners*, for the sake of making money, to assign the
highest honours in the power of the University to bestow, not
on *the most deserving*, but upon those who had been fortunate
enough to avail themselves of their instruction as Private Tutors.'
The picture he paints hardly suggests a society of republican
virtue and equality.

In fact we know that Wordsworth shared Gunning's view of
his University; his republic of learning was the Cambridge of his
dreams, little related to the bathetic reality. It might have been
the ideal he created before going up, but, rather than a continua-
tion of his earlier culture among the Lakeland 'statesmen', he
found his experience of the reality an experience of disillusionment—as elsewhere indeed he admits:

> . . . I had raised a pile
> Upon the basis of the coming time,
> That fell in ruins round me.
> (*Prel.*, III, 428-30.)

The truth is not that he was predisposed to accept political
republicanism because of his introduction to its academic shape
in Cambridge, but rather, I believe, that it was at Cambridge that
he first turned in anger against a system of privilege and prescription, a system of bigotry; what was stimulated there was
not the zeal for the principle of equality which he said the 'statesmen'[1] had implanted in him, so much as a discontent with
privilege and authority which he had already learned from the
Crackanthorpes and the Lowthers.

When he was writing *The Prelude* he was somewhat apologetic
for the violence of his youthful enthusiasm, and naturally preferred to emphasize those elements in his education which might
be interpreted as preparing him unconsciously for his subsequent
attachment to republican egalitarianism. He was anxious too
to stress the sympathetic rather than the antipathetic elements
in that attachment. Looking at his adolescence with such a
purpose, his experience of domestic persecution and social

[1] The local name given to freeholders of the Lake District.

injustice is passed by, and the emphasis placed on the benign influence of a rural democracy of a peculiar type; he tends to play down the hypocrisy, bigotry and pedantry of eighteenth-century Cambridge in favour of the image it so faintly presented to him at the time of a republic of learning.

Yet even in *The Prelude* there are occasions when, looking back to the Cambridge which he had really known and not to the one that he had only dreamed about when he was pining for any escape from the tyranny of his guardians, he does speak with ferocity and contempt of those other aspects of the University which he remembered with equal clarity. He laments the absence of

> A healthy sound simplicity . . .
> A seemly plainness, name it what you will,
> Republican or pious.
> (Prel., III, 399-401.)

What he found could only strengthen his existing spirit of independence and opposition; and if he admits that he saw there

> . . . in dwarf proportions . . . expressed
> The limbs of the great world,

even Labour and Hope were crowded out by—

> Idleness halting with his weary clog,
> And poor misguided shame, and witless Fear,
> And simple Pleasure foraging for Death;
> Honour misplaced, and Dignity astray;
> Feuds, factions, flatteries, enmity, and guile,
> Murmuring submission, and bald government,
> (The idol weak as the idolator),
> And Decency and Custom starving Truth,
> And blind Authority beating with his staff
> The child that might have led him; Emptiness
> Followed as of good omen, and meek Worth
> Left to herself unheard of and unknown.
> (Prel., III, 600-11.)

After the simple religious piety of the North he found (although he admitted it only in tentative manuscript form)—

... Folly and false seeming ... dizen'd out
In Superstition's cast-off garb; ...
... Dull thoughted mummery! that brings disgrace.
(*Prel.*, MS. 'M', III, 410 *et seq.*)[1]

The young undergraduate from the North was however not a
gloomy recluse. At least before his first vacation he was a sharer
in pleasures which, until recently, Cambridge has always offered
as a complement to or a substitute for its teaching:

... invitations, suppers, wine and fruit,
Smooth housekeeping within, and all without
Liberal, and suiting gentleman's array.

Though galled by the hypocritical discipline of the University,
and troubled, as indeed he well might be, 'Not seldom' with
'melancholy thoughts, From personal and family regards',[2]
and by 'some fears About my future worldly maintenance',[3]
the life probably typical of most of his Cambridge career was one
of idleness and pleasure in the company of fellow-spirits:

We sauntered, played, or rioted; we talked
Unprofitable talk at morning hours;
Drifted about along the streets and walks,
Read lazily in trivial books, went forth
To gallop through the country in blind zeal
Of senseless horsemanship, or on the breast
Of Cam sailed boisterously, and let the stars
Come forth, perhaps without one quiet thought.
(*Prel.*, III, 251-8.)

One of his main academic recreations was modern languages, and
he enrolled himself in the Italian class being conducted by
Agostino Isola. Isola had been appointed as assistant to the
professor of modern languages and modern history in 1764, and
as 'a modest and moderate man of unexceptionable morals' he
had made a considerable impression on Cambridge society.

[1] Quotations from all texts of *The Prelude* are from the ed. by E. de Selincourt (1928).
[2] *Prelude*, 1805, III, 75-6.
[3] *Prelude*, III, 78-9.

Charles Lamb's biographer, Thomas Noon Talfourd, in mention-
ing the friendship which later grew up between the Italian's
granddaughter[1] and the Lambs, said that her grandfather had
fled from Italy after a brush with the political authorities, and it is
perhaps significant that the diarist Henry Crabb Robinson
remembered him as 'the teacher of Garnham and others, the
liberals of that generation'.[2] It would of course be somewhat rash
to deduce from this that the Italian class was a centre of undergraduate Jacobinism.

From the notorious degradation of the University Wordsworth's College, St John's, was no exception. In 1794 Wilberforce
paid the Fellows a visit, and, no doubt remembering the assurance
which the teachers of the University had once given him that, as
a man of means, he had no need to study, he was not surprised to
discover of the Dons that 'they had neither the solidity of judgment possessed by ordinary men of business, nor the refined
feelings and elevated principles which become a studious and
sequestered life'.[3] But they were at least not lacking in political
zeal. With Wordsworth's tutor, Wood, prominent among
them, the Fellows of St John's were leaders in the indignant outburst of 1793 which followed the publication of a mild reforming pamphlet *Peace and Union*, by William Frend,[4] and Frend
classed them as members of that set who 'caring little for orthodoxy or sanctity, were zealous to recommend themselves to the
ruling powers'.[5]

The proceedings against Frend in 1793 are a reminder that the
close orthodoxy of Cambridge was not entirely undisturbed by
the ruffling breezes that blew from France after 1789. Indeed,
although the official tone of the place during Wordsworth's years
of residence was still that of High Church Toryism, it was more
susceptible to liberal ideas than Oxford, as Gibbon rather guard-
edly admitted. In 1824 Scott described Cambridge as 'infected

[1] Who married Wordsworth's publisher, Charles Moxon.

[2] *H.C.R. on Books and Their Writers*, ed. E. J. Morley (1938), 360.

[3] *q.* Gunning *op. cit.*, I, 326.

[4] Which contained a general though tentative plan for political and ecclesiastical reform as the best insurance against revolutionary violence.

[5] *An account of the Proceedings . . . against Wm. Frend . . . published by the
defendant*, (1793), p. ix.

long ago with liberalism',[1] but then his standards by that time were somewhat eccentric. Yet it is worth noting that by the end of the eighteenth century Cambridge had given a lead in toleration by permitting Dissenters at least to matriculate and reside. She had also been vocal in the anti-slavery agitation. In 1784 Vice-Chancellor Pickard had preached memorably against the slave trade in Saint Mary's, and as late as 1792 the Senate was petitioning for abolition. In 1789 the University joined in the general national rejoicing at the fall of the Bastille. Gunning says 'there was a proposal for a dinner to celebrate that event' made by some members of the Senate, and in 1790 the subject set by the Chancellor for the Latin Essay prize was 'Whether the French Revolution was likely to prove advantageous or injurious to this country'. Samuel Romilly in his *Memoirs* noted with approval that 'the prize was given to a dissertation written to prove that it would be advantageous to us'.

The acclamation which the undergraduates, with Coleridge prominent among them, accorded Frend in 1793, indicates a continuance of Revolutionary enthusiasm within the University long after the Senate had begun to see the danger of its initial reaction. Indeed, a revolt against an obsolete and tyrannical system of bigotry and privilege was bound to have repercussions in the Cambridge of the 1790's. To those whose eyes were opened, as we know Wordsworth's to have been, to the corruption and hypocrisy of the University, the appeal of the principles being put into effect by the French was obvious and direct.

One can point to a creditable number of Jacobins turned out by the University. Frend, Gilbert Wakefield,[2] Coleridge, and Wordsworth's friends Francis Wrangham and Basil Montagu are but a few of those enumerated by Gunning. It was only after Wordsworth's years that the University started to take active steps against the disaffected, but Gunning frequently testifies to the popularity of views rather more extreme than the

[1] q. Dicey, 'Wordsworth and the War', *Nineteenth Century Review*, May, 1915.
[2] Also the author of *A Reply to Parts of the Bishop of Llandaff's Address* (1798), which earned him a prison sentence.

University could condone among those who were the poet's contemporaries.

Now, while we know little of Wordsworth's political opinions at this early date, we do in fact know the political complexion of nearly all his Cambridge associates. His close friend James Losh was an early Jacobin and a consistent liberal;[1] Gunning mentions him as the friend of Tweddel, who was well known at Cambridge for his revolutionary opinions, and this Tweddel was also a friend of Wordsworth's, to judge from the poet's enquiry about him in a letter to Losh of 1798. In 1792 Losh and Tweddel were signatories of the intial declaration of 'The Society of the Friends of the People'. Further, it appears that Tweddel was a close friend of Francis Wrangham, whose opinions were so suspect that he was turned down for a Fellowship in 1793 because he was not 'idoneus moribus et ingenio', and Gunning again comes to our aid with the information that the basis of the rejection was political. Wrangham and Wordsworth we know to have been close friends by 1795, but I think that we may assume from this concatenation that they were acquainted at Cambridge, and that we can link Wordsworth with a circle of whose political complexion there is no doubt. Basil Montagu, another Jacobin whom we shall meet again, was intimate with Wrangham, Wordsworth and Tweddel in London after being their contemporary at Cambridge. William Mathews, with whom Wordsworth corresponded for many years, and whom he probably met at Cambridge, was also deeply affected by the political changes of the time, and Myers, the poet's cousin and friend at Cambridge, was, by 1794 at any rate, of the right colour, 'a patriot of unabated energy', as Wordsworth called him in a letter[2] to Mathews.

From a copy of the volume preserved at Dove Cottage we learn that in 1789 Wordsworth and Myers added their names to the list of subscribers to the edition, published in that year, of the *Elegiac Sonnets* of Charlotte Smith, one of the prominent Jacobin

---

[1] See E. Hughes, 'The Bishops and Reform 1831-33', in *English Historical Review*, July, 1941, p. 463, for details of Losh's consistent adherence to Reform principles.

[2] No. 44.

poets of the period. Indeed, Wordsworth's literary interests at this time are apposite to this study.

The predominance of Jacobin ideas in the popular verse of the 'eighties has not been unnoticed, and most of the contemporary poetry with which Wordsworth was familiar was politically liberal at least in implication. We know that he eagerly welcomed in 1786 the Kilmarnoch edition of Burns' poems. The lines written 'At the Grave of Burns, 1803', which proclaim that the Scots poet was one

> Whose light I hailed when first it shone
> And showed my youth
> How verse may build a princely throne
> On humble truth . . .

are supported by a letter from Dorothy to Jane Pollard in 1787, thanking her for the volume of Burns, which her brother had already read. In 1814 Wordsworth mentioned Burns and Cowper as the two modern poets to whom he owed most, and an 1842 note to the above poem reaffirms his early enthusiasm and his lasting debt.

This immediate acclamation, based ultimately on the fact that Burns wrote 'so humanely', is a further indication of the presence in the young Wordsworth of that active sympathy for the poor and oppressed to which his own situation and experience would naturally predispose him. For the humanitarianism of Burns is something considerably advanced beyond the vague sympathies of eighteenth-century literary convention. He not only sang the virtues of the poor, but openly indicted the tyranny and vice of the rich. However he hedged in plain prose when taken to task for his political opinions, he also had had experience of lordly injustice, and his poetry is flagrantly and bitingly democratic. The burning sense of injustice, the violent attacks on haughty lordlings and titled knaves, accusation and condemnation, these are endemic to Burns' inspiration, even in his mildest moods. In his hands the humble and overlooked aspects of nature are most often symbols of the humble and of the oppressed among men. Not content with Cowper to praise the simplicity of the rural poor, with Gray to defend them from scorn, or with Goldsmith to describe their pleasures with sympathy, Burns moves on in an age of revolution to complain of their oppression and to indict their oppressors. It is this indictment that distinguishes him.

The further evidence we possess of Wordsworth's youthful literary interests even more strongly suggests an early liberalism in political outlook.

In March 1787 the 'leftish' *European Magazine* published a 'Sonnet on Seeing Miss Helen Maria Williams Weep at a Tale of Distress', which was written by the schoolboy Wordsworth under the nom-de-plume 'Axiologus'. The later literary relationship between Wordsworth and this forgotten contemporary is rather more significant than has yet been suspected,[1] but there can be no doubt that they had not met in 1787. However, this proof of the interest shown by Wordsworth in the poetry of Helen Maria Williams, though less flattering to his poetic taste, is almost as significant as his enthusiasm for Burns.

Helen Maria Williams was another literary Jacobin, one of those writers who, continuing the strong eighteenth-century tradition of sentimental, humanitarian verse, found more and more in the actual events of the last years of the century to call forth their tears: instead of vague lamentation for the 'penurious swain' or the suffering poor, occasion for more justifiable weeping, whether for grief or joy, was discovered in the anti-slave movement, the American war, colonial expansion and exploitation, and finally in the French Revolution.

The American war, which caused such heart-searching among the thoughtful and such real misery among the people as a whole, along with the anti-slave trade movement which gave such unprecedented publicity to human suffering, these supplied practical and public outlets for what had been a merely conventional sentimentality, and helped to crystallize humanitarian benevolence into something like a political passion. Delicious tears flowed all the more readily when there was something concrete to shed them for, whether it was a soldier stretched 'on Bunker's charnel hill afar',[2] or the suffering negro.

So, from the general humanitarianism of the tradition, Helen Maria Williams, Charlotte Smith[3] and others moved on to a more

---

[1] See Appendix A.   [2] Wordsworth's 'An Evening Walk', 1793, 254.
[3] See Appendix A, pp. 219ff.

particular liberalism, concerned with the remediable injustice of existing conditions, and with the sufferings of the poor and the oppressed rather than with their virtues. It is true that their weapon was not the fierce indignation of Burns, but their lachrymose sentimentality applied itself more and more to actual events, and finally became the basis of the Jacobin poetry of the French Revolutionary era. Miss Williams wept in turn, and for varying reasons, over the peace with the United States, the Spanish exploitation of South America, the anti-slave trade legislation, and eventually and naturally over the promise of the French Revolution.

It is interesting and significant therefore, that the young Wordsworth, fresh from his reading of Burns and Cowper, should write to her his first published poem, and submit it to the liberal *European Magazine*.

The other minor poets whom we know Wordsworth was reading, Langhorne,[1] Beattie,[2] Darwin, Greenwood[3]—all were

---

[1] Wordsworth to S. C. Hall, 15 Jan. 1837: 'I must say how much I was pleased with your notice of our Westmorland Poet, Langhorne—the Critique is very judicious, both as to his merits and his faults—I do not wonder that you are struck with his poem of the Country Justice [1774-7]—you praise it and with discrimination—but you might have said still more in its favour. As far as I know, it is the first Poem, unless perhaps Shenstone's Schoolmistress be excepted, that fairly brought the Muse into the Company of common life, to which it comes nearer than Goldsmith, and upon which it looks with a tender and enlightened humanity—and with a charitable, (and being so) philosophical and poetical construction that is too rarely found in the works of Crabbe. It is not without many faults in style from which Crabbe's more austere judgment preserved him—but these are to me trifles in a work so original and touching.'

[2] *The Minstrel* (1771-4); a favourite poem of the agitator Thelwall's, as see his discourse in *The Peripatetic* (1793), I, 95, where he describes how he saw in the character of Edwin 'the faithful delineation of my own boyish years'. In fact this character seems to have given something of the same opportunity to Beattie's readers as the Byronic hero gave to those of a later generation. Dorothy Wordsworth too thought that 'the whole character of Edwin resembles much what William was when I first knew him'.

[3] *A Poem Written during a Shooting Excursion on the Moors*, by William Greenwood, Fellow of St John's, Cambridge (1787). Echoes of Langhorne, Beattie and Greenwood are to be found in Wordsworth's 'Evening Walk' and 'Descriptive Sketches'.

either concerned in their poetry with social questions, producing verse which was frankly humanitarian, or, for example, singing the praises of those sources of beauty and pleasure which are found in nature, and are therefore democratic, accessible to all, without restriction of birth, wealth or education.

It was in this literary fashion that Wordsworth was engrossed during his Cambridge years, imitating for example, and not only in poetry, its conventional melancholy,

> . . . that lov'd
> A pensive sky, sad days, and piping winds,
> The twilight more than dawn, Autumn than Spring.
> *(Prel.*, 1805, VI, 193-5.)

The mood went with him on his Swiss walking tour of 1790 as a

> Dejection taken up for pleasure's sake.
> *(Prel.*, VI, 551.)

Certainly this melancholy is an integral part of 'An Evening Walk' which he composed during his Cambridge period, and there too conventional sentimentality displays those humanitarian implications that were now so closely interwoven with what was no longer an entirely artificial literary pose. Thus he compares, with the natural domestic bliss of the swans, the plight of—

> . . . some wretch . . .
> Who faint, and beat by summer's breathless ray,
> Hath dragg'd ber babes along this weary way;
> While arrowy fire extorting feverish groans,
> Shot stinging through her stark o'er-labour'd bones.
> ('An Evening Walk', 1793, 242-6.)

The wretched wanderer

> . . . bids her soldier come her woes to share,
> Asleep on Bunker's charnel hill afar; . . .

where the very substitution of Bunker Hill for the Minden of an earlier version indicates the trend towards topical realism that was so typical of current sentimental verse.

On the basis of this evidence, and remembering the political ferment that was stirred up in the University during Wordsworth's years, it is difficult to resist the conclusion that it was at Cambridge that he was first attracted to the political principles of liberalism as the more practical complement to those vague sympathies and antipathies which his personal experience and his literary interests had already developed. When we re-examine *The Prelude* we can see that it plainly suggests that he was not only revolted by the corruption and seduced by the pleasures of the University. For example, in Book III he hints darkly at something else, which was—

> ... worst of all, a treasonable growth
> Of indecisive judgments, that impared
> And shook the mind's simplicity.

The last line of this quotation is especially noteworthy, for it was in just such terms that Wordsworth in later years usually condemned his youthful political enthusiasm, as impairing the 'simple', direct reaction of the feelings.

The *Memoirs*, compiled by Christopher Wordsworth, the poet's nephew, are hardly more enlightening on this aspect of Wordsworth's Cambridge years than they are on the obscurity of the year spent in France. But just as we can read more into their account of the year 1792 now that we are possessed of facts at which they only hint, so here too they may prove a complement to the evidence of the above pages. Christopher was at pains to point out that the freedom of the Hawkshead schooldays was little calculated to prepare Wordsworth for uncritical acceptance of the pedantic discipline of Cambridge. With a temperament eager, impetuous and impatient, he was all too 'liable to fall into a lower grade of society: to squander his time on aimless projects and desultory pursuits, to contract irregular habits ... and to become familiar with scenes which are unfavourable to his moral progress, and prey on his inward strength. His aspirations decline; and, being discontented with his own position, he is apt to look with sour and splenetic sullenness on the laws of the institution in which he lives.'

It is plain that Christopher is again concealing more than he

c

cared to reveal, but we too must tentatively restrict ourselves to the conclusion that the opinions which Wordsworth saw in 1804 as having shaken his 'mind's simplicity' were at least the precursors of that religious and political disaffection which was to typify such a vital part of his life soon after graduation.

.   .   .   .   .

The excursion which he made to the Continent with his Welsh friend Jones is not unconnected with the development which we have been tracing. It was made during his final vacation, at a time when he was expected to work his hardest for academic honours, and so was an act of defiance both of his family and of his University.

The plan was to make an excursion to Switzerland, but this entailed spending about one third of the holiday in crossing France. A decision (which, in any case, was originally Jones's) to make a walking tour through France in 1790 is not necessarily indicative of decided political views of any kind, but Wordsworth's own references to the venture do throw some light on his motives. We would agree with him that such a plan might have attracted 'In any age of uneventful calm',[1]—

> without an impulse sent
> From work of Nations and their goings-on,[2]

but he did not deny the powerful if supplementary attraction of a

> Europe . . . thrilled with joy,
> France standing on the top of golden hours,
> And human nature seeming born again;[3]

for it was the new political ideas and institutions, of course, and not the Swiss mountains, that were the 'mighty forms, seizing a youthful fancy' which 'Had given a charter to irregular hopes'.[4] It is clear in these lines of *The Prelude* that the 'Nature' then 'sovereign' in his mind was rather connected with the 'natural' society being established in France than with the scenery of the Alps.

[1] *Prelude*, VI, 336.   [2] *Prelude*, 1805, VI, 349-50.
[3] *Prelude*, VI, 339-41.   [4] *Prelude*, VI, 334.

There is, however, no reason to doubt the accuracy of his statement that the political turmoil of the France he crossed touched him 'with no intimate concern' as compared with the joy inspired in him by '. . . the ever-living universe . . . opening out its glories'.[1] When it came to the point, the pedestrian traveller was more concerned with scenery than with politics, and it is not surprising that the famed republicanism of the Swiss cantons inspired him less than the grand novelty of a mountain landscape. 'Among the more awful scenes of the Alps', he wrote back to his sister, 'I had not a thought of man, or a single created being. . . .'[2]

He did, of course, land in France on 13 July '. . . on the very eve of that great federal day', when France was celebrating the anniversary of the fall of the Bastille, and journeyed through a country replete with 'benevolence and blessedness' to a republican state long the inspiration of European liberalism. Yet, whatever his emotional reaction to the Revolution at the time, he recognized later that it was far removed from that intellectual conversion to complete support of the movement which was effected in him by Beaupuy: writing in 1804, he tended to see all his pre-1792 political sympathies as something insignificant by comparison.

However, we need not doubt the general influence of this tour upon his sympathy, however vague, for the Revolution. The movements of protest which he felt at the time against the more notorious aspects of the Revolutionary policy were significantly mild; especially so when we remember that our record of them comes from *The Prelude*, written up to ten or twelve years later, and more likely to emphasize than moderate such sentiments. The spoliation of the monastery of the Chartreuse he did regret, although, if *The Prelude* records his reactions as faithfully as it claims to, the terms of his condemnation are remarkably restricted; he would save only the Chartreuse:

> Perish what may—
> Let this one temple last, be this one spot
> Of earth devoted to eternity.

[1] *Prelude*, VI, 769-75.   [2] Letter No. 10.

And this was a weak reservation when compared with the pane-
gyric on the Revolution which followed it:

> Honour to the patriot's zeal!
> Glory and Hope to new-born Liberty!
> Hail to the mighty projects of the time!
> Discerning sword that Justice wields, do thou
> Go forth and prosper; and ye purging fires,
> Up to the loftiest towers of Pride ascend,
> Fanned by the breath of angry Providence.
> (*Prel.*, VI, 441-7.)

CHAPTER II

France

Graduation in 1790 faced Wordsworth with the problem of
his future. The Church was, of course, the obvious pro-
fession, but with two years to wait before he would be
of age to take Holy Orders, he was obliged to defer acceptance of
the preferment offered him by John Robinson of Harwich, his
father's cousin and an influential politician. Indeed, it is plain that
he did not relish the apparently inevitable prospect of a career in
the Church. His friend Mathews made the helpful and romantic
suggestion that the two of them should wander the country
together, and although Wordsworth prudently declined the
offer, he went on: 'I cannot deny that were I so situated as to be
without relations, to whom I were accountable for my actions, I
should perhaps prefer your idea to vegetating on a paltry curacy.'[1]
This was dangerous talk for a youth placed as he was, and the
correspondence of this period gives the impression that he had
been profoundly unsettled, and was, for whatever reason, unable
to think seriously about a career of any kind. He seems to have
been affected by something like that personal uncertainty which
Hazlitt noted as so typical of the contemporaries and early
supporters of the French Revolution.

For a few months he lived in London, a casual observer, as
he says in *The Prelude*, who 'pitch'd [his] vagrant tent . . . among
the unfenced regions of society'. We remember that, in *The
Excursion*, it was to London that the Solitary hurried after the
outbreak of the French Revolution, when the city had become—

> . . . an emporium then
> Of golden expectations, and receiving
> Freights every day from a new world of hope;

[1] Letter No. 16.

but we have no reason for inferring other motives in Wordsworth's case than mere curiosity, or for concluding that London
attracted him for any other reason than that it was a—

> vast metropolis,
> The fountain of my country's destiny,
> And of the destiny of Earth itself.
>
> (*Prel.*, 1805, VIII, 745.)

According to *The Prelude*, the people who swarmed about him
there were in themselves of more immediate interest than the
prospects of society or the French Revolution, and just as the
scenery of Switzerland had banished from his mind all other
thoughts, so in London he thrilled simply to the novelty of
humanity in the mass. He did attend the House of Commons,
listened to Burke, Fox and Pitt (whom he had already heard at
Cambridge), but spent more time at the theatre.

To a youth from the country, whose 'unconscious love and
reverence Of human nature' had been based on his acquaintance
with men 'Whose occupations and concerns were most Illustrated
by nature and adorn'd'[1] a sudden introduction to the degradation
of urban life was bound to come as something of a shock. But
it is interesting that he should claim, in *The Prelude*, that the
strength of such hopes as he already entertained for man and
society were unshaken; and this victory is recorded in terms which
strengthen our suspicion that his vague humanitarianism had at
Cambridge and on the Continent been already somewhat crystal-
lized. 'The deformities of crowded life', he says, provoked only—

> . . . still more elevated views
> Of human nature. Neither vice nor guilt,
> Debasement of the body or the mind,
> Nor all the misery forced upon my sight,
> . . . could overthrow my trust
> In what we *may* become.
>
> (*Prel.*, VIII, 644.)

This suggests that he was already thinking in those terms of
human progress and perfectibility which were so current with

[1] *Prelude*, 1805, VIII, 180.

advanced political philosophers at the time, and that his convictions were already strong enough to withstand these precursors of still more violent rebuffs to come. *The Prelude* plays down these early convictions for reasons already mentioned, but there is much to suggest the strength of the independent sympathies with which Wordsworth was endowed before he went to France.

The decision to spend a year abroad was a sudden one. He left London in May, 1791, to spend some three months with Jones in Wales, then settled at Cambridge until the opening of term. On the ninth of October Dorothy knew nothing of his intention to leave the country,[1] but by 23 November he was already at Brighton[2] awaiting a ship to start his journey to Orleans.

The motives for his journey are not quite clear. De Quincey had no doubts about the matter, and said plainly in his *Reminiscences of the English Lake Poets* that Wordsworth went to France because he 'felt himself so fascinated by the gorgeous festival era of the Revolution'. Indeed, he said that this was a fact 'well known to all who knew anything of his history'; but unfortunately De Quincey is not the most reliable of biographers, especially when he is dealing with the Lake Poets.

In his letter to Mathews, Wordsworth gave no reason; with a nonchalance typical of his correspondence at this time, he wrote merely: 'I am now on my way to Orleans, where I purpose to pass the winter.' His uncle, the Rev. Wm. Cookson, with whom Dorothy was now living at Forncett, in Norfolk, had advised a course of study in Oriental Languages, and 'to oblige him', William wrote, he had 'consented to pursue the plan upon my return from the Continent'; evidently it was still understood that he was to take orders. In Dorothy's letters to her Halifax friend Jane Pollard the object of the journey is given as the perfecting of William's French, in order to fit him for the post of a travelling tutor; if that plan fell through, then he was to turn to Oriental literature. The 'travelling tutor' explanation is a little dubious. Robinson's offer of the Harwich curacy was still open, and Uncle William, the incumbent of Forncett, was in any case prepared to have him as his own curate until the Harwich arrangements were concluded.

[1] Letter No. 17.   [2] Letter No. 18.

In the 1805 version of *The Prelude*, Wordsworth says of his journey that he was

> Led thither *chiefly* by a personal wish
> To speak the language more familiarly
> (IX, 36.) (My italics.)

but the final version, which may represent something in the nature of a correction, says simply and perhaps more frankly: 'France lured me forth' (IX, 34).

As in the case of the earlier excursion, we must beware of taking this somewhat confused testimony as evidence of motives about which Wordsworth did not care to be specific, but in which we are particularly interested. It is possible that Dorothy was merely inventing an excuse to cover up to Jane Pollard her brother's dangerous political sympathies; if that were the case then William continued the tale in the 1805 version of *The Prelude*, although, as Mathews was an associate who would need no explanation as to why a trip to France should be made, Wordsworth might have felt it unnecessary to invent any such excuse in the letter to him. This is interesting, possible, but hypothetical. We may at least remark that, if France did 'lure him forth', it was a France in revolution.

While waiting at Brighton, Wordsworth called on Charlotte Smith, whom we have mentioned above, and obtained a letter of introduction from her to Helen Maria Williams.[1] According to Mrs Smith's sister, Mrs Dorset, it was 'at Brighthelmstone, where she [Mrs Smith] formed acquaintances with some of the most violent advocates of the French Revolution, and unfortunately caught the contagion'.[2] Her *Elegiac Sonnets* of 1785 had gone through six editions by 1790, and her novels were about to obtain for her a greater popularity as a defender of the new order in France. Her friend and partner in the Jacobin cause, Miss Williams,

---

[1] See Appendix A, pp. 219ff.

[2] See the Biographical Note contributed to *The Miscellaneous Prose Works of Sir Walter Scott* (1847), Vol. I. Charlotte Smith's most extremely pro-Revolutionary novel, *Desmond*, appeared in 1792, and Wordsworth seems to have read it immediately, and with attention, for he borrowed a quotation from it, viz. the line from Smollett in 'Descriptive Sketches', 448.

had been quick to declare her Revolutionary sympathies in a volume of *Letters Written in France* (1790) which, incidentally, gave Wordsworth the story which he used as the basis of 'Vaudracour and Julia'[1]; in 1791 she too had announced, in 'A Farewell for Two Years to England' her intention of sojourning for two years at Orleans, 'Where the slow Loire, on borders ever gay, Delights to linger, in his sunny way'. Although these two years lengthened into a lifetime, Wordsworth's letter of introduction was never used, and a meeting was only arranged through the offices of Henry Crabb Robinson in 1820.[2]

Supplied therefore with a letter from one notorious supporter of the Revolution to another, Wordsworth crossed to Paris. There he made the acquaintance of a member of the National Assembly and was able to attend meetings of that body: a fact which indicates that his interest in the political events of the Capital had developed since his previous visit. But in Paris, as later in Orleans, he was, according to *The Prelude*, less moved by political events than by—

> novelties in speech,
> Domestic manners, customs, gestures, looks,
> And all the attire of ordinary life.

'Unprepared With needful knowledge' he—

> . . . stood 'mid those concussions, unconcerned,
> Tranquil almost.
>
> (IX, 82.)

Such an initial preoccupation with the more immediately striking elements of a novel environment is a natural one, as it had been in Switzerland and London. Wordsworth's further explanation, that his youthful experience made him see the Revolution as nothing out of Nature's common course, is less acceptable. We may legitimately doubt whether any upbringing could make such a revolution seem entirely 'natural'.

However, he did not feel himself so engrossed by the Parisian scene as to prolong his stay there, and after a few days he passed

---

[1] See Appendix A.   [2] *H.C.R. on Books and Their Writers*, p. 255.

to Orleans. Helen Williams had left for Paris before his arrival,
but his life in the smaller city passed pleasantly enough for three
months, among

> Routs, card-tables, (and) the formal haunts of men,
>   (*Prel.*, 1805, IX, 115.)

a style of existence very much in keeping with the tone of the
contemporary letters to Mathews.

Among this aristocratic set he was surprised to find no supporters of the Revolution, and the reason for his withdrawal to the
noisier world of Blois[1] from this tedious circle

> Where, through punctilios of elegance
> And deeper causes, all discourse, alike
> Of good and evil of the times, was shunned
> With studious care,
>   (*Prel.*, 1805, IX, 118.)

shows that this discovery was something of a disappointment,
and that he was already interested in making acquaintances for
other purposes than that of learning the French language.

In May, 1792, he announced to Mathews that it was still his
intention, faute de mieux, to take orders in the approaching
winter or spring, and in the same letter he writes so dispassion-
ately of the slight hopes of the Revolutionary armies that we can
only conclude that if, as he claims, he had already 'become a
patriot', he was still a rather pallid one. He did indeed resent the
'gloomy satisfaction' with which France's defeat was forecast by
many, and he was convinced that complete reaction was impossible: 'impossible to make any material alteration in the
Constitution, impossible to reinstate the clergy in their ancient
guilty splendour, impossible to give an existence to the noblesse
similar to that it before enjoyed'. Yet such a general satisfaction
with the destruction of French religious and aristocratic tyranny
is indicative of little more than an attitude common to most
Englishmen at this time.

The remarkable thing about the May letter is that it does not

---

[1] See G. M. Harper, 'Wordsworth at Blois', in *John Morley and Other Essays*
(1920).

mention Annette Vallon,[1] the mother of his daughter Caroline, who was to be born on December 15 of the same year. What is even more surprising is that it does not hint at any likely modification of his original plans. This fact does suggest some rather impertinent reflections and some rather obstetrical calculations which are not strictly relevant here, and which I have therefore consigned to an appendix.[2] They do however seem to indicate that the importance of the affair with Annette might have been over-emphasized.[3] It is of course possible and indeed likely that such an event's occurring at the height of Wordsworth's political fervour led to an association of the two experiences; so that, for example, his subsequent consciousness of guilt, his personal conviction of having sinned in France, helped to strengthen a wider condemnation of the other emotional influences which had been contemporaneously acting upon him. In looking back on his revolutionary youth, he could hardly have forgotten, in later years, that its most important personal event had been what he came to regard as the commission of sin; that republicanism in his own experience was closely connected, if only in time, with something which amounted in its outcome to seduction and desertion.

But it is hardly necessary to read into the later decline of revolutionary sympathies a psychological process of compensation and transference springing from an unwillingness on Wordsworth's part to fulfil his obligations. Something more like a valid explanation of his political development is readily available to us in circumstances with which we are much more fully acquainted. As we shall see, the political move can be explained without reference to Annette, at least as a primary influence; the affair might have given a personal implication to Wordsworth's political faith in the next few years that we must not overlook, but, had he never met Annette, there is no reason to believe that his political or poetic development would have been materially different.

At this stage at least the liaison is less important than Wordsworth's conversion to republicanism under the influence of

---

[1] See E. Legouis, *William Wordsworth and Annette Vallon* (1922).
[2] Appendix C. [3] See Herbert Read, *Wordsworth* (1930).

Michel Beaupuy, a French Army officer and an enthusiast for the new régime, whom he met at Blois.

Much is made of this association in *The Prelude*; as I have suggested, perhaps too much. If it was the conversion that Wordsworth suggests, then it was somewhat dramatically sudden, for Beaupuy left Blois on 27 July, and in the May letter to Mathews Wordsworth was still a typically English 'patriot' who, like Cowper, looked from all Continental states to his own 'free country, where every road is open, and where talents and industry are more liberally rewarded than amongst any other nation of the Universe'.

He also admits in *The Prelude*, that the blind royalism of the officers of the Blois garrison with whom he associated had pro-voked, independently of Beaupuy's influence and prior to it, an inevitable reaction. In a way typical of much of his political development, he was driven from vague liberalism towards ardent Jacobinism by the intransigence of his opponents, so that

> . . . zeal, which yet
> Had slumbered, now in opposition burst
> Forth like a Polar summer.
> (*Prel.*, IX, 254.)

What Beaupuy seems to have done was to give to this defensive reaction a positive and an intellectual basis; it was Beaupuy who kept the zeal awake, who made Wordsworth believe that political ideas were important, even paramount, that they might be allowed to dominate his life. It was Beaupuy who was respon-sible for Wordsworth's progress from the conventional social sympathies of 'An Evening Walk' to the political ardour of the 'Descriptive Sketches' and the *Letter to the Bishop of Llandaff*.

Yet it was through the poet's existing sympathies that he made his appeal, for

> . . . unto the poor
> Among mankind he was in service bound,
> As by some tie invisible, oaths professed
> To a religious order.
> (*Prel.*, IX, 303.)

In the midst of rational justification of revolutionary policy, he could be moved by the sight of poverty to recall that, after all, human misery was the real enemy.

Beaupuy was not a doctrinaire revolutionary. His discourses on 'the miseries of royal courts' did not preclude the appreciation of

> Custom and habit . . .
> . . . virtue in the few . . .
> . . . and ignorance in the labouring multitude.

Wordsworth testified to his own experience of the influence on 'the bigotry . . . of a youthful patriot's mind' of Beaupuy's imaginative attraction to and 'chivalrous delight' in the romance of the ancient; his teacher's mind was one 'to all intolerence indisposed'.

The relationship between the English poet and the French soldier has been so fully treated elsewhere[1] as to make further discussion superfluous, yet it should be realized that the republican was working upon material prepared to his hand. From Beaupuy Wordsworth gained intellectual backing for sympathies already fostered within him by his youthful life and experience, gained a determination to live up to, to live in accordance with ideals which until then he had held but vaguely, loosely. A great number of influences had made him a ready pupil: his orphanage and undisciplined youth, the injustice of his aristocratic debtor and the narrow bigotry of his university, his literary taste and his Cambridge associates. The influence of Beaupuy was the culmination of these others, but they all tended to the same end, and we must take account of them all, various as their degrees of influence were, and however their importance was depreciated or distorted by a Wordsworth naturally somewhat dazzled by an outstanding personality.

Beaupuy did make him a republican, but he was not acting alone, nor was his task a difficult one.

The 'heart-bracing colloquies' were interrupted by Beaupuy's departure, and Wordsworth himself was recalled, as he had not been before, to a realization of his personal responsibilities by the

[1] Bussière and Legouis, *Le Général Michel Beaupuy* (1891).

approaching confinement of Annette. After a few weeks in Orleans he evidently decided that, rather than wait with Annette until the birth of the child, his duty was plainly to return at once to England, there to make some provision for his new situation.[1] Nothing is more likely than such personal anxiety to drive from the mind of the enthusiast all thoughts on the progress of the species, and we can rest assured that the prospective father who went to Paris in October had few thoughts to spare for politics.

Before he left the Loire France's situation, and his own reaction to it, had changed considerably. The despotic armies whose advance and imminent victory he had a few months previously viewed with such equanimity, were now a 'presumptuous cloud' bursting 'on the plains of Liberty . . . innocuous'.[2] The Government had taken what was for Wordsworth the logical step—

> the body and venerable name of a republic,
> . . . as if to stamp the final seal
> On her security, and to the world
> Show what she was, a high and fearless soul.
> (*Prel.*, X, 31.)

In such a time of political confidence, violent excesses seemed only transitory and incidental, insignificant beside the noble work being accomplished, and as much the responsibility of the dying despotism as of the new-born democracy. The September Massacres had broken out the month before Wordsworth arrived in Paris, and although the actual power of the Parisian mob provoked misgivings, his faith was high: from—

> the least fear about the end of things
> I was as far as Angels are from guilt.
> (*Prel.*, 1805, X, 127.)[3]

---

[1] The 'Compell'd by nothing less than absolute want Of funds for my support' (*Prelude*, 1805, X, 191) may after all require only the change of the personal pronoun to make it accurate and honest.

[2] *Prelude*, X, 13.

[3] Wordsworth might well have made a closer acquaintance with revolutionary violence in the form of the murderous outbreaks in Orleans during September-October. See Lamartine, *History of the Girondists* (Trans. H. T. Ryde, 1913), II, 143.

The worst evils would be avoided, he felt, if a Hero could be produced. It was of course a consistent theme in his reflections on the political events of his time, that the great personality demanded by great events was so rarely forthcoming. He repeatedly lamented, in France, in Spain, and in England, that the great movements, the noble causes, so seldom called forth men of stature sufficient to fill the commanding role. So, at this stage of the Revolution, he did not doubt, and long after believed,

> . . . that the virtue of one paramount mind
> Would have abash'd those impious crests,
> . . . Have cleared a passage for just government,
> And left a solid birthright to the State,
> Redeem'd according to example given
> By ancient Lawgivers.
> (*Prel.*, 1805, X, 180.)[1]

Wordsworth looked in vain for his Hero, and we must beware of reading too much into these lines of *The Prelude*. Although he would no doubt

> . . . with willing heart
> Have undertaken for a cause so great
> Service however dangerous,
> (*Prel.*, X, 152.)

we must not assume, in contradiction to our knowledge of his more pressing personal anxieties, that he indulged in any political activity of a serious kind at this stage. In his unpublished biography[2] of the poet, his friend Barron Field went further than most investigators of this period in writing: ' . . . he is said to have become acquainted with many of the leaders of the revolutionary party, and to have lived in the same house with Brissot'; but Wordsworth wrote coldly on the opposite page of the MS.: 'There is much mistake here which I should like to correct in person.' Had he in fact formed any association with active politics,

[1] It was, of course, the same line of thought that developed in so many revolutionaries the longing for—or the fear of—the advent of a dictator.

[2] 'Memoirs of the Life and Poetry of William Wordsworth', B.M. Add. MS., 41,325-7.

presumably in the Girondin interest against the Paris-backed Jacobins, he could hardly have avoided meeting Helen Maria Williams, who was closely associated with the prominent members of that group in Paris during this very period. Especially as he had been given a letter of introduction to her, she would have been the obvious person through whom to establish a political connection. Any such activity on his part would at once have brought him under the notice of the British Government's spies and correspondents who were keeping close watch on expatriates like Miss Williams; but in their detailed reports[1] to the Foreign Office Wordsworth does not figure. So we can be certain that if at this time Wordsworth did think vaguely of taking an active part in the current political struggle, he did no more than think about it. *The Prelude*, after all, says merely that he *might* have become involved, had he stayed on; and *might* have perished too. Perhaps the possibilities became rather more vivid to him later, even frighteningly so. When he later refers to 'what had been escaped' by him in the days of his youthful enthusiasm, I fancy he is often thinking of this rather remote possibility. He could even see and pity himself on the scaffold (*Prelude*, X, 231.) as 'A poor mistaken and bewildered offering'.

It is true that the length of this final sojourn in Paris, in view of his personal situation, calls for some explanation. The final version of *The Prelude* says of the move from Orleans that he

> From the quiet of that scene passed on,
> Bound to the fierce Metropolis,[2]

which suggests a mere desire for a change of scene; we know this was not the motive for his leaving Orleans. However, the earlier version of the lines is more explicit; in 1805 he wrote: 'Toward the fierce Metropolis [I] turn'd my steps Their homeward way to England',[3] where it is at least plain that he was only passing through Paris en route for England, not moving there to spend the last few weeks of his stay in France.

Yet the many weeks that he did spend in Paris, and at such a crisis in his personal affairs, do present something of a problem.

[1] P.R.O., F.O., 27/40.   [2] *Prelude*, X, 10.   [3] *Prelude*, 1805, X, 7.

I think the explanation is that Wordsworth, although his withdrawal from France was 'unwilling',[1] was not able to return to
England as quickly as he would have liked.

William Lindsay, the British representative left in Paris after
the departure of the Ambassador, Lord Gower, wrote to Lord
Sidmouth on 2 September, 1792, that he had been unable to
obtain his passport from the French authorities, whose endless
delays had placed numerous other English travellers in the same
position.[2] Gower himself had experienced some difficulty,[3]
and Lord Kerry, abandoning all hope of satisfying the French
Government as to his nationality, had decided to content himself
with a passport 'pour l'intérieur', and thus at least get to Calais.
According to a letter from the Marquis del Campo to Mr Aust
of the Home Office, all applications from Englishmen for pass-
ports had been suspended for a time in August, and with the
closer approach of war the position undoubtedly deteriorated
thereafter. If Lindsay, with his official status, had to wait a fortnight for his passport in September, then we may conclude that
Wordsworth spent most of his weeks in Paris waiting for permission to leave.

. . . . .

Before he left for Paris, it was on the banks of the Loire
that Wordsworth wrote 'Descriptive Sketches', based on his
Swiss tour of 1790. It is essentially a poem of the revolutionary
years, reflecting the poet of 1792 rather than of 1790. It displays,
for example, an interesting change of opinion on the Swiss.
In his 1790 letter to Dorothy he had noted of them only that
he hoped they were more amiable than his experience of them
made him suspect, for, compared to the French and Italians, he
found little to admire in them. Since then, mainly through
reading Ramond De Carbonnière's 'translation' (1781) of
William Coxe's *Letters on Switzerland*, he had been reminded
that the people he had slighted were the traditional defenders of
republican liberty, 'simple, bienfaisant, brave, ennemi du faste,

[1] *Prelude*, XIV, 349.
[2] For this paragraph, see P.R.O., H.O., 42/23 and 32/2, and F.O., 27/40.
[3] See *The Dispatches of Earl Gower*, ed. O. Browning (1885).

D

ami du travail, ne cherchant point d'esclaves, et ne voulant point de maîtres'; a race of freemen 'sans doute le plus heureux de la terre, et le plus digne le l'être'.

So too, the melancholy which pervades the poem is in sharp contrast to the 'excellent health and spirits', 'the perpetual hurry of delight' of the 1790 letter to Dorothy, and Annette Vallon might have given point to a literary pose here. Further, if the Chartreuse passage in *The Prelude* really describes the poet's actual 1790 criticism of the Revolution's religious policy, ('The voice Was nature's, I heard it then, and seem to hear it now'[1]) then the corresponding passage of the 1792 poem shows that by that date this condemnation had been severely modified. His regret for

> . . . that Power whose frown severe
> Tam'd 'sober Reason' till she crouch'd in fear . . .[2]

brought forth only the expected 'sigh' and no longer prompted a plea for the preservation of the monastery.

The poem was clearly written by a poet now dominated by political opinion, as he was to be for the next three years. The invasion of Savoy, which Burns could not defend,[3] was to Wordsworth merely the 'emancipation' of 'the slave of slaves'. In the final lines, the shrill voice of political enthusiasm reaches its height, with a sweeping attack on all those who would oppose the advance of the waves of liberty from France.

. . . . .

Wordsworth returned to an England which had largely made up its mind on the French Revolution. The initial almost universal acclaim for what was thought to be another 'Glorious Revolution' across the Channel had been effectively countered by Burke's oratory, the September Massacres, and the execution of the King. With the blind loyalty of the 'people' revived by the approach and outbreak of war, the defence of the new order in France and the agitation for reform in Britain passed into the hands of a restricted group whose stronger sympathies had been more firmly

[1] *Prelude*, VI, 430.   [2] 'Descriptive Sketches' (1793), 55.
[3] Letter to Graham, 5 January 1793. *Letters*, ed. Ferguson (1931).

rooted. This group was of course a tiny minority, for political disaffection was not then the widespread sentiment that it was to become after the Napoleonic wars. The violent displays of popular loyalty against the reforming Dissenters in Manchester and Birmingham gave the lie direct to those radicals who claimed to be voicing the dissatisfaction of the people at large. The mobs who clamoured for war, who burned Priestley's home and attacked Thelwall, were obviously not on the side of the reformers. Jacobinism was an exclusive movement. Even popular societies like the London Corresponding Society were few in number, composed mostly of literate artisans, and they did not command wide support. Aristocratic groups like the Friends of the People were far more typical of the 'liberal' movement of the 'nineties and only in the era after Waterloo was its social complexion radically altered by its spread to an urban proletariat which was hardly in existence before the turn of the century.

Wordsworth was a member of this minority, and fully to appreciate the nature of his political sympathies during this period we must take account of the variety of appeals which the Revolution made to him and to his contemporaries.

Support of the Revolution was for many but an expression of domestic opposition, a corollary of their contempt for the Tories who were waging the war against it. In the eighteenth century one looked for political allies amongst the enemies of one's enemies, whether they were to be found inside or outside the country; hence the strange fascination which Jacobin policy seemed to have for the most substantial Whig magnates.

Yet it is also true that much support of the Revolution was ultimately based on pacifist sympathies of a more disinterested kind rather than on strictly political principles. They played a large part, for example, in the Jacobinism of the Dissenters, and it was not without justification that Burke saw in Price and his co-religionists the core of English disaffection.

Revolutionary France did seem to hold out the promise of an era of perpetual peace to an England which had not forgotten (as the Wordsworth of the 'Evening Walk' had not) the protracted bloodiness of the war against America. The renunciation of all war but that of defence was followed by the revocation of the Family Compact with Spain at the time of the Nootka Sound dispute which seemed to prove French sincerity. Liberals had long proclaimed that wars were solely the result of the ambitions and often of the whims of monarchical governments, and the converse of this thesis was being nobly sustained by the practice of Republican France. To Paine, democracy, in *The Rights of Man*, meant primarily peace, for 'if universal peace, civilization, and commerce, are ever to be the happy lot of man, it cannot be accomplished but by a revolution in the system of governments. All the monarchical governments are military. War is their trade, plunder and revenue their objects.' So, to many Englishmen, the new order in France had, as one of its strongest recommendations, a promise of peace for Great Britain and the world; as Samuel Romilly pointed out so categorically in his 1790 pamphlet, *Thoughts on the Probable Influence of the French Revolution on Great Britain*, France could now only wage war with the consent of the people, and, 'where such a consent must be obtained, no wars will be undertaken but what are just and necessary'.

This widespread pacifism is more particularly important because, while it was *one* of the bases of Revolutionary sympathies, it was almost the exclusive inspiration of the contemporary movement for British parliamentary reform. Demands for the extension of the suffrage, of course, antedated the Revolution in France, but it was the Revolutionary war which brought these demands to a head and gave them dramatic point. The argument of the reformers was that the war could only be declared and waged because parliament was not in fact representative of the people, and, indeed, because ministers were able to carry out the King's wishes in defiance of those of the parliamentary majority. So the 'ministerial war' gave the reformers their most convincing argument: reform was needed because only by means of reform could the country bring an end to the war and prevent its recurrence.

Pacifism then, at least of this modified kind, was at the root both of much of the contemporary revolutionary sympathy and of most of the reforming spirit in Britain. To a Wordsworth already schooled in a literary tradition radically opposed to militarism and concerned particularly with the sufferings of the poor in time of war, this pacifist appeal was a strong one. In *The Excursion* (III, 723) the song of the 'prophetic harps' which the Solitary heard 'in every grove ringing' upon the fall of the Bastille, proclaimed—'War shall cease; Did ye not hear that conquest is abjured'. He was long convinced that, but for the military ambitions of the continental despots and the shameful assistance given to 'Pride's perverted Ire' by the British Government, an era of perpetual world peace would have been ushered in by the Revolution. The outbreak of war was also more than a political blow; it postponed indefinitely his reunion with Annette, and his marriage, whether willing or dutiful. He had therefore a most compulsive personal reason for his hopes of peace, so that the pacifist basis of so much contemporary republicanism was a peculiarly real and personal element in his political attitude, an element strongly coloured by emotion.

Of course the more general emotional appeal of the Revolution as a whole was also a powerful influence, and not only on Wordsworth. It was not only a question of the government's legislative measures but rather of their phraseology, the very tone of its pronouncements. The Revolution was a rhetorical as well as a political one, and one which had indeed as remarkable an influence on manners as it had on the principles of government. Documents such as the Declaration of the Rights of Man, the reports of those incredible debates in the Assembly, the revolutionary calendar, the classical names affected by the republicans, the adoption of new modes of dress—all these by-products of the political revolt were to the guileless readers of Mackenzie and Beattie and Miss Williams irresistible appeals to the cherished emotions. The weeping and embracing deputies, the mass enthusiasm of the fêtes de fédération, the delegations from the races of the world—the whole naïve emotionalism of the Revolution was a source of attraction and enthusiasm that this more cynical and experienced age must beware of discounting.

To a generation which prided itself upon its sensibility, this emotional attraction of the event was often much stronger than the political. In her *Letters Written in France* Helen Maria Williams had defended her enthusiasm by claiming that 'if one is gifted with the least touch of sensitivity, it is very difficult to resist sharing in the general happiness. And my love for the French Revolution springs from that fellow feeling. My political feelings are purely emotional, and my head has never been called in to pass my judgment on matters which it can hardly comprehend.' In 1790 Wordsworth had also felt the strong influence of this national excitement, this 'joy in widest commonalty spread' which was sweeping France; and even after the intellectual conviction that came to him from Beaupuy, the exultation of the people in their revolt seemed to him one of the

> Arguments sent from Heaven to prove the cause
> Good, pure, which no one could stand up against,
> Who was not lost, abandoned, selfish, proud,
> Mean, miserable, wilfully depraved,
> Hater perverse of equity and truth.
>   (*Prel.*, IX, 283.)

In fact 'sentiment' became a preserve of Jacobin literature. 'La sensibilité' became a revolutionary slogan, and strong emotion was appropriated by the democrats as a part of the 'mœurs républicains'. To feel strongly was democratic, nor was it only a question of feeling strongly for the sufferings of the poor or of the blacks; strong sentiment of all kinds took a political colour. So in 1794 the pantisocrat Coleridge corrects himself in a private letter thus: ' . . . I took the liberty—Gracious God! pardon me for the aristocratic frigidity of that expression—I indulged my feelings by . . .'. Pierre Trahard, in his interesting study of *La Sensibilité Révolutionnaire* (1936) quotes the Jacobin Fabre d'Eglantine: 'Le modérantisme, . . . c'est à dire l'aristocrate moderne, ne veut pas que le peuple ait des sensations.'

In Wordsworth's particular case this emotional enthusiasm was strengthened by his actual experience in France, and above all modified by the fact that the liaison with Annette gave his contemporaneous revolutionary ardour a peculiarly personal context. His relationship with a Frenchwoman had developed

along with, and was possibly more closely related to, his acceptance of 'French' principles.[1] His defence of those principles often
echoes, we feel, his defence of the personal emotion which he had
experienced while under their dominion, just as subsequently, the
decline of his love for Annette, with the consequent increase in
the sense of guilt which he felt at having sinned with her, provoked him to an often abnormal condemnation, not so much of
the principles themselves, as of their country of origin.

It is important therefore to recognize the actual bases of
English Jacobinism and to appreciate Wordsworth's personal
contact with them at so many points. We have every reason to
suspect, as he did himself later, that these opinions were the
product of emotion rather than reason, and of the peculiar
coincidence of political and personal events. Significantly, when
his attitude to Annette changed so that the continuance of the
war became less of a personal issue, and when the rural peace of
Racedown removed him from the more feverish emotional
context of his early political convictions, their temper cooled, the
extremism disappeared. So while there is no point in denying the
violence of his 1793 republicanism, there is much to be said for
trying to understand its personal background.

There is one further point to be made. It is plain that the
extremer principles of republican democracy were more often
forced upon the 'Jacobins' than freely espoused. Under the lash of
Burke's unrestrained calumny, many reformers moved to a

[1] It is, after all, just possible that he formed the liaison at a time when he was
momentarily seduced by the more dubious tenets of the 'Revolutionary
morality', even though, in fact, Annette was a Royalist. In *The Excursion* (III,
797-805.) the Solitary admits, perhaps with suspicious precaution against mis-
understanding, that he—

> nor scrupled to proclaim,
> And propagate, by liberty of life,
> Those new persuasions. Not that I rejoiced,
> Or even found pleasure, in such vagrant course,
> For its own sake; but farthest from the walk
> Which I had trod in happiness and peace,
> Was most inviting to a troubled mind;
> That, in a struggling and distempered world,
> Saw a seductive image of herself.

republicanism which could at least provide a firm front of opposition. As Fox pointed out, speaking on an amendment to the address in reply to the King's speech of 13 December, 1792: 'One extreme naturally leads to another. Those who dread republicanism, fly for shelter to the crown. Those who desire reform and are calumniated, are driven by despair to republicanism.' With Burke and Reeves[1] convinced that all apologists for the French Revolution were guillotining republicans at heart, this polarisation of opinion was inevitable, although even the most violent of the English Jacobins were, when brought to the point, liable to make the most conservative reservations.

Events in France itself also forced the pace for English enthusiasts. Supporters of a limited monarchy, religious toleration and the reign of peace, found themselves under the necessity of justifying the deposition and execution of the King, a campaign against all traditional religious belief, and a policy of general European war. To Wordsworth, as to many, this change of footing was a bitter necessity, but the fear of apostasy and the very strength of their enemies enabled the transition to be effected. For if the ultimate aim of the contemporary liberal movement was reform in England, it could find no other significant expression for the moment except in terms of support for the French Revolution; on the justification and success of that event the English movement had based its arguments.

It is plain then that when we talk of Wordsworth's republicanism, a great many facts about his personal situation and about the political climate of the times need to be kept in mind. Our knowledge of the personal background at least should help to explain why his republicanism was something so different from the conventional and classical tyrannophobia of Southey, and from the shrill democratic frenzy of Coleridge. Connected as they were at so many points with his personal position, supplemented by a year's residence in revolutionary France, his liberal sympathies as a whole were far more profound, far more vital, and, fundamentally, far more difficult to subvert.

· · · · ·

[1] Chairman of the 'Association for Preserving Liberty and Property against Levellers and Republicans'.

In 1793 Wordsworth was still without a future. He had
returned to England to break the news to his family about
Annette, and his relations had promptly ostracized him, forbade
him to see his sister, and refused him assistance. Such treatment
only added to the sense of personal injustice which had before
now been a complement of his political sympathies.

But he had written two longish poems, 'Descriptive Sketches'
and 'An Evening Walk', and in an era when Church and King
men vowed that they could tell the political colour of a book as
soon as they knew the name of its publisher, he handed them to
Johnson, whom the Tory *Anti-Jacobin Review* described as 'the
favourite publisher and friend of the Priestleys, the Darwins, the
Godwins, and other *unprejudiced* authors'.

Johnson was popular among the disaffected, and he had
gathered about him a radical group which dined every week at his
shop in St. Paul's Churchyard. There is much to suggest that
Wordsworth's relationship with him was not merely the commercial one of author and publisher. The poet was no longer a
casual observer in the Metropolis, but an ardent liberal with the
most personal reason for supporting the most prominent of current
liberal demands; he would naturally relish the opportunity,
given him by his new status as a publishing poet, of making the
acquaintance of fellow spirits. His association with such people
may have directed official notice to him: the spy despatched by
the suspicious Home Office to Stowey in 1797[1] was under the
impression that Wordsworth was a name known to his superiors,
and it is possible that brother Richard's later misgivings[2] about
William's expression of his political views were related to this
notoriety.

In a note to *The Excursion*, Wordsworth mentions that he was
taken to hear the preacher Joseph Fawcett,[3] the original of his
character the Solitary, by a Mr Nicholson, whose acquaintance
he made in London about this time.[4] Nicholson was a

[1] See Appendix B.   [2] See below, p. 73.
[3] See A. Beatty, *Joseph Fawcett, The Art of War: Its Relation to the Early
Development of William Wordsworth* (1918).
[4] It is just possible that these visits took place in 1795, but the date does not
affect the significance of the acquaintance.

mathematician and engineer, connected in a business capacity
with the Wedgwoods, a friend of the radical Godwin, and one
of those with whom Godwin in 1792 discussed the principles of
Political Justice. It would seem likely therefore that to his association with Johnson Wordsworth owed an introduction to the
Godwinian circle of which Fawcett was also a member.

Fawcett's sermons in Old Jewry created something of a sensation in London during the 1790s, and his popularity among the
liberals is not surprising. His sermons were concerned primarily
with the social and political implications of Christian teaching,
and the reproduction of so much of their thought in *The Excursion* is proof of the young poet's reaction to them. Contemplation of humility brought him to remind the congregation that
'the tyrants that have trampled upon a people, before they set their
feet upon them, were led to look down upon them, as an herd of
insignificant and contemptible creatures. The lordly oppressor
of the rustic neighbourhood, the little tyrant of the poor man's
fields, has been ever in habits of looking upon them that have no
riches, as having no rights.' Charity to him meant above all love
of the poor, respect for their rights, anxiety to better their conditions. A vindication of Christianity 'in not particularly inculcat-
ing Friendship and Patriotism' introduces, in a very Godwinian
form, the thesis that Christ 'has inculcated an attachment to the
whole human race' irrespective of national boundaries; for
although local affections are natural, blind love of one's country
can be sinful, and the conscientious Christian must beware: 'if his
fellow-countrymen oppose the rights, set their face against the
welfare of their fellow-men; if they engage in unrighteous war,
if they go out to unjust battle; he has no God-speed to say to
their undertaking; his heart protests against their proceedings;
his prayers oppose the cry of their temples; his sighs accompany
the shout of their successes; and his song of thanksgiving ascends
for their defeat.' National enemies must be included within the
pale of Christian charity, for it demands benevolence to all men.

On Wordsworth, and on Fawcett's devotees generally, the
actuality of sermons such as these would not be lost; and how
Lonsdale's victim would have warmed to a condemnation of the
vices of the nobility, with particular reference to their 'defrauding

industrious creditors of their due'. From the 1795 edition of
these sermons it is plain that Fawcett was developing the democratic implications of Christianity as the Jacobin school of poetry
was developing those of sentimentalism; he was preaching the
equality of all men before God, the dignity and the rights of the
poor, the indisputable evil of war. His sermons were patently
directed against the existing government of England and its
policy towards France.

Further light is cast on Wordsworth's life during these months
by his reference, in a 1794 letter to Mathews, to his personal
acquaintance with Perry and Gray, the editors of the Whig-
Radical *Morning Chronicle*. Perry had been editor of the liberal
European Magazine in which Wordsworth had published his
sonnet on Helen Maria Williams, and his political opinions were
to bring him into court for the publication of a seditious libel
before the end of the year. So this chance reference, proving a
connection with the editors of the leading liberal journal in the
country, is at least a precious addition to our scanty knowledge of
the poet's acquaintance during this crucial year.

Of his political opinions we have, of course, more evidence.
Before he left London two books were published, one of which
was to exert a powerful influence on his political and intellectual
development, the other to provoke him to a full avowal of the
political position which he had reached by 1793.

CHAPTER III

The Republican

The first of the two books mentioned at the end of the previous chapter was William Godwin's *Enquiry concerning Political Justice*, published in February, 1793; the second was Bishop Watson of Llandaff's *Strictures on the French Revolution and the British Constitution*, printed as an appendix to his sermon on '*The Wisdom and Goodness of God in having made both Rich and Poor*'. Wordsworth's 'Letter to the Bishop of Llandaff, on the extraordinary avowal of his political principles, contained in the appendix to his late sermon; by a Republican',[1] is as much an abstract of the first as it is a reply to the second.

The Letter was never published in the poet's lifetime, and indeed the MS. has only recently been rediscovered.[2] We assume that the traditional dating is accurate, and it is unlikely that such a letter could have come from Wordsworth's pen at any time but 1793, when his experience of the past year and his personal situation at the time combined to produce in him a fervent political enthusiasm that he was seldom to know again.

To the liberal minority of 1793 *Political Justice* was a godsend. At a time when military violence had clouded the issue in France, when the superficial materialism of Paine could afford such little inspiration to the enlightened, when the cause of reaction seemed to be triumphant on all sides, there appeared *Political Justice*, a full-scale and uncompromising justification of just that extreme of republicanism to which so many of the liberals had been often

[1] See E. M. Hooker, 'Wordsworth's Letter to the Bishop of Llandaff', in *Studies in Philology* (July, 1931).

[2] Miss Darbishire found the MS. among papers bequeathed to Dove Cottage by the late Gordon Wordsworth; she is of the opinion that it is in Wordsworth's hand.

unwillingly driven. At last the disaffected had produced a man and a work fit to stand against Burke, fit even to balance the deadly progress of the French Revolution. For them at least the philosopher made the statesman seem a childish babbler, for he had raised the argument from the level of the debates in the Commons, above that of a mere defence of the Revolution, even above the sphere of historical principles, to the stratosphere of pure reason.

The sensation caused by Godwin's book is a matter of wonder to modern critics. His rather arid volumes, following the same theme to its most exasperating conclusions, the redundancy, the endless exemplifications, the dry, pulse-less spirit of the work seem little calculated to excite that enthusiasm[1] which Hazlitt describes in *The Spirit of the Age*. To understand that we must realise that its initial popularity was due to its author's humanitarianism rather than to his rationalistic philosophy. As Godwin said in his preface to the second (1796) edition, his purpose, initially at least, was: 'to prepare the enlightened to sympathize with the just claims of the oppressed and humble', and to condemn 'the imposition of that self-regard which would represent our own interest as of as much value as that of all the world beside'. So that Crabb Robinson's was apparently the expected reaction, for he said of the book: 'it made me feel more generously. . . . I had never before felt so strongly the duty of not living to one's self, but of having for one's sole object the good of the community'.[2]

It was precisely this (as he thought) spurious philanthropy that moved Charles Lloyd, a friend of Coleridge and Southey, to write his novel *Edmund Oliver* in 1798, 'to present arguments against *unrestrained sensibility* and abstract philosophy of *the Godwin school of general benevolence*, and to plead on behalf of stoicism and private virtue'.

In his 1795 sonnet Coleridge saw Godwin as 'form'd t'illume a senseless world forlorn', and went on to describe his own reaction:

> Pleas'd have I mark'd oppression, terror-pale,
> Since, through the windings of her dark machine,

---

[1] Although, as Shelley learned, it did not make its author's fortune.
[2] *Henry Crabb Robinson on Books*, etc., p. 3.

Thy steady eye has shot its glances keen,
And bade the all-lovely 'scenes at distance hail'.
    Nor will I not thy holy guidance bless,
And hymn thee, Godwin, with an ardent lay,
For that thy voice, in Passion's stormy day,
When wild I roam'd the bleak heath of distress,
Bade the bright form of Justice meet my way—
And told me that her name was Happiness.

In the following year he abandoned Godwin, but he did so, surprisingly enough, because he now considered him 'a pander to sensuality'.

It is significant that so many of Godwin's readers applauded or abused him not because of his rationalism but because of his humanitarianism. So there is no need to see in Wordsworth's immediate acceptance of the political arguments of the new philosopher any implied rejection of the emotional bases of his revolutionary enthusiasm. The Letter to Llandaff shows that he extracted just as much from Godwin as applied to his current opinions, for while drawing on *Political Justice* for almost every argument he uses, he does not advocate atheism or anarchy, does not advert to the evils of charity or the invalidity of promises or the irrationality of domestic affections, and does not turn his back on that sentimental humanitarianism which was so much a part of his republicanism. This deeper influence was a later growth.

The Letter to Llandaff contains little that is not in Godwin, and even Godwin's extensive borrowings from Paine and others were taken over into the work of his disciple. The Letter has indeed every appearance of having been written immediately after a hasty reading of the newly published *Political Justice*, and borrowings are made almost exclusively from the second volume.

These borrowings account for almost every argument in the pamphlet, and they are so often indicated by a close verbal echo that enumeration would be tedious.[1] Even arguments not exclusively Godwinian are expressed in language and in a spirit so close to Godwin's that their immediate source is indisputable.

[1] See C. W. Roberts, 'The Influence of Godwin on Wordsworth's Letter to the Bishop of Llandaff', *Studies in Philology*, Vol. 29, 1932.

Thus, in *Political Justice* p. 415, Godwin makes an additional reflection on the subject of monarchy: 'another of the evil consequences attendant upon this species of government (is) the existence and corruption of courts'. And Wordsworth, introducing the point in the same supplementary way, writes, 'I shall not pursue this topic further, but . . . I cannot but remind you of that atmosphere of corruption without which it would seem that courts cannot exist'.

In specifying the advantages of a democratic franchise and the removal of electoral qualifications, Godwin points out: 'we ought to have no pecuniary qualifications, or in other words no regulation requiring the possession of a certain property as a condition to the right of electing or the capacity of being elected'; which Wordsworth echoes in foreseeing that 'in the choice of its representatives a people will not immorally hold out wealth as a criterion of integrity, nor lay down as a fundamental rule, that to be qualified for the trying duties of legislation a citizen should be possessed of a certain fixed property'.

Even details, incidental to the main argument, are often taken from Godwin; in condemning the limitation inherent in specific legislation, the philosopher wrote: 'We may institute sumptuary laws, limiting the expense of our citizens in dress and food. We may institute agrarian laws, forbidding any man to possess more than a certain annual revenue, but how far are we really advanced?' And in the same context Wordsworth follows suit with 'I am not an advocate for the agrarian laws, nor for sumptuary regulations. . . .'

For reasons mentioned above, elucidation of Wordsworth's debt to Paine is not always easy. For example, both Paine and Godwin make much of the separation of the interests of the governor and the governed under undemocratic constitutions, and both emphasize the illogicality of the limited intellect of the monarch possessing unlimited power. To Paine rather than to Godwin does Wordsworth probably owe his particular reference to the danger of the hereditary principle, his attack on the unnaturalness of the law of primogeniture, and his defence of the behaviour of the mob in England and France while under the residual influence of monarchical corruption. But the tone of the

Letter to Llandaff is much more Godwinian than Painite, reflecting the calm logic of the former rather than the clamant defiance
of the American. Paine's continual plea for economy, his preoccupation with the burden of taxation, his rather petty and
materialistic concern with the cost of things—these find no place
in Wordsworth's argument. Paine was arguing for suffrage
co-extensive with taxation, while to Wordsworth and Godwin,
all the unfranchised were social helots; Paine could be content
with a limited monarchy, and agreed to retaining Louis as an
amiable servant of the people; but to Wordsworth Louis was a
convicted murderer, and, with Godwin, he insisted on the
essential incompatibility of democracy with any form of privilege.

This Letter then is little more than a résumé of the outstanding
work on political theory of the time. On the question of inequality before the laws, on the French Revolution, and on the
Swiss republics, it is plain that Wordsworth is speaking from
experience,[1] and the reference to 'the miseries entailed upon the
marriage of those who are not rich' is not unconnected with it.
Elsewhere the author is a pure enthusiast, a true perfectionist,
who could look forward to the democratic republic of the future
as a state where the laws 'being but the expression of the general
will, would be enacted only from an almost universal conviction of their utility, and any resistance to such laws, any
desire of eluding them, must proceed from a few refractory
individuals'.

Despite its lack of originality, the Letter is a valuable document
in Wordsworth's biography. In it he declares himself without
reserve an extreme republican, a supporter of universal suffrage
and frequent elections; he does insist, however, on the prime
necessity of education as the prelude to the transference of power
to a people long debased by oppression. Rather more significantly
for our purpose, Wordsworth here announces his absorption with
political enquiry as 'the most fruitful field of human knowledge'.

. . . . .

Unpublished pamphlets were not solving the problem of
profitable activity, but in the middle of the year the unsettled

[1] See p. 18 above.

republican was once again able to defer the vital decision on his future. William Calvert, another liberal, asked for his company during a tour in the West Country, Calvert bearing all expenses. Apparently this diversion brought initially little relief to the depression which political events and their fatal effect on his personal happiness had forced upon him. The sight of the fleet preparing for sea off the Isle of Wight filled him with gloom; at the sound of the sunset cannon, he wrote:

> The star of life appears to set in blood
> And ocean shudders in offended mood,
> Deepening with moral gloom his angry flood.[1]

He was in this morbid condition when Calvert separated from him on Salisbury Plain, and during his solitary wandering through the desolate countryside on his way north to visit Jones, the companion of the Swiss tour, he conceived the story of 'Guilt and Sorrow', a poem on the 'calamities, principally those consequent upon war, to which, more than any other classes of men, the poor are subject'.[2] He was in fact developing that reference in the Letter to Llandaff to the misguided enthusiasm of the 'popular mind' crying out 'as with one voice, for a war from which not a single ray of consolation can visit them to compensate for the additional keenness with which they are about to smart under the scourge of labour, of cold, and of hunger'. Probably at the same time his earlier prose reflections on 'the vices of the penal law' were also given poetic expression in 'The Convict', a poem purely Jacobin in its sympathy for the criminal, and purely Godwinian in its plans for his reformation.

If we are to believe the reference in 'Tintern Abbey', and if lines 66 to 83[3] in that later poem do refer to the 1793 visit and not to some earlier period 'when first I came among these hills', it appears that by the time Wordsworth reached the Wye on his way to Jones in North Wales, the spirit which was responsible for 'Guilt and Sorrow' had given way to a far less desperate state

---

[1] 'At the Isle of Wight, 1793'. (See de Selincourt ed. I, 307.)
[2] Advertisement to 'Guilt and Sorrow'.
[3] Which talk of 'aching joys' and 'dizzy raptures'.

of mind.[1] The change, if there was a change, was certainly a sudden one, and, judging by his subsequent experience, not a permanent one, but it is not, for all that, incredible. If he was in fact anxious for reunion with Annette more out of a sense of duty than of affection, then there must certainly have been occasions when he saw the war as a not unrelieved catastrophe. As long as it continued his plans for Annette and Caroline did not constitute a real problem; whatever he hoped to do, the war would not allow him to do anything, and the longer it continued the less pressing and attractive his duties presumably seemed.

So we can allow for temporary breaks in the gloom, especially for bursts of the sort of frantic irresponsibility which 'Tintern Abbey' suggests. It is not difficult to imagine that the political and personal despondency which had pursued him from the Isle of Wight across Salisbury Plain was temporarily lightened by a more radiant countryside, and by the prospect of a return to the pleasant company of Jones and his family. It is feasible that the agitation of a mind always susceptible to the restorative influence of natural beauty should have been calmed by the 'sylvan Wye', and that in Wales, as in Switzerland three years before, the glory of the scenery drove all thoughts of man from his mind. It is also possible that in 'Tintern Abbey' Wordsworth was once again idealizing his past.

·   ·   ·   ·   ·

There is a legend that Wordsworth stole to France in October[2] after a tour in North Wales with Jones, but for want of conclusive evidence the journey must remain hypothetical. It is based primarily on Carlyle's assertion that Wordsworth told him that he had witnessed the execution of the Girondist Gorsas, which took place in that month. Carlyle's circumstantial testimony[3] is

[1] Although, of course, the references in 'Tintern Abbey' are to a delight somewhat extravagant, possibly to something that we might call an escapist reaction. Wordsworth talks of 'fleeing' from something unspecified; this might be peculiarly significant.

[2] See G. M. Harper, 'Did Wordsworth defy the Guillotine?', *Quarterly Review*, May, 1930; 'Wordsworth in Paris', *Times Literary Supplement*, 1 May, 1930. J. R. Macgillivray, 'Wordsworth in Paris', *T.L.S.*, 12 June, 1930.

[3] *Reminiscences* (1881), pp. 330 *et seq*.

hardly decisive, and the mere fact that such a number of years elapsed between the supposed visit (1793) and Wordsworth's statement (*c.* 1840), and between Carlyle's hearing the story and actually recounting it (1867), is enough to make us dubious. It is strange that Carlyle does not seem to have realized that, if Wordsworth *had* witnessed the execution of Gorsas in October, 1793, he must have been in Paris at a particularly perilous time. He ran the risk of execution on both sides of the Channel, under a French regulation and the British Traitorous Correspondence Act. With the recent British action at Toulon affecting official French policy towards alien residents as it did, October was the worst possible time for an Englishman to cross the Channel. In the face of the evidence at our disposal, we can only say that the possibility of such a visit is extremely slight. The third-hand and conflicting story quoted by Alaric Watts[1] is of no value, even in corroboration.

.   .   .   .   .   .

From Wales Wordsworth passed north to pay a visit to Dorothy, now staying with more amenable relatives at Halifax. His future was still uncertain, but he was, of course, no longer thinking of the Church. 'All professions', he wrote to Mathews in February, 1794, 'I think are attended with great inconveniences, but that of the priesthood with most.' Mathews had planned a European journey, and in the same letter Wordsworth enquires after his impressions of the Portuguese: 'In what state is knowledge with them? and have the principles of free government any advocate there? or is liberty a sound of which they have never heard? Are they so debased by superstition as we are told, or are they improving in anything?' Such questions indicate that his political interests, if subdued during his stay in Wales, were soon revived. There is significantly no indication here nor in any

[1] A. A. Watts, *Alaric Watts: A Narrative of his Life* (1884), II, 280. Watts was apparently acquainted with a certain Stewart, who was in turn acquainted with 'an old Republican named Bailey, who had been confined in the Temple with Pichegru. He had met Wordsworth in Paris, and having warned him that his connection with the 'mountain' rendered his situation there at that time perilous, the poet, he said, decamped with great precipitation.'

of the 1794 letters that, as was the case with Crabb Robinson and
others, the extinction of the Girondin Party and the reign of
terror in France had fundamentally affected his revolutionary
sympathies.

During the spring William and Dorothy took a house at Windy
Brow, near Keswick. After three years of wandering and anxiety,
Wordsworth at last found himself in the sympathetic company
of one who had never turned against him, and the experience
strengthened his resolution to make this domestic relation a
permanent one. 'We please ourselves', wrote Dorothy, 'in calculat-
ing from our present expenses for how very small a sum we could
live.' The virtue and simplicity of their neighbours were also an
attraction to Dorothy, and no doubt to her brother: 'I have
never been more delighted with the manners of any people. . . .
They are the most honest cleanly sensible people I ever saw in
their rank of life—and I think I may safely affirm, happier than
anybody I know. They are contented with a supply of the bare
necessaries of life, are active and industrious and declare with
simple frankness unmixed with ostentation that they prefer their
cottage . . . to any of the showy edifices in the neighbourhood.'
In reply to her aunt's misgivings, she wrote: 'I am convinced
that there is no place in the world in which a good and virtuous
young woman would be more likely to continue good and
virtuous than under the roof of these honest, worthy, and un-
corrupted people.'

At Windy Brow Wordsworth turned once more to his poetry.
In a passage now added to 'An Evening Walk' he claimed that
he had already found that the 'sober charms' of nature—

> 'can chase with sweet control
> Each idle thought and sanctify the soul,
> And on the morbid passions pouring balm,
> Resistless breathe a melancholy calm';

but most of the additions and emendations made at this time to
'An Evening Walk' and 'Descriptive Sketches' reflect that closer
acquaintance with human suffering, that political and social
consciousness and that more real melancholy which the last three
years had brought him. In fact the consistent morbidity of

their tone suggests that his state of mind was becoming critical.

After the episode of the vagrant mother whose lot, in 'An Evening Walk', he had contrasted so unfavourably with the domestic bliss of the swans, a 1794 insertion goes on to describe a parallel incident, relating to 'the catastrophe of a poor woman who was found dead on Stanemoor two years ago with two children whom she had in vain attempted to protect from the storm in the manner described'.[1]

In a similar vein he added to his lines on the quarry, the picture of a maiden 'led by terror' passing—

> Through the dull gloom, inaudible and slow
> To that sad spot her bosomed pain to tell
> Where crushed by falling rocks her lover fell.

Even the description of the summer noon is expanded to display an almost morbid sense of discomfort:

> When he who long with languid steps had toiled
> Across the slippery moor, oppressed and foiled
> Sicks down and finds no rest, while as he turns
> The fervid earth his languid body burns,
> Nor can his weak arm faintly lifted chase
> The insect host that gather round his face
> And join their murmurs to the tedious sound
> Of seeds of bursting furze that crackle round
> While his faint dog extended on the heath
> Pants in his ear,

and so on.

His political fervour is directly reflected in the Godwinian address to the sun:

> Spirit who guid'st that orb and view'st from high
> Thrones, towers, and fanes in blended ruin lie,
> Role to Peruvian vales thy gorgeous way
> See thine own temples mouldering in decay
> Roll on till hurled from thy bright car sublime
> Thyself confess the mighty arm of Time;
> Thy star must perish, but triumphant Truth
> Shall tend a brightening flame in endless youth.

[1] Wordsworth's note to the poem.

So too, in the calm radiance of the moon he now sees a suggestively personal image of that Miltonic virtue which—

> fallen on times to gloom consigned,
> Makes round her path the light she cannot find,
> And by her own internal lamp fulfills
> And asks no other star what Virtue wills,
> Acknowledging though round her Danger lurk,
> And Fear, no night in which she cannot work.

The borrowed picture of the crowing cock becomes an excuse for an attack on the luxurious:

> Blush ye not—ye who that high soul employ
> To fire your savage breasts with barbarous joy?
> Learn at his call to rise from slumber pure
> And meet him early at your opening door . . .
> . . . From love of Nature love of Virtue flows
> And hand in hand with Virtue Pleasure goes.[1]

This same spirit is at work in the contemporaneous emendations of the 'Descriptive Sketches' preserved in Wordsworth's copy of the 1793 edition now in the Huntington Library. The anxiety of the bereaved wife of the chamois hunter is expanded into nineteen lines from the mere six of the early version, and the terrors of the hunter's plight are correspondingly heightened. The poet's pity for the Ensiedlen pilgrims is also more fully developed, in a passage concluding:

> So I forlorn dejected weary slow
> A pilgrim wandering round the world of woe
> Oft as I meet a brother on whose cheek
> The fading gleams of dawning gladness break
> Feel once again the balm of life bestowed
> And press as now with joy my (   ) road.

In these same months Wordsworth wrote most of 'The Female Vagrant', later to be expanded into 'Guilt and Sorrow'.[2] The

[1] The final couplet is an interesting if rather naïve expression of his developing attitude to Nature.

[2] See O. J. Campbell and P. Mueschke, 'Guilt and Sorrow', *Modern Philology*, February, 1926.

origin of this poem and the circumstances of its conception have already been mentioned, but its first MS. form, entitled 'Salisbury Plain', dates from the Windy Brow period.

The didactic political tone of the poem is established in the second stanza, with the theme that sorrow owes its bitterness not only to remembered pleasures, but also to—

> reflection in the state
> Of those who on the couch of affluence rest,
> By laughing Fortune's sparkling cup elate,
> While we of comfort reft, by pain depressed,
> No other pillow know than Penury's iron breast.

These opening stanzas, and other portions of MS. I, later cancelled, express a deeper melancholy, a more intimate concern with human suffering and a more violent social and political protest than that form of the 'Female Vagrant' published later in the *Lyrical Ballads*. The sixty-eight lines which, in the Windy Brow poem, follow the line corresponding to line 185 of 'Guilt and Sorrow', conclude:

> And are ye spread, ye glittering dews of youth,
> For this—that frost may gall the tender flower
> In Joy's fair breast with more untimely tooth?
> Unhappy Man! Thy sole delightful hour
> Flies first; it is thy miserable dower
> Only to taste of joy that thou may'st pine
> A loss which rolling Suns shall ne'er restore.
> New suns roll on: nor any rest is thine
> Nor hope, till on the tomb thy willing limbs recline.

The theme of social injustice is also prominent, as exemplified in the history of the vagrant's father:

> . . . by cruel chance and wilful wrong
> My father's substance fell into decay
> Oppression trampled on his tresses gray
> His little range of water was denied
> Even to the bed where his old body lay
> His all was seized; and creeping side by side
> Turned out on the cold winds alone we wandered wide.

The accusatory tone of this passage was considerably modified
in 1798, when—

> To cruel injuries he became a prey,
> Sore traversed in whate'er he bought and sold:
> His troubles grew upon him day by day,
> Till all his substance fell into decay.
> His little range of water was denied
> All but the bed where his old body lay
> All, all was seized, and weeping side by side
> We sought a home where we uninjured might abide.

The war experiences of the female vagrant gave Wordsworth
an opportunity of proclaiming his pacifism in terms that he did
not retract until 1805, when such a creed had far different implications for him; but in the early version the stanza inserted
between lines 297 and 298 of the completed 'Guilt and Sorrow'
reads:

> 'Oh! dreadful price of being to resign
> All that is dear *in* being! better far
> In Want's most lonely cave till death to pine
> Unseen, unheard, unwatched by any star,
> Better before proud Fortune's sumptuous car
> Obvious our dying bodies to obtrude,
> Than dog-like, wading at the heels of war
> Protract a curst existence, with a brood
> That lap (their very nourishment!) their brothers' blood.

The conclusion of this early version does not relieve its oppres-
sive melancholy: the two wanderers become symbols of wretched
humanity straying over the plains of life, for—

> . . . life is like this desert broad,
> Where all the happiest find is but a shed
> And a green spot mid wastes interminably spread.

But the guilt of human misery lies not at the door of the suffering:

> For proof, if man thou lovest, turn thine eye
> On realms which least the cup of Misery taste;

For want how many men and Children die;
How many, at Oppression's portal placed,
Receive the scanty dole she cannot waste;
And bless, as she has taught, the hand benign.
How many, by inhuman toil debased,
Abject, obscure, and brute, to earth incline
Unrespited, forlorn of every spark divine!

And to individual suffering from injustice is now added the curse
of war, with all its train of misery:

Nor only is the walk of private life
Unblessed by Justice and the kindly train
Of Peace and Truth, while Injury and Strife
Outrage and deadly Hate usurp their reign.
From the pale line to either frozen main
The Nations, forced at home in bonds to drink
The dregs of Wretchedness, for empire strain;
And when by their own fetters crushed they sink
Move their galled limbs in fear, and eye each silent link.

In the final stanzas Wordsworth again rises to the shrill invective
of the conclusion of 'Descriptive Sketches', but he now adverts
not only to 'kingbred rage', but also to the violence of the
Revolutionary Terror:

Say, rulers of the nations, from the sword
Can aught but murder, pain, and tears proceed?
Oh, what can war but endless war still breed?
Insensate they who think, at Wisdom's porch,
That Exile, Terror, Bonds, and Force may stand;
That Truth with human blood can feed his torch,
And Justice balance with her gory hand
Scales whose dire weight of human heads demand
A Nero's arm.

Wordsworth sees more clearly now, more clearly even than in the
Letter to Llandaff, that the regeneration of man can only come
from education, from an attention to the lessons of the Godwinian philosopher:

> . . . Whence but from the labours of the sage
> Can poor benighted mortals gain the meed
> Of happiness and virtue, how assuage
> But by his gentle words their self-consuming rage?

It is not, as in 'Descriptive Sketches', to the Revolutionary armies that he now looks for victory, but to the 'Heroes of Truth':

> . . . pursue your march, uptear
> The oppressors' dungeon from its deepest base;
> High o'er the towers of Pride undaunted rear
> Resistless in your might th' Herculean mace
> Of Reason, let foul Error's monstrous race
> Dragged from their dens start at the light with pain
> And die! pursue your toils till not a trace
> Be left on earth of Superstition's reign
> Save that eternal pile which frowns on Sarum's plain.

Indeed, the author of these lines saw himself now as one of those 'Heroes of Truth', and set about making plans for his own contribution to the contest. At Whitehaven in May, he combined with Mathews, a youth 'indefatigable in his search after knowledge' as his sister-in-law described him,[1] to plan a periodical which was to give full expression to those political opinions with which, as we have seen, his 1794 poetry was concerned. A plan for joint literary activity had been proposed by Mathews as long ago as 1792, but now the proposal took more definite shape. *The Philanthropist*, as the periodical was to be called, was to be a monthly miscellany, but Wordsworth demanded a clear avowal of each other's political opinions as an essential prerequisite for the two editors: '. . . here at the very threshold', he wrote, 'I solemnly affirm that in no writings of mine will I ever admit of any sentiments which can have the least tendency to induce my readers to suppose that the doctrines which are now enforced by banishment, imprisonment, etc., are other than pregnant with every species of misery. You know perhaps already that I am of that odious class of men called democrats, and of that class I shall forever continue. In a work like that of which we are speaking,

[1] In her edition of the *Memoirs* of his brother, Charles Mathews, 1838-9.

it would be impossible (and indeed it would render our publication worthless, were we to attempt it) not to inculcate principles of government and forms of social order of one kind or another.'

Richard Wordsworth, now a struggling London lawyer, had evidently seen enough of his brother during 1793 to make him apprehensive that the young republican would voice too openly his unwelcome democratic notions. He urged William to be prudent, and was no doubt relieved to hear from Dorothy at this time that she could '. . . answer for William's caution about expressing his political opinions. He . . . seems well aware of the dangers of a contrary conduct.'

This caution was certainly not evident in his private correspondence. In June he replied to Mathews' 'explicit avowal' with this declaration: 'I disapprove of monarchical and aristocratic governments however modified. Hereditary distinctions and privileged orders of every species, I think must necessarily counteract the period of human improvement. Hence it follows that I am not amongst the admirers of the British Constitution.' This extreme democracy is an echo of the Letter to Llandaff, but he goes on in a vein that indicates a somewhat closer acquaintance with the fundamental Godwinian precept that the only desirable change can be wrought by the essentially gradual process of education: 'Now there are two causes which appear to me to be accomplishing the subversion of this constitution; first the infatuation, profligacy, and extravagance of men in power; and secondly the changes of opinions respecting matters of government, which within these few years have rapidly taken place in the minds of speculative men. The operation of the former of these causes I would spare no exertion to diminish, to the latter I would give every additional energy in my power. I conceive that a more excellent system of civil policy might be established amongst us; yet, in my ardour to attain the goal, I do not forget the nature of the ground where the race is to be run. The destruction of those institutions which I condemn appears to me to be hastening on too rapidly.' This emphasized condemnation of the rapidity of the current change—in 1794—is revealing. He recoils, certainly, 'from the bare idea of a revolution', but goes much further in deprecating the rapid subversion of institutions which, though stopping short of revolution, would, as he saw it, make that catastrophe inevitable. To avoid this ever-present danger he was prepared to modify the public expression of his opinions. He would not preach the full gospel of republicanism as he had done in the Letter to Llandaff. *The Philanthropist*, despite the extreme opinions of its editors, was to advocate merely economic retrenchment and 'bit-by-bit' reform; 'it seems to me', wrote Wordsworth, 'that a writer who has the welfare of mankind at heart should call forth his best exertions to convince the people that they can only be preserved from a convulsion by economy in the administration of the public purse, and a gradual and constant reform of those abuses which, if left to themselves, may grow to such a height as to render even a Revolution desirable'.

In practice, therefore, his aim was to be as much the averting revolution as the forwarding reform; the method was to be the orthodox Godwinian dissemination of political and moral truth, letting slip 'no opportunity of explaining and enforcing those general principles of the social order which are applicable to all times and all places; (of diffusing) by all methods a knowledge of those rules of political justice, from which the further any government deviates the more effectively must it defeat the object for which government was ordained.' Wordsworth had evidently already learned the lesson which the French Revolution was fated to teach him, and, deploring the 'miserable situation' of the French, he was now 'a determined enemy to every species of violence'. But even at this stage France could not be completely written off: '. . . we should belie our title if we did not hold up to the approbation of the world such of their regulations and decrees as are dictated by the spirit of philosophy'.

Nevertheless, it is clear that the emotional enthusiasm of Wordsworth's political convictions came now not from that 'country in romance', but from a less obvious source, from a Godwinian faith in the irresistible might and final triumph of Reason and Truth: 'Freedom of enquiry is all that I wish for; let nothing be deemed too sacred for investigation. Rather than restrain the liberty of the press I would suffer the most atrocious doctrines to be recommended: let the field be open and unencumbered, and truth must be victorious.' As we saw in the concluding stanza of the Windy Brow MS. of 'Salisbury Plain', the field of battle had now been removed from the plains of France to the mind of man.

With its editors strong in condemnation of 'all inflammatory addresses to the passions of man, even when it is intended to direct those passions to a good purpose', *The Philanthropist* was to be no popular organ of propaganda. It sought support only among 'the dispassionate advocates of liberty and discussion', and Wordsworth was convinced of success; even stylistic shortcomings would be attended to by 'an ardent wish to promote the welfare of mankind'.

This letter is a complete statement of Wordsworth's political position in 1794—or at least in May of that year. Its hopeful tone may not be unconnected with the fact that the dying Raisley Calvert, apparently to compensate him for Lonsdale's continued default,[1] had made provision for Wordsworth in his will, so that the most pressing cause of personal anxiety was now removed.

In July came the death of Robespierre, an event profoundly significant in the history of the Revolution, and of almost equivalent importance in Wordsworth's own biography. As the persecutor of the Girondins and the inspirer of the Terror, Robespierre had been the author of those 'execrable measures' to which the would-be editor of *The Philanthropist* had attributed 'the miserable situation of the French'. It was the Jacobin tyranny which had fulfilled those forebodings which had troubled Wordsworth during his last weeks in Paris, and Robespierre's rule had seemed to fulfil the most grisly prophecies of the anti-Jacobins.

For this reason the effect on Wordsworth of the news of Robespierre's fall must not be underestimated, and certainly the prominence given the event in *The Prelude* justifies our particular attention:

[1] So Wordsworth's friend Basil Montagu said, in referring to the case in the evidence he gave before the Commission on Bankruptcy and Insolvency in 1840.

> . . . few happier moments have been mine
> Than that which told the downfall of this Tribe
> So dreaded, so abhorred.
>
> (*Prel.*, X, 511.)

Immediately, the whole contest became transfigured. France was again the field of conflict for the future of the world, and again those early hopes which had been long so fatally contradicted by reality were given new impetus:

> . . . Authority in France
> Put on a milder face; Terror had ceased . . .
>
> (*Prel.*, XI, 1.)

Although he soon saw that

> . . . everything was wanting that might give
> Courage to them who looked for good by light
> Of rational Experience, for the shoots
> And hopeful blossoms of a second spring:
> Yet, in me, confidence was unimpaired;
> The Senate's language, and the public acts
> And measures of the government, though both
> Weak, and of heartless omen, had not power
> To daunt me; in the People was my trust
> And in the virtues which mine eyes had seen.
> I knew that wound external could not take
> Life from the young Republic; that new foes
> Would only follow, in the path of shame,
> Their brethren, and her triumphs be in the end
> Great, universal, irresistible.
>
> (*Prel.*, XI, 3.)

It is clear that after the fall of Robespierre Wordsworth again strove to recapture that faith in France, in practical politics, which the proscription of the Girondins, the reign of Terror, and the militarist policy of the Jacobins had taken from him; but again the facts played him false, and again he had to admit to 'unreasonable expectations'. For the faith which was revived by this event was a faith in that phase of the revolution to which that very event had decisively put an end. The rule of Robespierre, however repulsive to English Jacobins, did not entirely preclude justification; at whatever price, some progress was being made under his rule, and the success of the Revolutionary armies at the frontiers seemed to justify the rigour of Jacobin policy. The Terror did at least appear to achieve its ends, and if the Jacobins 'did not spare others, neither did they spare themselves, and compromise and corruption were as unknown to them as fear and mercy'.[1]

Wordsworth was certainly not unaware of this aspect of Jacobin tyranny. In the worst days of the Terror he was conscious of a strange and sympathetic exaltation when—

> Uplifted from the vantage-ground
> Of pity and sorrow to a state of being
> That through the time's exceeding fierceness saw
> Glimpses of retribution, terrible,
> And in the order of sublime behests.

At this elevation he could feel, and still felt ten years later,

> . . . daring sympathies with power,
> Motions not treacherous or profane, else why
> Within the folds of no ungentle breast
> Their dread vibration to this hour prolonged?[2]
>
> (*Prel.*, X, 449.)

In the rule of Robespierre's successors, even these compensations were impossible; if the poet had detected a deeper, less repulsive meaning beneath the violent expression of the Terror, he looked in vain beneath the shallow corruption of the subsequent regime. With the death of Robespierre, the idealistic period of the Revolution also passed away; the preoccupation of the rulers became plainly the retention of power, and the noble struggle against the leagued despots became the mere concomitant of a domestic policy of bankruptcy. Because of the revival of hope which had preceded it, I believe the disappointment which was produced by this realization to have been particularly violent.

[1] Cole and Postgate, *The Common People* (1938), p. 160.

[2] See also Southey's vindication, at least as quoted by Hazlitt in 'A Letter to Wm. Gifford' (1819) (*Works*, ed. Howe, 1930-4, Vol. ix): 'It was a phrase common in (Southey's) mouth, that Robespierre, by destroying the lives of thousands, saved the lives of millions.'

It is then not unworthy of attention that, in Book XI of *The Prelude*, the account of the famous mental crisis which Wordsworth said he experienced as the catastrophe of his hopes of the Revolution follows immediately after the description of the effect on him of Robespierre's death. The chronology of *The Prelude* is not of course completely reliable, but it is more than possible that the critical despondence which overtook him was directly connected with his bitter disappointment at the failure of France to complete the regeneration which the execution of Robespierre seemed to prelude. There is no evidence in the correspondence or elsewhere to support the common location of the crisis at the Racedown period, (where, indeed, the letters refer continually to a Wordsworth in the best of spirits) and if, as seems probable, the opening lines of *The Prelude* were the poet's installation ode to Racedown, we may reasonably infer that the crisis was then passed.

The perverse habit of rationalism which he describes as the immediate cause of the crisis was due, he said, to an attempt to extend Godwin's analytical method to the entire range of human belief, and we have already noted in the June letter to Mathews a much closer acquaintance with the philosophy of the author of *Political Justice* than the Letter to Llandaff displays. The Letter to Llandaff shows the original response, the immediate impact; there Wordsworth was using *Political Justice* simply as a mine of republican arguments. But *The Prelude* chronicles the whole story of Godwin's growing influence. The supporter of the French Revolution in 1793 found himself in a difficult position when every day—

> . . . events
> Brought less encouragement, and unto these
> The immediate proof of principles no more
> Could be entrusted, while the events themselves,
> Worn out in greatness, stripped of novelty,
> Less occupied the mind, and sentiments
> Could through my understanding's natural growth
> No longer keep their ground, by faith maintained
> Of inward consciousness, and hope that laid
> Her hand upon her object.

The cause now demanded positive but theoretic justification, divorced from the intractable facts of reality:

> . . . evidence
> Safer, of universal application, such
> As could not be impeached.
> (*Prel.*, XI, 194.)

It was this demand that *Political Justice* in fact supplied with a philosophy

> That promised to abstract the hopes of man
> Out of his feelings, to be fixed thenceforth
> For ever in a purer element.
> (*Prel.*, XI, 224.)

To Wordsworth and others even Godwinism, properly understood, seemed at first an optimistic philosophy:

> How glorious! in self-knowledge and self-rule
> To look through all the frailties of the world,
> And, with a resolute mastery, shaking off
> Infirmities of nature, time and place,
> Build social upon personal liberty,
> Which, to the blind restraints of general laws
> Superior, magisterially adopts
> One guide, the light of circumstances flashed
> Upon an independent intellect.
> (*Prel.*, XI, 236.)

These lines express precisely the spirit of the letters to Mathews, the concluding stanzas of 'The Female Vagrant', and two of the more significant passages added at the same time to 'An Evening Walk'.

Then came, I believe, the death of Robespierre, with the elation and then the despondency which followed it. It would seem that it was in reaction against this dashing of his 'practical' hopes that he returned to Godwinism and moved on, by stages incompletely described, to a complete rationalism which forced him to subject all opinion and belief to the test and judgment of reason. This led to mental confusion and doubt, and then to 'the

crisis of the strong disease', that despair which he describes in
The Prelude:

> . . . our blessed reason . . .
> The lordly attributes of will and choice . . .
> What are they but the mockery of a being
> Who hath in no concerns of his a test
> Of good and evil; knows not what to fear
> Or hope for, what to covet or to shun.

Complete and exclusive trust in reason had led not unnaturally
to the complete mistrust of it.

From this crisis he recovered quickly, if we interpret *The
Prelude* correctly, and he was helped in this recovery by Dorothy
and, of course, by nature. Now if we assume, as I feel we must,
that the crisis was past before Wordsworth left London later in
the year to go to Racedown, his earlier period at Windy Brow
seems to be the inevitable location for the crisis and the beginning
of the recovery: there his Godwinism and his political enthusiasm
were at their height, there he was in the country, his own country,
and with Dorothy. In the *Memoirs*, Christopher Wordsworth
described the 'crisis' simply as a consequence of Wordsworth's
political hopes, making no mention of the influence of Godwinian
rationalism. It was, he says, simply a 'vortex of doubt', in which
'the crimes of the professed partisans of liberty . . . shook his
faith in the existence of human virtue, and almost compelled
him to sit down in misanthropic sadness and sullen despair'.
If this simpler view is more accurate, and if the poet was in fact
complicating the story for effect, then the chronology I have
suggested would seem even more acceptable. The course of events
in France after the death of Robespierre constituted the catastrophe of Wordsworth's passionately renewed hopes of the
Revolution, and that death did occur while he was at Windy
Brow.

The abandonment of *The Philanthropist*, to which Wordsworth
so readily agreed in a November letter to Mathews, suggests
certainly that something important had happened to temper the
enthusiasm of five months before. In the same letter occurs the
notorious opinion that 'cataracts and mountains are good

occasional society, but they will not do for constant companions';
and this may very well be a symptom of that subversion of his
taste for natural beauty, of that preoccupation with 'meagre
novelties' which was one expression of the crisis.

There is also a sentence in the following letter to Mathews
of December, 1794, or January, 1795, that may be significant.
This letter was not posted until a fortnight after it was completed,
and in the apologetic postscript Wordsworth wrote: 'I have
lately undergone much uneasiness of mind; but I have had sufficient *time* on my hands to write a folio volume.' It is tempting
to see this considerable 'uneasiness of mind' as in fact the climax
of the crisis, the final 'Yielding up moral questions in despair'.
In any case, however slight and ambiguous this reference is, it
is the only reference in the correspondence to anything approaching the experience described in *The Prelude*.

But although *The Philanthropist* was to be abandoned, Wordsworth still hoped to contribute something to the struggle of
opinion by journalistic service—on an opposition paper, he
insists, but in explaining this preference to Mathews he displays
now an understanding and a tolerance far removed from his early
intransigence: 'I am far', he writes, 'from reprobating those
whose sentiments on this point differ from my own. I know that
many good men were persuaded of the expediency of the present
war, and I know also that many persons may think it their duty
to support the acting ministry from an idea of supporting the
government, even when they disapprove of most of the present
measures.' This unwonted readiness to see the viewpoint of the
supporters of the war not only indicates a tempering of his
political ardour, but may well be the result of that much wider
self-mistrust, that more fundamental suspicion of his political
faith which was so important an aspect of his crisis.

His reaction to the 1794 treason trials displays the same tendency carried a degree further. He naturally joins in the liberal
joy over the acquittal of Hardy and his colleagues, though he is
frankly reserved on Horne Tooke, whom he describes as 'a man
much swayed by personal considerations, one who has courted
persecution, and that rather from a wish to vex powerful individuals, than to be an instrument of public good'. But the

outcome of the trial has two implications for him: not only will it 'abate the insolence and presumption of the aristocracy', but by it 'bigoted enemies of our present constitution' will be convinced 'that it contains parts upon which too high a value cannot be set'. The acquittal was then as much a triumph for the British Constitution as for the Jacobins, and above all a justification of moderation: 'To every class of men occupied in the correction of abuses it must be an animating reflection that their exertions, so long as they are temperate, will be countenanced and protected by the good sense of the country.' The Wordsworth who wrote this letter was no longer the author of the conclusion of 'Descriptive Sketches', nor of the Letter to Llandaff.

CHAPTER IV

Racedown and Alfoxden

After Raisley Calvert's death in January, 1795, Wordsworth went to London, presumably to engage in the political journalism which he had discussed with Mathews. But we have remarked the decline in his political fervour which had taken place even before he left the North, and the experiment was not a happy one. In the opening lines of *The Prelude* it is the London of this period that he describes as 'the vast city' where he 'long had pined a discontented sojourner'. Dorothy lamented sympathetically 'the unsettled way' in which her brother lived there,[1] and the original plan made for her to join him was never put into effect. Plainly, political journalism did not turn out to be that noble crusade against error which he had envisaged, but rather a galling imprisonment in a completely antipathetic environment.

He made or renewed his acquaintance with Francis Wrangham at this time, planned a political satire with him, read him 'Salisbury Plain', and was probably introduced by him to a law student of the same political opinions, Basil Montagu.

Montagu's account, in his manuscript autobiography,[2] of Wordsworth's impact upon him is interesting. He described himself in 1795 as 'perplexed and misled by passions wild and strong' as the consequence of personal misfortunes. But Wordsworth, whose acquaintance he considered 'the most fortunate event of my life', 'unremittingly . . . endeavoured to eradicate my faults and to encourage my good dispositions'. Now, that Wordsworth was able at this time to play such a role, was able to effect in another despairing spirit a regeneration so similar to his

---

[1] Letter No. 48.   [2] *q*. de Selincourt, *Early Letters*, p. 138.

own, would seem to indicate that he had already passed the crisis
of his own despair.

This would seem to support the earlier dating of the crisis
suggested above, and the poem 'Tintern Abbey' also makes it
clear that at least before leaving London if not before arriving
there, he had been made aware of those influences which even
'in lonely rooms', and 'mid the din Of towns and cities' could
counter 'the heavy and the weary weight Of all this unintelligible
world'. These influences were, of course, his memories of nature,
his memories of a peculiar experience of nature whose significance
had now been made clear to him. If they had been revived at
Windy Brow, misery in London only served to make their
significance more vivid. Dramatically, it would seem, he decided
to return to the country, to the nature that had been the context
of the only period of peace and joy he had known in his life. He
obtained a house, arranged for Dorothy to join him, and the
enthusiast who had a few months before spoken so cavalierly of
cataracts and mountains now celebrated the removal which
Calvert's legacy made possible with the exultation of the opening
lines of *The Prelude*.[1]

The withdrawal from London, as we can see in *The Prelude*,
appeared tremendously significant to Wordsworth, for he saw it
as a physical expression of his abandonment of the life, activities
and interests of the preceding three years, the shaking off of—

> That burthen of my own unnatural self,
> The heavy weight of many a weary day
> Not mine, and such as were not made for me.
> (*Prel.*, I, 20.)

He was rejecting these years and the mental culture which
typified them. He saw that ultimately his crisis, his despair, was
the result of an attitude of mind, the result of allowing political
opinions and aspirations to

[1] There has been some debate as to whether these lines refer to the departure
from London in 1795 or to that from Goslar in 1799. The similarity of the
expressions in 'Tintern Abbey' (which plainly refer to the poet's stay in London
in 1795) to those in Book One of *The Prelude* help to place the matter beyond
doubt.

> Grow into consequence, till round my mind
> They clung, as if they were its life, nay more,
> The very being of the immortal soul.
>   (*Prel.*, XI, 220.)

Despair had been the consequence of his political life, of his becoming too closely involved in the struggle of political ideas. With this life he had been able at Windy Brow to compare another, which he had indeed known before the period of his political preoccupation. When he fled with exultation to Racedown I fancy that he knew only that he had experienced nothing but misery or the prospect of misery since he had left school at Hawkshead, since he had left the world of nature for the world of men. He decided to go back. It was almost an intuitive reaction, later to be explained and justified in terms of a 'philosophy' tailored to fit the facts.

At Racedown his only real task was the education of Montagu's son, and it seems to have left him with considerable time for composition. When in London he had planned with Wrangham an imitation of the democratic eighth satire of Juvenal, and continuing the poem at Racedown until as late as 1797, he made it the vehicle for his most outspoken condemnation of aristocratic and courtly corruption. But it was to some extent a labour of friendship, and it is significant that he never published it.

The lines 'At the Isle of Wight, 1793' also date from this period, and prove that the retirement to Racedown did not entail a modification of his attitude to the Revolutionary War. Following the line adopted by the *Morning Chronicle* and by liberal opinion generally, Wordsworth was still convinced that the war forced on France by the jealous monarchs had been the main cause of the subversion of the Revolution, and that peace could still be had for the asking. This was a conviction that he never abandoned.

Similarly, the final lines of the fragment 'Incipient Madness' hark back to an earlier period, echoing the vagrant episode in 'An Evening Walk', and the plot of 'Salisbury Plain'. Wordsworth was still troubled by the sufferings of the poor, the injustice of the war, and the degradation of the aristocracy.

In this spirit he turned again to 'Salisbury Plain', and by the introduction of the account of the injustice suffered by the sailor, the social force of the poem was considerably strengthened. This new extension characterizes the sailor as the naturally benevolent man of the Jacobin novelists driven to crime by an unjust state of society and finally murdered by that society in the name of something it calls justice. The emendations made in the second MS. are in almost every case more accusatory than the version of 1793-4. The incident of the 'ruffian pressgang', the sailor's pleadings before 'the slaves of office', these are typical of the spirit in which the poem was revised and extended. The world formerly symbolized by the dreary waste of Salisbury Plain is now a jungle, where 'Each prowls to strip his brother of his fleece', and where death is the only relief. 'Why should you grieve,' asks the vagrant; 'a little while And we shall meet in heaven.' But significantly the moral is not political. Man can find felicity in domestic peace and indeed it is to point this lesson that the poet introduces, with such apparently gratuitous abruptness, that sordid episode of the family quarrel; for peace is made with this advice:

> Much need have ye that time more closely draw
> The bond of nature, all unkindness cease,
> And that among so few there still be peace:
> Else can ye hope but with such numerous foes
> Your pains shall ever with your years increase?

So while the tone of most of the emendations to 'Salisbury Plain' indicates the bitterness of Wordsworth's attitude to the world he was rejecting, the important thing was that he was now beginning to look elsewhere than to political action for the solution to the problem of human happiness.

His play 'The Borderers'[1] which dates from the same period, is indicative of the same change. It owes a great deal in the first place to Schiller's 'Die Räuber', for it is one of the many examples of the current taste for 'German' melodrama. But it is also a document in Wordsworth's biography.

Hitherto it has been universally interpreted simply as a statement of Wordsworth's rejection of Godwinian rationalism.

[1] See O. J. Campbell and P. Mueschke, 'The Borderers', *Modern Philology*, May, 1926.

However, especially if the Prefatory Essay is given the attention it obviously calls for, the significance of other neglected aspects is made plain. It is worth pointing out to begin with that Wordsworth is not here concerned fundamentally with political or social questions; the play is carefully set in a region and a time which leave the actors free from all social influences and restraints. They are free agents who are at liberty to do good or evil: the significant fact is that, given such freedom, they do commit evil.

Oswald, the villain who persuades Marmaduke to murder, is no Godwinian; he is no more a rationalist than Iago, and he belongs in fact to the Machiavellian category of villains if to any. His significance as a character is that he is an evil man bent on the propagation of evil. His aim is not to preach truth, to conquer prejudice by the might of reason, nor to reform society, but to seduce Marmaduke into sin. To achieve this end he will use any weapon, but the one especially suitable in the case of a robber chief who has renounced the irrational and traditional institutions of an artificial society is a specious appeal to the independent judgment, an exaltation of reason over sentiment.

The tragedy of the play, and its significance in a study of the author's development lie in the obvious power of the evil man, in the ease with which he can ensnare the virtuous. The point was not, as Marmaduke lamented, that the world was poisoned at the heart;[1] his own character, that of Eldred the peasant, Herbert and Idonea are all innately virtuous. But in a society of such virtue, one evil man can still work tremendous destruction, can turn benevolent altruists into murderers.[2] And this lesson Wordsworth had learned not from the pages of *Political Justice*,

---

[1] Although this conviction of the supreme necessity of an 'internal', a spiritual and moral regeneration starting in the heart of the individual was significantly to strengthen in Wordsworth. It is of course orthodox Godwinism, and typical of Shelley's mature position.

[2] See Arnold, 'Empedocles on Etna', I, ii, 262-6.

> And, lastly, though of ours
> No weakness spoil our lot,
> Though the non-human powers
> Of Nature harm us not,
> The ill deeds of other men make often *our* life dark.

but from the history of the French Revolution.[1] Had Marmaduke been the perfect Godwinian, had he insisted on the irrefragable proof that could never have been given him, the crime would never have been committed; even if he had remembered Godwin's strictures on violence and retribution of all kinds, and particularly his mistrust of all man's judgments on man, of all punishment, then he would have been preserved.

'The Borderers' therefore is not an indictment of the reason per se; as its author pointed out in the Prefatory Essay,[2] he was concerned with 'the dangerous use which may be made of reason *when a man has committed a great crime*'. He saw in the abuse of reason by the wicked one of the means by which the virtuous might be subverted, one of the means by which man might be prevented from reacting to his natural and intuitive promptings to virtue. Marmaduke is completely taken in not so much by rationalism as by '. . . a few swelling phrases, and a flash of truth, enough to dazzle and to blind', and is led by them to murder and crime as so many had been led between 1789 and 1794.[3]

The fact that Wordsworth was drawing on his experience of the French Revolution in this portrayal of the power of evil gives the play its political point. The history of France was proving that the progress of truth, man's advance towards perfection, could be and was being thwarted by an active power[4] that had been largely ignored. In the vaunted reason this power of evil could possess a lethal weapon, but the significant discovery embodied in the play is the poet's realization that the real source of evil was in the

[1] See the references to the influence of his memories of the French Revolution in the 1842 and Fenwick notes to the poem.

[2] See de Selincourt, 'The Preface to Wordsworth's Borderers', (*The Nineteenth Century*, November, 1926).

[3] Thus Hazlitt on Godwin, in *The Spirit of the Age*: ' . . . with the unlimited scope of private opinion, and with a boundless field of speculation . . . there was danger that the *unseasoned novice* might substitute some pragmatical conceit of his own for the rule of right reason, and *mistake* a heartless indifference for a superiority to more natural and generous feelings'. (My italics.)

[4] It is not extravagant to point out that this conviction of an active power of evil at work in the world, this conviction of a rampant devil, of sin, was the beginning of Wordsworth's return to orthodox Christianity. The novels of Mr Graham Greene might appropriately be invoked as exemplifying the relevance of such a conviction to such a (re-) conversion.

individual, not in the society; the consequence of this discovery was a growing concern rather with the regeneration of the individual than with that of the society. The over-simplified picture of the political reformer, of the revolutionary, gave way to the complex awareness of the poet. An awareness which had been forced upon him, and which was in the end fatal, as such an awareness must always be, to the simple faith of his youthful enthusiasm, fatal to the revolutionary spirit and in the end fatal or nearly so to the reforming spirit in politics. What the tortured preface of 'The Borderers' is really trying to convey, is merely the poet's new found conviction of the unsuspected complexity of the human scene, of the possibility of the best intentions being perverted, of man's essential fallibility.

'The Borderers' is then significant as displaying, in its concern with the obscurities of motive and character as well, the first stirrings of that awareness of complexity which was to become so typical of Wordsworth's mature political position. He no longer saw the problem of human happiness in simple terms, political or social; he is not here concerned with man's sufferings from injustice, inequality or privilege. The question is now a much deeper one, and the working of the evil mind is one of its inescapable aspects.

The Preface and the poem are the work of a chastened poet, whose early vision has clouded. From this disillusionment he rose to find a surer basis for hope, for life and work.

. . . . .

It was in 'The Ruined Cottage'[1] that Wordsworth gave full expression to that state of mind, to that new attitude to human suffering which it was peculiarly the work of the Racedown period to develop. The story is significantly parallel to that of the 'Female Vagrant': the sorrows of Margaret, like those of the vagrant, are caused by economic distress—'a time Laden, for them and all of their degree, With care and sorrow'—which drives her husband to war. But there is no political indictment here, no suggestion that Margaret is at issue with society. The tale is told, not as an example of social injustice, but purely as a

[1] Later incorporated in Book I of *The Excursion*.

sympathetic study of human suffering, and for a purpose not
political but moral:

> We have known that there is often found,
> In mournful thoughts, and always might be found,
> A power to virtue friendly.

The aim is to provoke not indignation, but pity and benevolence: to stir up not a hatred of injustice, but an admiration
for the strength of human affection. The scope of the story is
never widened beyond that of personality, for the theme is that
elemental suffering common to all men and to all societies. War
comes to Margaret's household not as a political or social imposition, but, like the bad harvests, as another plague which 'it
pleased Heaven to add' to the afflictions of humanity. And its
sufferings were not confined to her class, for 'many rich Sank
down, as in a dream' at the same time.

The artistic merit of this poem is a proof of the profound
effect upon Wordsworth of the renovation wrought in his spirit
and in his mental habits by the Racedown retirement. He had
abandoned his passionate enthusiasm for political reform, and
with it his preoccupation with those tales of distress which were
propaganda in the cause; he told now 'a common tale, An ordinary sorrow of man's life, A tale of silent suffering' which betrayed
only a preoccupation with humanity for its own precious sake,
an enthusiasm for the virtue and fortitude of man, not for his
rights. That he was enabled thus early to move from the im-
mature conventionalism of 'The Female Vagrant' to the full
power and clarity of his own vision and inspiration is proof to us
of the reformation effected at Racedown, as it must have been, to
him, proof of the efficacy and validity both of the rejections and
the acceptances which this reformation had involved.

It is plain from this poem that before the Alfoxden period
and before the close association with Coleridge, Wordsworth
had already freed himself from the 'morbid passions' inherent in
his previous attitude to man and society; he had, in practice,
divorced his humanitarianism, his faith in and affection for the
unfranchised, from that direct indictment of society which had
been, until then, its concomitant. Which is to say that the

political propagandist had become the mature and distinctive poet. The intuitive joy with which he had greeted his return to nature had now been buttressed by a reasoned justification of his action and an explanation of the power which he felt nature had over him. This 'philosophy' he soon began to set forth, probably for his own satisfaction in the first place, if later for Coleridge's, in *The Prelude*.

There he explains how, having abandoned the world of men because his concern with it had brought him only despair, he returned to nature to find again the joy and peace which it had given him in his childhood. But he found in Racedown that his own experience of a communion with the benevolent spirit of nature, though perhaps unusually powerful and unusually self-conscious, was not unique. It seemed to him that people who lived close to nature shared in its harmony and peace, and bene-fited from its moral influence. For when he inspected 'the basis of the social pile' and moved among the rural poor, he heard

> . . . truths
> Replete with honour; sounds in unison
> With loftiest promises of good and fair.
> (*Prel.*, XIII, 183.)

In the fruits of this enquiry he found the solution to the mis-anthropic aspect of his crisis of doubt,

> Hope to my hope, and to my pleasure peace
> And steadiness, and healing and repose
> To every angry passion.
> (*Prel.*, XIII, 180.)

He found, not political animosity nor social hatred, but a depth of peace and joy in perfect sympathy with the central theme of universal nature.

The circumstances of this discovery were responsible for that unity of purpose which typifies his mature verse. Despairing of man's political and social progress he had turned to the un-deniable lesson of joy which natural processes and natural beauty proclaimed; but he had found that such a transference need imply no misanthropy, no real abandonment of man, for when freely reacting to his natural environment, man could also be an object of faith and hope; viewed against his proper background, he was an essential part, a supreme embodiment, of the benevolent spirit of universal nature. He became convinced that any poet who saw life whole and saw it clearly must sing of peace and joy, not of conflict and resentment.

His conviction of the validity of this cosmic optimism led him away from his early poetry and away from the political discontent which was its basis. For

> What we feel of sorrow and despair
> From ruin and from change, and all the grief
> That passing shows of being leave behind

came to seem but

> an idle dream, that could maintain
> Nowhere, dominion o'er the enlightened Spirit.
>   (*Exc.*, I, 949.)

He determined to close 'the restless oblique eye, That looks for evil like a treacherous spy', for poetry must be essentially 'a joy, a consolation, and a hope'[1] and its aim must be 'To exhilarate the spirit and to soothe The heart of human-kind';[2] it was not to provoke disaffection and accusation, but to indicate to man the true sources of his substantial happiness.

Wordsworth's own discovery of these sources acted directly on the root of his crisis of despair, for it indicated that man need not be at the mercy of the Oswalds, the Robespierres (or even the Pitts?) of the world. For there was available to all a source of virtue and strength and happiness, a source of joy divorced entirely from man's social and political existence. Hence, the discovery that the voteless were wise and virtuous did not revive demands for the franchise nor attacks on privilege. What it did mean was the end of that

> . . . confusion of the judgment, zeal decayed,
> And utter loss of hope itself.[3]

His association with Coleridge brought him confirmation of his tentative philosophical conclusions. To Coleridge he owed

---

[1] *Prelude*, 1805, V, 109.   [2] *Prelude*, MSS. A4 and C, V, 108.
[3] *Prelude*, Opening of Book XII.

his introduction to the little known philosopher Hartley, who, in his *Observations on Man* (1749), had proclaimed the doctrine of optimism with logical certainty, insisting that pleasure predominated over pain in any general view of the universe, that happiness must inevitably outweigh suffering. Coleridge himself had long been convinced that—

> 'Tis the sublime of man,
> Our noontide majesty, to know ourselves
> Parts and proportions of one wondrous whole.
> This fraternises man, this constitutes
> Our charities and bearings.
>   ('Religious Musings', 1794.)

And like Wordsworth at Racedown, he had in Pantisocracy early turned, though more symbolically than practically, from man's social and political aspirations to a more individual and personal sphere for reforming ambition; looking back on the scheme in 1818[1] he explained it in these terms: 'What I dared not expect from Constitutions of Government and whole nations, I hoped from religion and a small company of chosen individuals.'

It was in Coleridge's enthusiasm, in his unshaken and fervent optimism, and in his intellectual and philosophical superiority that Wordsworth found the buttresses which he needed; needed more than ever as his political hopes were more and more confounded. In 1797 England's position vis-à-vis France had changed dramatically and significantly. By the defection of her continental allies, she was no longer the head and purse of a despotic league against the French Republic, but a deserted and embattled nation at the mercy of a great and unscrupulous military power. In the face of imminent invasion from France, the English Jacobins were obliged to reconsider their cosmopolitan disregard for national loyalty; with England itself threatened by the ravages of war, domestic disagreements among Englishmen began to appear pathetically academic. In 'Fears in Solitude', Coleridge at least was not slow to proclaim his reaction to the new position.

Then when nothing stood between England and defeat but her navy, the sailors' revolts gave the position an ominous

[1] *The Friend*, Section I, Essay VI.

complexion. The revolt at Spithead was the result only of specific
grievances and ill-treatment, but the blockading of London by a
'Floating Republic' at the mouth of the Thames at such a mili-
tarily critical moment was enough to bring any Jacobin to his
senses.

It is not surprising then that in the early days of their association Coleridge found Wordsworth ready to converse on almost
any topic but the painful one of politics. Such evasion was
typical of other disappointed patriots, and does not of course
imply any abandonment of liberal opinions. Like Coleridge in
'France' and 'Recantation', Wordsworth had still no doubt of
British guilt: if France had betrayed his hopes, she had been
driven to betrayal by 'pride's perverted ire' and 'King-bred rage'.
If we can believe Hazlitt, the poet had not forgotten Pitt's share
in this guilt, nor that of the British Government[1], although
bitterness of feeling became less and less a part of his political
sympathies. As Coleridge wrote of him to his friend Estlin in
1798: 'It is his practice and almost his nature to convey all the
truth he knows without any attack on what he supposes falsehood, if that falsehood be interwoven with virtues and happiness';
and in thus modifying the temper and the nature of his political
enthusiasm, Wordsworth was consciously bringing it into line
with his peculiar experience of nature. Because his return to an
affection for and fervent interest in nature had been so vital a part
of the restoration of his own spiritual balance, he was inevitably
anxious to extend the application of her lessons to every sphere of
his interests. He had turned to nature for consolation, as the
supreme embodiment of joy, of peace, and of permanence. In a
period of social and personal turmoil, bitterness and change, he
found in the natural scene a balancing vision of repose; a 'counterpoise' of 'secret happiness' outweighing the 'distracted times'.[2]

---

[1] Hazlitt, in 'A Reply to "Z"', quotes Wordsworth's comment on the Pitt-
Tierney duel (27 May, '98): '. . . That he wished Tierney had shot out Mr
Pitt's tongue, to put an end to his gift of the gab. . . .' At this time, he said,
Wordsworth desired to make 'an example of the whole House of Commons for
being the echoes of the King's speeches for carrying on the war against the
French Revolution' (*Illustrations of the Times Newspaper*: On Modern Apostates).

[2] *Prelude*, XII, 40-3.

Subsequently, nature was always for him a consoling, a modifying, a restraining force, and on the basis of these ideals he remodelled his political attitude.

It is difficult to overestimate the reality of this process for Wordsworth, the literalness with which he carried it out, the force of his conviction that nature afforded instruction not only to the eye and ear, but that, in his own experience, it spoke in even more commanding tones, to 'social reason's inner sense'; for him it was logically inevitable that

> the Man
> Who . . . communes with the Forms
> Of nature, who with understanding heart
> Both knows and loves such objects as excite
> No morbid passions, no disquietude,
> No vengeance, and no hatred—needs must feel
> The joy of that pure principle of love
> So deeply, that, unsatisfied with aught
> Less pure and exquisite, he cannot choose
> But seek for objects of a kindred love
> In fellow-natures, and a kindred joy.
> Accordingly he by degrees perceives
> His feelings of aversion softened down;
> A holy tenderness pervades his frame.
> . . . he looks round
> And seeks for good; and finds the good he seeks:
> Until abhorrence and contempt are things
> He only knows by name; and, if he hear,
> From other mouths, the language which they speak,
> He is compassionate, and has no thought,
> No feeling, which can overcome his love.[1]

This toning down of aversion, which was one of the most significant political aspects of the new moderation, was not an easy nor a sudden transition for the author of 'The Female Vagrant', for the poet who, at the end of 1797, was still engaged on a topical imitation of Juvenal; but it was assisted by his environment and his associates. Coleridge admitted in the Argument

[1] These lines, later incorporated in *The Excursion*, IV, 1207, were written in 1797 or 1798; Coleridge quoted from them in a letter to his brother George in April, 1798.

G

to 'France: An Ode', that 'those feelings and that grand ideal of freedom which the mind attains by its contemplation of its individual nature, and of the sublime surrounding objects . . . do not belong to men, as a society . . . but belong to the individual man, so far as he is pure, and inflamed with adoration of God in Nature'. Even the reformer Thelwall who visited the poets at Nether Stowey had announced his withdrawl from '. . . the vain effort to redeem a race Enslaved because degenerate'.[1] Whatever the suspicions of the authorities,[2] the circle at Stowey devoted itself, as Coleridge wrote to his brother, 'to such works as encroach not on the anti-social passions—in poetry, to elevate the imagination and set the affections in right tune by the beauty of the inanimate impregnated as with a living soul by the presence of life'. A concern for the superficialities of day to day politics was plainly alien to a reverence for—

> . . . A power
> That is the visible quality and shape
> And image of right reason; that matures
> Her processes by steadfast laws; gives birth
> To no impatient or fallacious hopes,
> No heat of passion or excessive zeal . . .
> . . . but trains
> To meekness, and exalts by humble faith;
> Holds up before the mind intoxicate
> With present objects, and the busy dance
> Of things that pass away, a temperate show
> Of objects that endure; and by this course
> Disposes her, when over-fondly set
> On throwing off incumbrances, to seek
> In man, and in the frame of social life,
> Whate'er there is desirable and good
> Of kindred permanence.
>
> (*Prel.*, XIII, 20.)

---

[1] 'Lines written at Bridgewater . . . on the 27th July, 1797', in *Poems Chiefly written in Retirement* (1801). In the same poem Thelwall refers to Wordsworth, significantly, as 'Alfoxden's *musing* tenant'. (My italics.)

[2] A spy was, of course, despatched to Stowey by the Home Office, but after some misgivings about Wordsworth and 'the woman he calls his sister', the group was apparently cleared of a suspicion of espionage. See Appendix B.

In such an attitude there is no taint of misanthropy; the Nature to which Wordsworth had turned in despair of man had led him back to renewed faith in and affection for man the part of that nature, man the partaker of that universal spirit of bene-volence and virtue. Despite the obtuseness of the critics, nature *had* taught Wordsworth more of man than all the sages; and it was in this new humanitarianism that he found the inspiration of his greatest poetry. He now looked no more to the jarring and the disconsolate for the source of his personal faith or his poetic inspira-tion—not to the Oswalds and the vagrants, not to the disfranchised and the oppressed as such, but to humble man as he knew him against his natural background. Inevitably then, he came to mistrust those who continued to concern themselves with man in that warp-ing context which he had rejected; he was now and for ever after

> ... prepared to find
> Presumption, folly, madness, in the men
> Who thrust themselves upon the passive world
> As Rulers of the world; to see in these,
> Even when the public welfare is their aim,
> Plans without thought, or built on theories
> Vague and unsound ...
>
> (*Prel.*, XIII, 65.)

Wordsworth's poems in the *Lyrical Ballads* of 1798 express this new found faith in man, this new affection for his virtue and courage. How different it was from his earlier, pre-Racedown enthusiasm we can see by comparing the rest of his contributions with the two poems which deal with human suffering in its 'social' aspect, with what 'man has made of man', both of which belong to that earlier period. Unwilling to publish 'The Female Vagrant' in its entirety because of the morbid conclusion which it still retained,[1] he did accede to Coleridge's request to publish a truncated version; significantly, the 'wilful wrong' suffered by the vagrant's father was modified to 'cruel injuries', and the incident of his dispossession was generally toned down in accord-ance with the author's aversion to the stimulation of 'morbid passions'. The sailor's story, with its more direct indictment of injustice, is of course omitted.

[1] See Fenwick Note to 'Guilt and Sorrow'.

'The Convict' is something of a companion piece to Coleridge's 'Dungeon', and it too was the product of the earlier Godwinian discipleship.

Apart from these poems, the tales of suffering in the *Lyrical Ballads* are essentially of the same kind as 'The Ruined Cottage'. 'The Last of the Flock', 'We are Seven', 'The Mad Mother', 'The Complaint'—these are told to demonstrate the power of affection among the lower classes, not to lament their oppression. The 'Old Man Travelling'[1] is indeed journeying to his son 'Who from a sea fight has been brought to Falmouth, And there is dying in an hospital', and these lines were later perhaps significantly removed; yet even here the bereavement, however topical, is only used to emphasize the resignation, the composure of the bereaved: he is—

> . . . one to whom
> Long patience hath such mild composure given,
> That patience now doth seem a thing of which
> He hath no need. He is by nature led
> To peace so perfect that the young behold
> With envy, what the Old Man hardly feels.

In no poem is the poet's new attitude even to *social* injustice more prominent than in the direct morality of 'Goody Blake and Harry Gill', where a tale, which earlier would have been used to far more pointed effect, is told instead in a tone objective and dispassionate, and is rather Wordsworth's answer to 'The Ancient Mariner' than a companion piece to 'The Female Vagrant'.

Even the tales of suffering and sorrow were not typical of the vein Wordsworth was to develop, and they owe more to his personal misfortunes than to his new inspiration. It is in the 'Lines written in Early Spring', 'Expostulation and Reply', and 'The Tables Turned', the 'Lines written at a small Distance', and 'Tintern Abbey', that he proclaims the new 'philosophy'; it is in them that he gives full expression to the cult of joy that was to become the fundamental inspiration of the man and the poet. As he said in the Advertisement, his purpose was simply the 'natural delineation of human passions, human characters, and

[1] Later called 'Animal Tranquillity and Decay'.

human incidents'. His poems were meant to declare his faith in humanity, more especially in the virtues and wisdom of the poor and humble, in the unsophisticated strength of their affections; he was giving poetic expression to his discovery of the 'depth of human souls', in 'souls that appear to have no depth at all To careless eyes' (*Prel.*, XIII, 166). He was consciously warring against those who attend merely to—

> Extrinsic differences, the outward marks
> Whereby society has parted man
> From man,[1]

against the exclusive and aristocratic taste of his age, against the 'judgments of the wealthy few, who see By artificial lights' (*Prel.*, XIII, 209). He had therefore no illusions concerning the reaction of those who insisted that poetry was the preserve of the learned, who could not admit

> How little those formalities, to which
> With overweening trust alone we give
> The name of Education, have to do
> With real feeling and just sense.
>   (*Prel.*, XIII, 169.)

His theory of poetic diction, his claim that the language of the 'middle and lower classes of society' should be the model for the poet, was both the least important and the least original part of his ideas on poetry. One suspects that it was indeed more closely related to his political opinions, if only in so far as it was an act of defiance against literary tradition, persisted in somewhat wilfully. It plainly had little influence on the composition of the *Lyrical Ballads* themselves, and hardly any at all on his other poems.

It was perhaps Rousseau who gave him the idea, or at least the germ of it, in a passage in *The Confessions*, which announced that: 'Parmi le peuple, ou les grandes passions ne parlent que par intervalles, les sentiments de la nature se font plus souvent entendre. Dans les états plus élevés ils sont étouffés absolument, et, sous le masque du sentiment, il n'y a que l'intérêt ou la vanité qui parle.'[2]

Condorcet too had pointed out, with all the undocumented confidence of his age, that in the 'pastoral' stage of social development,

---

[1] *Prelude*, XIII, 218.   [2] *Confessions* (Flammarion ed., n.d.), Vol. I, p. 149.

the Golden Age of the poet, 'languages were enriched without becoming less figurative or less bold. The images employed were more varied and more pleasing. They were acquired in pastoral life, as well as in the savage life of the forests, from the regular phenomena of nature, as well as from its wildness and eccentricities.'[1]

D'Holbach, and even Godwin in his *Enquirer*, had shown an interest in the question. Godwin was convinced by 1797 that 'the cause of political reform and the cause of intellectual and literary refinement, are inseparably connected'; yet he did not follow the 'party line' on the question of style and diction. In fact he opposed those literary liberals who were proclaiming, before the advent of the *Lyrical Ballads*, that 'the mode of writing which is now practised . . is dazzling and gaudy, not of intrinsic value. Our language is infected with a motley train of foreign phraseology. We hunt after unreal beauties. The dignified simplicity which characterized the language of our forefathers is no more.' Godwin could not accept these strictures, but he was in a minority among his political comperes. The usual liberal conviction, which Wordsworth shared and carried to far more extreme conclusions, was that the rural poor, the most unspoilt class in society, were the preservers of true linguistic as of other virtues.

On this question of diction at least, I feel we can accept Christopher Wordsworth's explanation in the *Memoirs* that 'the clue to (the) *poetical* theory, in some of its questionable details, may be found in his *political* principles; these had been democratical, and still, though in some degree modified, they were of a republican character. At this period he entertained little reverence for ancient institutions as such; and he felt little sympathy with the higher classes of society. He was deeply impressed with a sense of the true dignity of the lower orders, and their sufferings; and his design was to endeavour to recover for them the rights of the human family, and the franchise of universal brotherhood, of which . . . they had been robbed by the wealthy, the noble and the few.' It is certainly more flattering to Wordsworth to assume that his theory of diction was the product of his political and social beliefs rather than of his critical judgment.

[1] *Outline of an Historical View of the Progress of the Human Mind* (pub. Johnson, 1795), p. 35.

CHAPTER V

To Grasmere

The Wordsworth's had moved from Racedown in 1797 to Alfoxden, in North Somerset, mainly to be near Coleridge at Nether Stowey. They were anxious to stay longer, but in midsummer 1798 their landlord refused them an extension of tenancy, apparently because of their political reputation. Their friend Poole, a local squire of considerable property and advanced opinions, interceded for them, but without success.

Coleridge suggested that, instead of separating, they should all spend two years in Germany, 'in order', as William wrote to Losh, 'to acquire the German language, and to furnish ourselves with a tolerable stock of information in natural science'.[1] We have met this passion for foreign languages before, but it is possible that Germany offered other attractions besides the educational.

The affection of the English Jacobins for the fatherland of Schiller and Kotzebue was notorious, and after the decline of France's popularity the 'revolutionary' literature of the German school[2] had been readily acclaimed by the liberals, expecially as the literary record of revolutionary France had proved so dismal. It was against the Jacobinism and infidelity of German universities and against the Jacobin literature of Germany that the loyal English periodicals fulminated, for they were aware of the political implications of the *Sturm und Drang*. After 1793 many Jacobins looked to Germany for the replanting 'in hardier soil', as Southey called it, of that tree of liberty to which the French had proved so false.

---

[1] Letter No. 75.

[2] Wordsworth later admitted the influence German literature had on him, which indeed 'The Borderers' proves; see also the 1842 note to 'Thoughts suggested the Day Following', the sequel to 'At the Grave of Burns'.

Although Wordsworth later denied knowledge of the spy's visit to Stowey,[1] that event had at least made Coleridge aware of the 'spirit of secret defamation' which typified the England of the Revolutionary period. In any case, the suspicious attitude of his landlords, the St Aubyns, must have seemed to Wordsworth something like persecution, and a period of exile might well have appealed to him as one way of avoiding a repetition of it.

There are then a number of reasons for thinking that there were again other factors at work more significant than a mere desire for a change of scene, and even that Wordsworth might have gone to Germany in something like the same despairing spirit that drove the reformer Holcroft there a year later.[2] He was still of course a defender, if a chastened one, of the French Revolution, still an opponent of the War; and it is necessary to correct the accepted idea that the Directory's invasion of Switzerland in 1798 had an effect on his sympathies comparable to that which it had on the Coleridge of 'France: an Ode'. It is plain from Wordsworth's letter to Losh of December 1821 that it was Napoleon's 1802 invasion, and not the earlier one, that finally disillusioned him.

The Anti-Jacobin Review and Magazine was certainly in no doubt of his motives for the German visit. Although it had published a most suspiciously favourable review of the *Lyrical Ballads* in Vol. V,[3] it included in the appendix to Vol. VI a letter from 'An Honest Briton' dated from 'Upper Saxony, 28th April, 1800'. This correspondent opens with an illuminating reference to the popularity of the German universities among the disaffected. 'Nothing of late years', he writes, 'has been more frequently the object of abuse among the English Jacobins than the English universities. We have been repeatedly told that they are sinks of vice, of ignorance and prejudice. And it has been more than insinuated that learning and virtue are only to be acquired

[1] See Appendix B.

[2] See his *Memoirs*, ed. Hazlitt (Howe ed. of *The Works of Hazlitt*, Vol. III).

[3] P. 334 (April, 1800): the reviewer singled out for praise 'The Ancient Mariner', 'Foster Mother's Tale', 'Simon Lee', 'Idiot Boy' and 'Goody Blake', applauded the volume for its 'genius, taste, elegance, wit', and was convinced that 'the author possesses a mind at once classic and accomplished'; I do not think that he had read the book.

in Dissenting Academies or German Universities.' He then goes on to a paragraph which deserves to be quoted in full:

'I heard lately . . . from a friend, of two gentlemen, formerly well-known at Cambridge, who, feeling the restraints of law and religion somewhat irksome, left the university and became philosophers. It seems these worthy men finding the Church of England totally unfit for them agreed with four others to go to America and put their philosophy in practice. It was agreed that each of the six should engage a woman to accompany them and that these women should be common to the whole. . . . Two of these gentlemen who, it seems, were the projectors of this admirable colony for America, and who are writers in the *Morning Chronicle*, and other publications of Jacobinical notoriety, came afterwards to Germany, to enable themselves, by acquiring the language and philosophy of this favoured country, to enlighten more completely the ignorant people of England.'

The garbled reference to Pantisocracy is enough to identify the 'two gentlemen' as Wordsworth and Coleridge.

Before leaving England, Wordsworth made enquiries, through Losh, from Tweddel (both of whom have been mentioned above in connection with the political tone of Wordsworth's undergraduate days) concerning conditions in Germany. He even suggested that Losh and his wife join the party. The publisher Johnson again figures in the scheme; Wordsworth had not severed his connection there, had apparently introduced Coleridge to him, and requested his nervous Bristol publisher Cottle to transfer to Johnson his right to the *Lyrical Ballads* 'on account of its being likely to be very advantageous to me'. From Johnson the travellers now received an order on Remnant, his Hamburg representative.

When they arrived at Hamburg, they hastened to make the acquaintance of Klopstock,[1] whose famous Odes had been the most considerable tribute paid to the Revolution in Europe. The aged author of the 'Messiah' had travelled far from the fervour of 'Les Etats-Généraux', but he still retained his firm liberal sympathies. He too had undergone a crisis of misanthropic doubt, described in 'Der Sieger', and, like Wordsworth, he had been forced to

[1] Also visited by Holcroft. See Hazlitt, *ed. cit.*, III, 229.

abandon his early political enthusiasm in favour of the settled calm of a less passionate humanitarianism.

The man Klopstock was something of an anti-climax to Wordsworth: Germany itself was a tremendous disappointment. Immediately after his arrival he bewailed to Poole: 'Money, money is here the God of universal worship, and rapacity and extortion among the lower classes, and the classes immediately above them. . . .' Dorothy's Journal is an unbroken account of cheating landlords and tradesmen, bad manners, personal discomfort, revolting food, disgusting habits, poor roads, unpleasant conditions and vexing experiences of every kind. Instead of the twelve months that Wordsworth and Dorothy planned to spend at Goslar preparatory to William's taking a university course they were decided after one month to return to England, and only the worst winter of the century delayed them. Like his 1795 scheme in London, the German venture was to Wordsworth a supreme disillusionment; but again it was at least not without its lesson.

In London he had learnt that he was not meant for an active political career, even on the journalistic fringe of politics, and that he must seek his future in other activities and in other interests. In Germany he discovered that he was no cosmopolite: it was there that he recovered that patriotic feeling (now strengthened and expanded by the nostalgia of the exile) which had been taken from him and from most of the Jacobins by England's role in the anti-French coalition.

That temporary exile, however willingly planned, should in the event have stimulated a patriotic reaction is such a normal process that explanation is unnecessary; Southey and even Shelley, at times when they were both true citizens of the world, testified to its reality. In France in 1791 Wordsworth had not been immune from this influence, and now he had been prepared for a more powerful reaction by the change in England's international position which had taken place even before his departure. Her desertion by her allies, her momentary paralysis by naval mutiny, and the transformation of her enemy effected by the coup of Fructidor, these events must have had something of the influence on Wordsworth that they had on the author of 'Fears in Solitude'.

Coleridge, who four years earlier had proclaimed that 'in reality the government of Turkey is more free in its forms than the British' now admitted that a brief residence among the 'unlovely race' of Germany made him a loyalist, 'almost a Pittite'. If he experienced this reaction amidst the distractions and pre-occupations of a novel society, far more profound was its effect on William and Dorothy in the solitude and confinement of that snow-bound Goslar of which Coleridge could 'never think but with dejection'; an 'ugly, silent old desert of a city' as he described it to Poole. A stranger indeed in a strange land, Words-worth looked back to England as an 'indulgent parent, to whose arms even they who have been imprudent and undeserving may, like the prodigal son, betake themselves, without fear of being rejected'.[1] Both brother and sister, said Coleridge in April, burned 'with . . . impatience to return to their native country', and the poet occupied his enforced idleness by giving verse expression to his nostalgia, stimulating within himself that fervour of affection for the land of his birth which was to become an integral part of his inspiration. His heartfelt yearning taught him that he was not merely a poet of nature, but a poet of that nature which he had known at Racedown and Alfoxden, and in his youth in the North. So he fed on his memories of England, of his boyhood among the Lakes, even creating a fictitious English mistress from whom he imagined himself separated by death, further to point his patriotic affection and longing. His devotion for Lucy was a part of his love for those mountains among which he had felt 'the joy of his desire', and she was remembered

Beside an English fire.

Whatever his initial motives for leaving England, the plan now seemed 'a melancholy dream', sufficiently so at least to make him resolve:

Nor will I quit thy shore
A second time.

[1] 1835 Postscript. See *Works*, ed. de Selincourt, II, 447.

A resolution expressed in those terms may be sufficient to confirm our earlier tentative interpretation. He could not mean simply that he would never go abroad again; surely the correct implication is that he could never again abandon his homeland in that frame of mind which had led to this particular journey, perhaps in a spirit of defiant cosmopolitanism; that he would not again turn to a foreign country in disgust at his own, hoping there to find compensation for the shortcomings of England. It was now that he realized his debt to England, to that specifically English countryside which had been such a formative influence upon his youth.

He found also, among the liberal faction in Germany, a counter to his own suspicion of England's international position; with them it was England who was the hope of the world, the only bulwark against French military ambition. England was to Germany 'The Great Nation', and Coleridge found that Nelson's victories only increased the enthusiasm of the continental Anglophiles. Klopstock, Bürger and Wieland had all turned from France to England as the nation which now held out the only hope for the lovers of rational liberty, and the only model for reformers.

Thus Wordsworth's growing affection for the homeland he had abandoned and perhaps rejected, was stimulated by its reputation in Germany, by seeing for himself what the very name 'England' connoted for a Europe under the shadow of the French armies. As soon as it could be arranged, he abandoned his plans for enrolment at a university, returned to England, and wrote to Cottle: '. . . we are right glad to find ourselves in England, for we have learnt to know its value'.

.   .   .   .   .

In view of their different experience in Germany, it is not surprising that Wordsworth and Coleridge went different ways on their return. The student from the 'infidel' University of Göttingen forgot his aversion for 'local and temporary' politics, and joined the *Morning Post*; the homesick prisoner of Goslar returned to settle in complete retirement among his 'native hills', among those scenes of his youth which had come to mean so much to him in the 'melancholy dream' of his exile.

A great deal of the significance of the retirement to the Lakes lies in the fact that it was a return home, a physical expression, similar to the flight to Racedown, of his deliberate reaching back over the years of his early manhood and the experiences which typified them, to establish again a connection with 'the feelings of (his) earlier life'.[1] It symbolized the firmer repudiation of much of that past which had led him away from his youthful simplicity, and which he could now regard only as a period of delusion, of spiritual sickness, provoked by an unnatural and dangerous intellectual and emotional culture. Germany had convinced him not only that he was an Englishman, but that before all things he was a poet, and one whose source of power and widsom was a peculiar experience of nature. The continuance of this experience depended on a complete devotion to it, a devotion which would brook no divided, no spasmodic obser-vance, no homage paid merely in 'the lucid intervals of life'.

This realization had already made him reject the plan of joining Coleridge in the life and society of a German university, and it now decided him on a complete retirement aimed at removing what he thought was the last shadow of contradiction between his way of life and the basis of his poetic inspiration, at giving his life that 'lovely harmony with his poetry' to which Felicia Hemans paid tribute so many years later.[2]

The withdrawal, physical and spiritual, involved sacrifices of which Wordsworth was only too conscious. It was a con-tradiction of the 'wild appetites and blind desires', of those 'motions of savage instinct'[3] which were more typical of his spirit than most of his critics have acknowledged, and as one biographer[4] has pointed out, while the retirement meant on the one hand an escape from 'those sufferings which exceptional natures must needs derive from too close a contact with this commonplace world', it also meant 'a life which most men would have found austere and blank indeed: . . . poverty and retire-ment, . . . long apparent failure, and honour that came tardily at the close'.

This practical and complete self-dedication was possible only

[1] *Prelude*, 1805, X, 925. [2] See *Memorials*, ed. H. F. Chorley (1836).
[3] 'The Recluse', I, 706. [4] F. W. H. Myers, *Wordsworth* (1881) p. 59.

because of the intense reality of his confidence in his inspiration, of his literal belief in its lessons.

.   .   .   .   .

To the second edition of the *Lyrical Ballads* in 1800 Wordsworth added the famous Preface, in which he gave to his poetic theory a much fuller and more purposeful exposition than had been attempted in the brief Advertisement. As compared with the simple directness of the earlier proclamation, the Preface evinces primarily a desire to give to this theory a more philosophic tone, and to achieve an accuracy of expression rather more defensible than the generalizations of its brief precursor. Inevitably this involved in places a withdrawal from the bland assertions of 1798. Thus the sentence in the Advertisement, 'they [the poems] were written chiefly with a view to ascertain how far the language of conversation in the middle and lower classes of society is adapted to the purposes of poetic pleasure', becomes in 1800: 'it [the volume] was published as an experiment which, I hoped, might be of some use to ascertain how far, by fitting to metrical arrangement a selection of the real language of men in a state of vivid sensation, that sort of pleasure and that quantity of pleasure might be imparted, which a poet may rationally endeavour to impart'. The change of expression from 'the language of conversation in the middle and lower classes of society' to 'a selection of the real language of men' is in itself striking, for it represents Wordsworth's attempt to remove from the enunciation of his theory the political and sociological terms which suggested its origins.

He sent a copy of the new edition to Fox, along with a letter which is something of a supplement to the Preface, and which brings to light the more practical implications at the back of the Preface's aesthetic doctrines. Wordsworth could hardly have sent the book with Coleridge's approval, for in January, 1800, his collaborator had written of Fox and his party that he knew 'enough of them to know that more profligate and unprincipled men never disgraced an honest cause'.

Because the letter[1] is from a poetic liberal to a political one,

[1] Wordsworth's comment when it was published without his permission in 1836 was simply that he was not aware 'that any reason exists why I should particularly regret that it has seen the light'.

it is often more revealing than the Preface, more direct in its statement. It is there that we are told (though we need not believe) that 'The Brothers' and 'Michael' 'were written with a view to show that men who do not wear fine clothes can feel deeply'.[1] But the more significant parts of the letter are those which expound Wordsworth's views on the effect of the new industrialism upon men not considered 'in bodies and in classes' but as individuals. This and not political injustice or disfranchisement is the sort of thing he wishes to discuss with the Whig leader. He is concerned at 'the increasing disproportion between the price of labour and that of the necessaries of life', but more particularly at the attack that the new order is making on the dignity and importance of the individual personality. For this he sees a remedy not in political reform, but in a revival (to which Fox and his party will, he hopes, contribute) of that 'independent domestic life' which appeared to be confined at the time to the 'statesmen' of the Lake District.

The letter makes clear Wordsworth's new preoccupation with spiritual and personal rather than political and public reform, and to that extent it confirms the implications of his poetry. While it is plain, if only from the name of the addressee, that he was still a liberal in politics, it is equally clear that he now sees the political question as but one aspect, and possibly a minor one, of a larger aspiration.

Yet we learn from Dorothy's Journal that she and her brother could still relish 'a pleasant conversation about the manners of the rich—avarice, inordinate desires, and the effeminacy, unnaturalness, and the unworthy objects of education'. Their friends were liberal neighbours like the Speddings, the Loshes, the Calverts and the Clarksons and when Coleridge revived in 1801 a plan of emigration faintly reminiscent of the old Pantisocracy, he was sure Wordsworth would make one of the party.

It is unfortunate that we have little record of his attitude to events in France at this stage, or of his reaction to the early career of Napoleon.[2] It is possible that he did not at once give

[1] Cf. the quotation from Fabre d'Eglantine, p. 52 above.
[2] See K. Coburn, *Inquiring Spirit* (1951), pp. 277-88, for Coleridge's contemporary opinions.

way to that anti-Napoleonic revulsion which so characterized his later attitude. The man who had felt 'strange sympathies' with the Terror may well have been attracted by the undeniably heroic stature of the young general who made such short work of the effete and hypocritical Directory and of the enemies of the Republic. The poet who had so long lamented the absence of 'one paramount mind' in France would not have been the only liberal who found fresh hope in Napoleon's advent. Coleridge admitted that his later hatred of the First Consul was largely the result of his 'having hoped proudly of an individual and the having been miserably disappointed'. There is ample evidence in Southey's correspondence that he suffered from the same process of inspiration and disappointment, while to younger men Napoleon was always the reformer, the regenerator, who had saved the Revolution from the degradation of the Directorate. This role he always filled in the imagination of Hazlitt, whose memories did not go back, as did Wordsworth's, to an earlier period before the Directorate and even before the Terror. Hazlitt could only compare the Consul with the Directors, whereas Wordsworth had not forgotten Roland and Vergniaud.

In any case, Bonaparte did at least restore to France a stable and a comparatively reputable government which removed England's most plausible objections to a renewal of peace negotiations. Liberal opinion still condemned England's participation in the war, and Napoleonic rule made her ultimate success still more unlikely; and only too truly could there be now little pretence that England was combatting world revolution. But even to those who still pretended to see in French military aggression objects basically defensive, the terms under which peace was finally restored came as something of a shock: they were indeed an effective rebuke to Whig insistence that at all times peace might have been had for the asking. The Peace of Amiens shattered many illusions. Sheridan admitted that 'This is a peace which all men are glad of, but no man can be proud of', and Coleridge echoed: 'We, i.e. Wordsworth and myself, regard the Peace as necessary, but the Terms as most alarming.' In Wordsworth's case at least, the events of the next year were materially to strengthen that alarm.

CHAPTER VI

1802

At the beginning of 1802 his theory of poetic diction at least was unmodified, and he wrote a direct résumé of it to his youthful admirer John Wilson. In this letter he expands the converse, the offensive side of his repudiation of poetic convention in terms far less equivocal than he had permitted himself in the *Lyrical Ballads* Preface. He is plainly aware that his democratic theory will arouse opposition from those who 'cannot bear to see delicate and refined feelings ascribed to men in low conditions of society, because their vanity and self love tell them that these belong only to themselves and men like themselves in dress, station, and way of life; others are disgusted with the naked language of some of the most interesting passions of men, because either it is indelicate, or gross, or vulgar'.

He is openly in conflict with 'ladies and gentlemen', and in stressing the attack on convention and prejudice which his theory involves, he connects his own revolution in diction with other revolutions in political and social opinion already effected, and in their success he finds hope for his own: 'What excessive admiration was paid in former times to personal prowess and military success. . . . So with regard to birth, and numerous other modes of sentiment, civil and religious.'

This political or at least sociological background to his poetic aims is further sketched in by his June letter to Sara Hutchinson on 'Resolution and Independence', in which he points out that the Leech-Gatherer is to be considered as 'carrying with him his own fortitude, and the necessities which an unjust state of society has entailed upon him'; and this despite the fact that 'an unjust state of society' is no obvious or necessary part of the setting for the poem itself.[1]

So too the Preface to the third edition of the *Lyrical Ballads* in the same year, although it stresses once more that 'a selection of the language really used by men' is used only 'as far as was possible', adds also a long passage on the poetic character, which is, typically, concerned with attacking the received opinion of the superiority of the poet above common humanity. To Wordsworth the poet is essentially 'a man speaking to men, . . . nothing differing in kind from other men, but only in degree', and dealing with the 'passions, and thoughts and feelings' of ordinary men. As Paine and Godwin had planned to do with kings and princes, so Wordsworth wished to remove the poet from the unnatural, the superhuman eminence of his imagined superiority, in order to elevate him to the truer dignity of common humanity.

In fact, the opposition which Wordsworth had so industriously analysed in the letter to Wilson had not been notable before 1802. But in July of that year Coleridge reported to Southey his disagreement with the extremer doctrines of his collaborator, and in October came the more ominous inaugural onslaught of the *Edinburgh Review*.

In the *Memoirs*, Christopher Wordsworth pointed out that it was 'remarkable that some critics, entertaining democratical opinions, should have been among the bitterest censors [of Wordsworth's poems]. . . . It would seem', he went on, 'as if, in pronouncing judgment on poetry, they forgot or abandoned the tenets of their political creed.' It is indeed not without significance in this study that the principal organ of a party with which Wordsworth was still in close sympathy, should, from the appearance of its very first number, have singled out his democratic poetic theory and practice for its especial condemnation.

---

[1] By comparing Wordsworth's reaction to his meeting with the leech-gatherer in 1802 with his description of his earlier encounter with the peasant leading her cow on the banks of the Loire (*Prelude*, IX, 509), we can measure the magnitude and significance of the change in his outlook which had intervened. The poor were no longer seen, as they had been in the Letter to Llandaff, as social 'helots', nor were mendicants now a 'class of wretches' whose existence shocked the 'feelings of humanity'.

It is hardly fair to impute Wordsworth's later dislike of the
Whigs to his annoyance at their notorious rejection of his poetry,[1]
but it is true that the critical opinions of Jeffrey and Brougham
exemplified many of the essential characteristics of contemporary
Whig philosophy to which Wordsworth was gradually to realize
himself opposed: the disagreement over poetry was only one
aspect of a much wider difference of opinion, although the
Edinburgh Reviewers perceived it before the poet.

The Whig Party and its famous review were in many ways
typically eighteenth-century institutions, prolonging into a new
age political conventions and critical precepts inherited from the
past. They repudiated Wordsworth as an innovator, one who
endeavoured to destroy the poetic conventions, just as they
scorned the radicals, who attempted to carry out political reform
outside the traditional party divisions. They had no time for the
idealist in art or politics, nor for the poet who found his inspiration outside the traditional cultivation of urban society. They
suspected the recluse of the Lakes because he was something
beyond their ken, an 'anti-social' and unnatural being divorced
from the traditions of English literature. Parliamentary reform,
the limited extension of the franchise, the education of the
masses—these aims they understood; but a general dissatisfaction
with the new industrial society, a suspicion of the whole basis of
national life, these were to the Whigs of the *Review* merely
'hankerings after some unattainable state of voluptuous virtue
and perfection'; while to proclaim the supremacy of the lower
classes in the question of poetic diction was to form a 'most
considerable conspiracy . . . against sound judgment in matters
poetical'. For the Edinburgh Reviewers were men of eminently
sound judgment in an eminently superficial way, and they were
precluded from sympathy with Wordsworth's poetry for exactly
those reasons which precluded them from sympathy with the
Spanish revolt, and paralysed them before the obvious military
genius of Napoleon; the new romanticism was as bewildering to
them as the new nationalism.

Despite the appearance of this formidable opponent, 1802 was

[1] Although in 1818 he accused the Whigs of indifference to English literature
as well as to English 'religion, laws, morals and manners'. See below, p. 177.

a year of considerable poetic activity on Wordsworth's part. It is impossible to say whether this outburst was directly related to the Peace and its restoration of a healthier political atmosphere in Britain; it was however simultaneous with his renewed interest in political affairs which no doubt appeared more attractive to him now that the war had finished. In February Dorothy noted in her Journal: 'The papers came in soon after I laid aside the book—a good thing for my William'; and in March she was busy at the task of filing two months' accumulation of them.

In the history of Wordsworth's poetic development, the year 1802 is above all significant as the year of his adoption of the sonnet, and even this event is not without its interest for our specific purpose. Among the verse reformers of the Revolutionary period, Wordsworth was not alone in his initial opinion of the sonnet as a species of composition 'egregiously absurd'; to many it was typical of those artificial and conventional forms of aristocratic verse whose subversion was to be effected. In Thelwall's miscellany, *The Peripatetic*, published in 1793, Ambulator commentated as follows on a blank verse sonnet recited to him by his friend Sylvanus Theophrastus: 'I am happy . . . you soon relieved me from the dread which the *name* of your little poem excited, of having my ear tortured by the quaint recurrence of the same tedious rhymes. I must own I consider the sonnet as the only species of affected versification retained in use among us; and I cannot but lament the growing popularity of a kind of poetry so little congenial with the genius of our language.'

It is significant therefore, that, in the poetic sphere at least, the charms of order were by 1802 already appealing to a poet who had until that time claimed complete freedom from formal restraint and convention. Wordsworth found a new pleasure in the obligatory restriction exercised by a set poetic form, and hoped that he might transmit this delight,

> pleas'd if some souls
> Who have felt the weight of too much liberty,
> Should find short solace there as I have found.

And to this discovery must be related an incipient suspicion of his way of life:

My whole life I have lived in pleasant thought,
As if life's business were a summer mood;
As if all needful things would come unsought
To genial faith, still rich in genial good;
But how can he expect that others should
Build for him, sow for him, and at his call
Love him, who for himself will take no heed at all?
                    ('Resolution and Independence.')

In the regularity of the sonnet form he found an artistic counterpart to that personal discipline for which he was beginning to
yearn; and the appeal of the ordered verse form was the precursor
of those imperious demands which the principle of duty was later
to make on him. The conflict between freedom and order was as
real in Wordsworth's mind as it is in the minds of all men, and in
1802 he made this limited but significant movement towards the
standard of order.

Not only the fact, but the circumstances of the adoption of the
sonnet are significant. His interest was revived when Dorothy
read him the sonnets of Milton, and he tells us that he was struck
above all by their 'Republican austerity'. Now a revived interest
in Milton the *English* republican was common among the disillusioned English supporters of the French Revolution at the turn
of the century. Describing his disappointment in France to Rick-
man in 1800, Southey wrote: 'Buonaparte has made me anti-
Gallican; and I remember Alfred, and the two Bacons, and
Hartley, and Milton, and Shakespeare, with more patriotic pride
than ever.' Now that France had failed the liberals, they turned
perforce to England, though, naturally enough, to England's
past rather than her present. So with Wordsworth; he looked
back, not to the eighteenth century, not to the 'fair Albion' of the
'Glorious Revolution', but to the English republic of the seven-
teenth century, and to its champions, Milton, Sidney, Marvell
and Vane. It was when she was thus matched that France indeed
seemed 'Perpetual emptiness, unceasing change . . .' with—

        No master spirit, no determined road,
        But equally a want of books and men.

From a continental perversion of liberty, Wordsworth turned to
the native tradition, to 'the flood of British freedom', which he

had neglected, but which, despite misgivings, he must believe not wholly swallowed up in 'bogs and sands', not wholly unable still to send forth its 'freights of worth to foreign lands'; *must* believe it, because he could not allow himself to descend again into despair for want of a tangible basis to his hopes. So he called on the spirit of Milton and his peers to revive England as a worthy object of his hopes for liberty.

This growing faith in the essentially *English* tradition of liberty was strengthened by his journey to France. He crossed to Annette and Caroline at Calais in August, before his marriage to Mary Hutchinson; to close, as it were, one chapter of his life, to terminate even his personal connection with France and what it represented in his experience before a step which was to link him even more closely with England. From this journey he returned as the poet of the clarion sonnets 'dedicated to National Independence and Liberty'.

His disappointment with Napoleonic France was inevitable, and perhaps preconceived. William Taylor of Norwich,[1] a Whig friend of Southey's, during a visit roughly contemporaneous, delighted in what he saw: a system of economic, political and social order, combined with an apparent absence of oppression. Hazlitt too wondered at the magnificence of a Paris embellished with the pillage of a continent. But Wordsworth looked for something other than high wages, domestic prosperity and well-stocked galleries. With the rule of Napoleon Hazlitt could compare only the corruption of the Directory, but the enthusiast who had walked with Beaupuy when Hazlitt was a boy of fourteen had older memories too vivid to be erased. To him Napoleon was merely that military despot whose advent had been so ominously foretold by Burke, and whose mission it was to bring the Revolution to its melancholy catastrophe of absolutism. To him the coldly formal fêtes of the Consulate only the more forcibly recalled 'Festivals . . . that were not names', when 'The senselessness of joy was . . . sublime'.

The disappointment did not drive him to despair, mainly because he was prepared for it, and had long before formed a firmer basis for his hopes of man than the political development

[1] See J. W. Robberds, *A Memoir of the Life and Writings of Wm. Taylor* (1843).

of France. By now he had sounded 'himself to know The destiny of man', cared not 'for Pope, Consul or King', and could still 'live in hope'. So he proclaimed:

> ... despair ... I feel not,
> Fair seasons yet will come, and hopes as fair.[1]

No longer could he be affected by the news of Napoleon's appointment to the Consulship for life as he had been by the earlier events of the Revolution.

With this opinion of Napoleon, he could not but be revolted by the adulation which his contemporaries, with the liberals to the fore, showered on the military autocrat. In September there were ten thousand Englishmen in Paris, and even the Whig Romilly admitted that he was 'disgusted at the eagerness with which [they] crowded to do homage at the new court of a usurper and tyrant'. Most prominent among the throng was Wordsworth's erstwhile hero Fox, and if Burdett and Romilly were unwilling to meet Napoleon, Fox knew no such scruples. It is probable that he and Wordsworth reached Calais on the same day, and the poet would naturally be acquainted with the purpose of the visit of his famous fellow-traveller. Indeed, the latter's presentation to the Consul and the fraternization which was said to have followed caused something of a stir in England, and Coleridge devoted an entire article to strictures on his conduct.[2] Only when the sonnet 'Calais, August, 1802' is read in conjunction with the letter to Fox of January 1801 is the full significance of the poem's condemnation apparent.

Wordsworth did not resent 'a seemly reverence ... to power', but he did lament the very unseemly haste with which his countrymen flocked to prostrate themselves before a nearly victorious enemy. Napoleon the soldier, the autocrat and the parvenu was little calculated to excite the admiration of the mature Wordsworth who had not forgotten his republicanism or his pacifism, and was now becoming increasingly conscious

---

[1] 'Composed near Calais ... Aug. 1802.' These lines, though later emended, were at least retained until 1815.

[2] *Essays on his Own Times* (1850), p. 572. See also Creevey's aspersions, *Creevey*, ed. Gore (1942), p. 6.

of the influence of tradition on the formation of loyalty and patriotic attachment.

But if he had found in France the proof of the final annihilation of his hopes in the Revolution, he saw also positive indications of the national might of his country's enemy. The Peace of Amiens was to Napoleon merely a breathing space, an opportunity to pursue undisturbed his European ambitions, and few Englishmen were deceived as to the inevitability of a resumption of hostilities. Wordsworth returned to England impressed above all with the threat to his country which he saw inherent in the unprecedented power and military organization of her enemy. He saw plainly that the very existence of England would soon be in jeopardy, and his vision haunted him. For that reason, when he returned to verse of a directly political inspiration, he wrote not of the rights of man, of legislative or legal reform, of republics or monarchies, but of national independence and liberty.

His poems were calls to arms, exhortations to his country to fit herself for the struggle by self-regeneration and moral reform. He saw that the coming conflict could only be finally won by moral superiority expressing itself in physical energy and determination. In France he saw the magnitude of the peril, and his conviction brooked no half-measures.

After his two years' retirement, this return to political reality filled him again with the old fervour in a new cause, and many of the mental habits acquired and fostered in Grasmere were swept away or greatly weakened by the pressure of actuality which descended upon him in Calais and London. However he had decided that evil was not poetic material, that joy, not indignation must be his inspiration, the peril now threatening his country was too real, too vital to be scouted. To awaken England by Miltonic outbursts, it was necessary to point the danger, to describe the peril, to stress the essential viciousness of the enemy's aims; it was not enough to remind his countrymen of England's great traditions, her record in the cause of freedom; he had also to anathematize the degradation and slavery that defeat by France would entail for England and the rest of Europe. In taking upon himself the expression of this indictment, Wordsworth of necessity abandoned much of that benevolence and that moderation which he had cultivated in Grasmere. It was in the struggle against the evil threat of French aggression that he contracted that tone of acerbity too often typical of his later political utterance, and so much a contradiction of his earlier principles.

He did not turn from France to Britain in a spirit of complacent and insular patriotism. Returning to Dover, he had again learned to know England's value:

> Europe is yet in bonds; but let that pass,
> Thought for another moment. Thou art free,
> My country!
>   ('Composed in the Valley near Dover.')

Yet his devotion was still somewhat comparative; if England was now the only bulwark of freedom, she gave every indication of her complete unworthiness to champion the great cause against the power of tyranny.' Oh grief', he wrote, 'that Earth's best hopes rest all with thee!' In the very adulation of Napoleon by the English he saw 'the most melancholy evidence of degradation in the British feeling and intellect which the times have furnished' and, eager as he was for 'hope to his hope', he often found himself ignorant 'which way I must look For comfort'. His liberal political convictions were still strong enough to prevent him closing his eyes to his country's shortcomings, to the injustice of the rich, the sufferings of the poor, the craven spirit of the 'moneyed worldlings', to all the 'mischief engendered and fostered among us by undisturbed wealth'. He was aware of the chinks, even of some gaping holes, in the armour of the champion of liberty, and although he insisted now on personal regeneration rather than political or social reform, he did not overlook the superficial expression of the deeper degradation of spirit in the unfair distribution of wealth and in the sufferings inflicted on the poor. In her Journal of the Scotch tour of 1803, Dorothy found a sympathetic place for the complaints of the peasantry: 'In talking of the French, their language was what most people would call Jacobinical. They spoke much of the oppression endured by the Highlanders . . . of the absolute impossibility of their living in any comfort, and of the cruelty of laying so many restraints on emigration.' In October of that year Wordsworth was still seeking in vain signs of that regeneration for which he had prayed, finding only

> . . . nothing great:
> Nothing is left which I can venerate;
> . . . such emptiness at length
> Seems at the heart of all things.

The very anomalous complexities of the British Constitution seemed to promise little hope of success in a struggle against the ordered military discipline of France.

It was in dissatisfaction with the present state of his country that he turned to the promise of its glorious past. His aim was now to restore the spirit of this past, to revive in his countrymen the virtue and the fortitude of their ancestors, so that they might be capable of the supreme task, the defeat of tyranny as embodied in France and her leader. This ambition was not the result of conventional patriotism or narrow nationalism, but of heartfelt conviction, a purpose undertaken initially with doubt and misgiving, but destined to become the complete preoccupation of the man and the poet for the next thirteen years. To this aim he sacrificed a great deal more than the blessings of his spiritual retirement.

In October came the French invasion of Switzerland, and the key was turned in the lock. As he later wrote to Losh: 'After Bonaparte had violated the independence of Switzerland, my heart turned against him, and against the nation that could submit to be the instrument of such an outrage.' In this time of 'sorrowful reverse for all mankind', England was indeed the 'last spot of earth, where Freedom now Stands single in her only Sanctuary'. The conflict between love of England and love of liberty which had formerly wrought such havoc in Wordsworth's spiritual integrity was now finally resolved; for the next thirteen years his hopes were centred on and his entire outlook modified by the imperious necessity of French defeat.

·   ·   ·   ·   ·

The central theme of Wordsworth's subsequent political development is his gradual movement away from the Whig sympathies evinced in the letter to Fox of 1801; and the initial cause of this movement was his disagreement with them on the question of the war against Napoleon. As he wrote to Losh, the Napoleonic invasion of Switzerland in 1802 was not only the occasion of his final abandonment of the French, but: 'Here it was that I parted, in feeling, from the Whigs, and to a certain degree united with their adversaries, who were free from the delusion (such I must ever regard it) of Mr. Fox and his party, that a safe and honourable peace was practicable with the French nation, and that an ambitious conqueror like Napoleon could be softened down into a commercial rival.' By its condemnation of the first war, of whose injustice Wordsworth was permanently convinced, the Whig Party had earned his admiration, and its leader his affection; by its refusal to modify this condemnation when the war had for Wordsworth profoundly altered its complexion, the same party earned his contempt.

Apart from the dismal futility of the secession from Parliament, the record of the Whig Party during the Revolutionary war had been an imposing one. A contemporary pamphleteer wrote thus of their conduct after the outbreak of hostilities in 1793: 'It was on this occasion, when all was dismay and confusion, when the noisy partisans of democracy were reduced to insignificance and silence, that the firm body of the Whigs, headed by their immortal leader, stood forth to rescue the nation from madness and ruin; to restore the confidence of the public; to support the freedom of the press, and the unrestrained intercourse of sentiments and opinions. They laboured to avert the widespreading evils; they deprecated the destructive consequences of the war . . . they disclaimed against the crooked policy of alarm, which alone, to a reflecting mind, will appear to be the cause of the present miseries. Unsupported by popular favour, their constancy, their dignity, and their temper were exposed to a severe trial.'[1] This is not perhaps the 'impartial statement' which its author promised, but it is true that in the years before the Peace of Amiens, Whig opposition to the war had been dignified and creditable. Their arguments against the conflict

[1] S. Fleming, *An Impartial Statement of the Merits and Services of the Opposition*, n.d.

were not the fruit of mere partisan hostility, but were based consistently upon an essentially moral condemnation which was as evident in the speeches of Fox as it was in the writings of Frend and Fawcett. The war to them, as to Wordsworth, was unjust, unchristian in its aims, while the stupidity of the administration made even the attainment of these aims impossible, as indeed the terms of the final settlement conclusively proved. English intervention in the war seemed only to give increased justification and opportunity to French military ambition.

The domestic inquisition which was part of the war effort, was to Wordsworth, as to the Whigs, a fantastic campaign against what the imitator of Juvenal called inoffensive 'fireside treason-parties *en famille*'. And however the Whigs (with understandable caution in view of their own hopes of the Prince of Wales) failed to make full use of the fact, the cause of the opposition was further strengthened by the fact that Pitt's War Ministry was initially a Royal appointment made against the wishes of the Parliamentary majority.

In these circumstances, and largely protected from the charge of disloyalty by the precedent of the righteous national condemnation of the ministerial campaign against America, the old Whigs of the Revolutionary war were able to sustain their opposition and condemnation on the highest level of morality and reason.

This was certainly not true of the general tone of their opposition to the Napoleonic War. Especially under the influence of a younger political generation, their arguments, whether economic or political, were criminally short-sighted and anachronistically superficial. The party gave no evidence that it even faintly shared Wordsworth's perspicacious realization of the significance and importance of the military contest; they were aware only that the war was bad for trade, that the Tories were waging it, and that it must therefore be concluded.

They wanted peace, and that at any price. Even after the failure of the Coalition Ministry of the Talents to effect an understanding with France in 1807, the Whigs persisted in their assertion that peace could still be had for the asking. It was this pitiful illogicality which was responsible for the aberrations of their policy on the war. As an historian of the period has written: 'The general effect produced by a study of the Whig criticisms of the war is not flattering to the intelligence and judgment of the Whigs as a party. They proved to be wrong on almost every point of policy, and upon many points of fact. They prophesied too darkly and too often; and apparently no confounding of their predictions could convince them of their errors . . . their inability to rise above purely destructive criticism condemned them in the eyes of the nation. Their attacks on the Government were too constant, too petty, and too unproductive of useful ideas, to convince the country of their sincerity or utility. The Whigs had nothing to substitute for the policy of Castlereagh and the Wellesleys.'[1]

The party was, in effect, pleading for an eighteenth-century settlement for a nineteenth-century war; and to Wordsworth the war was the supreme political question. Whig inability to grasp the significance of the Napoleonic contest was as indicative of the falsity of their political principles as the *Edinburgh Review's* condemnation of Wordsworth's poetry was to him proof positive of the degradation of their poetic taste; he spurned Whig critics as he spurned Whig politicians. As his condemnation of the Revolutionary war had helped to make him a Republican, so his mature conviction of the vital necessity of Napoleon's defeat was even more influential in making him a Tory.

His change was not merely the result of that impatience with partisan opposition in times of national peril with which we are all familiar. The ardent Grasmere volunteer ('surely', wrote Dorothy, 'there was never a more determined hater of the French nor one more willing to do his utmost to destroy them if they really do come') was bitterly critical of 'the ministry and their servants' who did little but thwart the national patriotic spirit.

Criticism of administrative debility he could more than tolerate in Fox as in Burke; when the former, referring to French activities in the West Indies, and to their conduct 'towards the blacks, and particularly towards Toussaint', complained of 'the little attention which was paid to these events in England, under the vulgar supposition of their being foreign to British interests', he was voicing the sentiments of a more notable poetic tribute

[1] M. Roberts, *The Whig Party, 1807-12* (1939), p. 163.

already published by his former admirer. But it was not to such strictures that the Whigs confined themselves. As Southey complained, they did not stop at opposition to the Government, but took part 'against their country . . . they always sided with the enemy, pleading his cause, palliating his crimes, extolling his wisdom, magnifying his power, vilifying and accusing their own government, depreciating its resources, impeding its measures, insulting its allies. . . .' And come Melville or York, come Cintra or Walcheren, this attitude neither Wordsworth nor the country would tolerate.

A preoccupation with the necessity of military victory inevitably entailed a modification, a relegation of other aspirations. Wordsworth had recognized, in the threat of national subjugation, 'a bondage worse than death'; the averting this peril must therefore be the immediate aim, for some time the only aim, of all Englishmen, whether of those who, in the event of a dispute merely civil,

> . . . would take your stand,
> . . . by the monarch's side,
> And, like Montrose, make loyalty your pride . . . ,

or of those—

> who, not less zealous, might display
> Banners at enmity with regal sway,
> And like the Pyms and Miltons of that day,
> Think that state would live in sounder health
> If kingship bowed its head to Commonwealth. . . .

Naturally enough, with a French army embarking at the Channel ports, differences of opinion on the franchise seemed criminally academic; however real the need for constitutional reform, the immediate necessity was to 'Save this honoured land from every Lord but British reason and the British sword'.[1]

It was then their differing views on the war and on the urgency of domestic reform that provided the point of cleavage between

---

[1] Cf. Burns, 'The Dumfries Volunteers':

> For never but by British hands
> Maun British wrangs be righted.

Wordsworth on the one hand, and the Whigs (as representing English liberalism in its articulate, parliamentary form) on the other. The Whigs and radicals were never entirely free from a sneaking conviction that Napoleonic conquest of an unreformed Britain would not be an unmitigated catastrophe; at least they consistently implied that a Tory government had no right to call on the unfranchised for the defence of an obsolete constitution. They insisted on reform first; Wordsworth on the defeat of France, the removal of the national danger as a prerequisite to the setting of Britain's house in order. The two views were ultimately irreconcilable, and we need hardly debate their relative merits. So, although in December, 1804, the *Morning Chronicle* was still 'wished for very much' at Dove Cottage, the prospect earlier in the year of a Whig accession to power under the wing of the Prince of Wales did not attract that household. 'We pray', wrote Dorothy, 'for the King's life, for we think that we shall be having a peace with the new ministry before we have drubbed the French.'

By 1804 Wordsworth had at least become aware of a modification of his opinions on man and society sufficiently significant to warrant the extension of the autobiographical section of his magnum opus to include the story of that modification. The story of *The Prelude* is, as we should expect, one of his redemption from ignorance by the spirit of nature, of his passage from the half light of superficial knowledge to the knowledge of fundamental truth. He did not decry his early sympathies, saw much to praise in their vigour and benevolence, but condemned them because they were based on a partial knowledge and an oblique vision which inevitably led him to a catastrophe of despair and disillusionment. In describing the violence of his youthful opinions he was honest and unflinching, rarely clouding the picture by the qualifications which his later convictions would suggest. He was still convinced that the Revolution had only just failed, perhaps merely for the want of that 'one paramount mind' which might have led it to success.

This is the fidelity of the early version of *The Prelude*, and it is also that of the final published form. There is much loose talk about the supposed toning-down of *The Prelude* over the last forty years of Wordsworth's life that a comparison of the MSS. does not in any way justify. It is well to remember that Macaulay wrote of the 1850 publication: 'The poem is to the last degree Jacobinical, indeed Socialist. I understand perfectly why Wordsworth did not choose to publish it in his lifetime.'[1] Far too much has been made of occasional, rarely significant emendations; the value of many of them consists only of their being evidence of Wordsworth's movement from a vague pantheism (of whose implications he was at first possibly unaware) to a more orthodox religious position.

This religious development does not directly concern us here, but it was to become closely related to the growth of his political opinions. The poet of the war sonnets had called on God to clothe 'in deeds His curse of the oppressor' and to bring victory to Britain, but the exact nature of Wordsworth's religious position at the time is obscure. It is perhaps not insignificant that the Wordsworths were not yet regular churchgoers; in 1832 Dorothy reread her Journal of the Scotch tour of 1803 and remarked: 'I find that this tour was both begun and ended on a Sunday. I am sorry that it should have been so, though I hope and trust that our thoughts and feelings were not seldom as pious and serious as if we had attended a place devoted to public worship. My sentiments have undergone a great change since 1803 respecting the absolute necessity of keeping the Sabbath by a regular attendance at Church.'

The Prelude's references to the religious hypocrisy of Cambridge were outspoken enough, and it is possibly significant that the aspersions on the despoliation of the Chartreuse are not found in MS. A. Coleridge claimed at least that he had cured his friend of necessitarianism by 1804, but the year before he complained that both Hazlitt and Wordsworth 'spoke irreverently [and] malignantly' on the question of Divine wisdom.[2] From this we may infer that in the early years of the Grasmere retirement Wordsworth's independence in religion, as in politics, was largely unshaken.

The first inroads made into this self-sufficiency were, as we

[1] Life and Letters, ed. G. O. Trevelyan (1876), II, 279.
[2] See H. House, Coleridge, (1953), p. 43.

have seen, the result, initially at least, of 'No disturbance of my
soul, Or strong compunction in me wrought'. He had not
abandoned the cult of joy, the conviction of pleasure, and in 1804
he could still re-dedicate himself completely to the joyful spirit of
nature:

> [I] to pleasure will be true;
> Spite of melancholy reason,
> I will have my careless season.[1]

But the brief interruption of his retirement in 1802, the events
of the succeeding years, and even the hostages he gave to fortune
in his wife and child, these gradually brought him to a realization
of other no less questionable realities. His earlier misgivings about
his seclusion were confirmed, and in the 'Ode to Duty' he proclaimed his readiness to submit to a rule of discipline and service:

> I, loving freedom and untried;
> No sport of every random gust,
> Yet being to myself a guide,
> Too blindly have reposed my trust;
> Resolv'd that nothing e'er should press
> Upon my present happiness
> I shov'd unwelcome tasks away:
> But henceforth I would serve; and strictly if I may.

[1] MS. version of 'The Kitten and the Falling Leaves' (1804).

CHAPTER VII

The Death of John

The death of John Wordsworth at sea at the beginning of 1805 was a bereavement of the most profound importance in William's development as a man and a poet. The affection and admiration which he felt, along with so many others, for his brother, who had planned shortly to retire to Grasmere, help to explain the devastation which the bereavement wrought at Dove Cottage. Southey wrote that he had 'never witnessed such affliction as his and his sister's', while Dorothy was convinced that she could 'never again . . . have *perfect*—that is an unchastized—joy in this world'.

The first reaction which this event caused in the poet was a crystallization and a strengthening of his formerly vague religious sentiments, expressed at once in a new certainty of a future existence. He turned to the translation of the religious sonnets of Michelangelo, and in the fragment 'Yes, it was a mountain echo', he gave expression to his conviction that those instinctive promptings to virtue of which he had been so long aware, were now to be prized above all because 'Of God, of God they are'.

This religious reaction, though immediate and obvious, was rather one expression of a much more general modification which we have noted as already preparing in the 'Ode to Duty', and hinted at even earlier in a vague suspicion of the bases of his life and its inspiration. The poetic preoccupation with joy and the sources of pleasure in Nature to the virtual exclusion of all distraction, the seclusion of a life withdrawn from 'the heavy and the weary weight Of all this unintelligible world', had never been entirely without concomitant doubts and self-searchings. John's death came as a sudden and shocking personal reintroduction to that anguish and suffering which he had hoped to avoid by withdrawing from the world: he had withdrawn himself from the obvious scenes of human sorrow, but sorrow now came to search him out.

He was forced again to take stock, again to re-assess the validity of his self-justification. Earlier he had sought this justification only in his personal judgment: his life had been lived by his own lights, without conformity to institution or prescription. The world's society he had rejected, the world's religion he had ignored. Yet when the blow came he turned at once, not to the God of nature, not to the 'Spirit of the universe', but to the judge and redeemer of the scriptures who promised eternal life.

In the 'Ode to Duty' he was already questioning this intellectual self-sufficiency, this spiritual independence, in the conviction that submission to an external law, to a higher prescription, could lead him to greater achievement and fulfilment. It was as confirmation of this opinion that he interpreted the lesson of his brother's death. In words which Dorothy used of her own reaction, but which plainly applied with equal force to him: '. . . I did not know what sorrow was till now, which made me over secure in what I loved and rejoiced in, and think it too good and too perfect.' That self-satisfaction Wordsworth now rejected, for he had 'submitted to a new control: A deep distress hath humaniz'd my soul'. His grief was not cheerless, because of his very knowledge that he 'must grieve', that in his grief he was re-establishing his connection with the sorrow of humanity, and bidding farewell to—

> . . . the heart that lives alone,
> Hous'd in a dream, at distance from the kind!
> Such happiness, wherever it be known,
> Is to be pitied; for 'tis surely blind.
> But welcome fortitude, and patient cheer,
> And frequent sights of what is to be borne!
> Not without hope we suffer and we mourn.[1]

Indeed, in thus rejecting that self-sufficiency which stands in no need of support from any external or institutional guide outside its own security in joy, Wordsworth was but carrying further that rejection of the Godwinian independent judgment

[1] 'Peele Castle.'

which he had proclaimed eight years before. He realized now that at Racedown and Alfoxden he had not cut deeply enough, and that he still preserved traces of a culpable intellectual self-confidence which his seclusion from the world had only fostered.

The sudden blow to his hopes and the religious reaction which followed his bereavement combined also to give new force to those exhortations to restraint, to that condemnation of temporal expectation which he had already heard in the voice of nature:

> Oh do not thou too fondly brood,
> Although deserving of all good,
> On any earthly hope, however pure . . . ;[1]

this was the moral he drew from his calamity, and to it is due the increasingly spiritual tone of his life and work in subsequent years. He found it hard to revive that interest in practical and temporal events which had been typical of the previous two years since the visit to France. Writing to Sir George Beaumont of the political events of the day soon after John's death, he said: 'I have asked myself more than once lately, if my affections can be in the right place, caring as I do so little about what the world seems to care so much for. All this seems to me "a tale told by an idiot, full of sound and fury, signifying nothing" '; and this lack of interest is typical of his attitude right up to the outbreak of the Spanish revolt. The larger international scene gradually reclaimed his attention, but it was some time before even the European contest could make him forget that 'lamentable change' which had brought home to him so vividly, even 'in the bosom of our rustic cell', the realization that 'bliss with mortal man may not abide'.[2]

His poetic activity in the year of bereavement was not considerable. The fourth edition of the *Lyrical Ballads* appeared, including 'The Female Vagrant', but omitting the stanza on 'the brood that lap (their very nourishment!) their brothers' blood'. Such a correction we would expect in view of the modification of Wordsworth's pacifism after the outbreak of the Napoleonic

---

[1] 'Elegiac Verses in Memory of My Brother.'
[2] Dedication to 'The White Doe of Rylstone'.

War. In the same year he paid his famous tribute to the ideal military character in a poem, 'The Character of the Happy Warrior', which drew on his memories of his dead brother and of Beaupuy. The poet who had come to see in poverty and mendicancy opportunities for the exercise of human benevolence which did much to justify their existence, now proclaimed the unparalleled scope given to that same benevolent sentiment by the very nature of the military life.

The death of Pitt found Wordsworth unchanged in his condemnation of that minister's policy. Aware that his correspondent would think otherwise, he wrote to Beaumont frankly: 'Mr Pitt is also gone! by tens of thousands looked upon . . . as a great loss. For my own part, as you probably know, I have never been able to regard his political life with complacency. I believe him, however, to have been as disinterested a man, and as true a lover of his country as it was possible for so ambitious a man to be. His first wish (though probably unknown to himself) was that his country should prosper under his administration; his next, that it should prosper: could the order of these wishes have been reversed, Mr Pitt would have avoided many of the grievous mistakes into which I think he fell.'

The subsequent change of Government left him unmoved; the Whigs he had now abandoned, and even in a Cabinet including Fox he found 'no true honour or ability'. The coalition of Fox and the arch-sinecurist Grenville was not an inspiring one, and was indeed all too likely to recall that earlier alliance with North which Fox had perpetrated to the disgust of the country and of his supporters alike. Southey, with whom Wordsworth's friendship had ripened considerably since the death of John, said of the Ministry of All the Talents that it was 'such a damned scramble for places—so completely everything which it ought not to be— that I am out of heart, and have lost all hope of any beneficial change to any extent'. The Whig tenure of office at least proved to the satisfaction of everyone but the Whigs themselves the fallacy of their pacifist delusions, and after the death of Fox Wordsworth looked at the ministry which had to face up to the catastrophe of Jena with all too justifiable a doubt whether

> . . . they who rule the land
> Be men who hold its many blessings dear,
> Wise, upright, valiant; not a servile band,
> Who are to judge of danger which they fear,
> And honour which they do not understand.[1]

Southey, inveighing against the 'base and cowardly feeling . . . which would humble this country at the feet of France', added that as Wordsworth was in complete agreement with him, 'I require . . . no other sanction to convince me that I am right'. The two poets had other opinions in common. In 1807 a wide-eyed De Quincey heard them 'giving utterance to sentiments which seemed utterly disloyal. . . . I heard', he goes on, 'opinions avowed most hostile to the reigning family; not personally to them, but generally to a monarchical form of government.'[2]

Yet the republican was a gloomy and disconsolate one. He still claimed ('Stray Pleasures', 1806) to find in nature a 'beauty ministrant to comfort and to peace', but plainly more effort was required now, more conscious turning away from the 'unholy deeds' which 'ravage the world'. The true note of this period is struck rather in the 1805 lines on 'Rob Roy's Grave' with its lament:

> Of old things all are over old,
> Of good things none are good enough.

At the same time his resentment at his own neglect found sharper expression. If the aristocratic taste of the critics prevented the public's appreciating 'Peter Bell', he was sure that 'the people would love the poem', if only he could get it to them. He toyed with the idea of printing his poems in chap-books, and even as late as 1840 he was still considering the same expedient, though with hardly the same necessity. In a letter to Lady Beaumont in May, 1807 he abandoned his philistine critics, 'all worldlings of every rank and situation' and any hopes he might have had of influencing them.[3]

'What have my poems', he asks, 'to do with routs, dinners,

---

[1] 'November, 1806.'

[2] *Reminiscences* (Everyman, 1929), 178.

[3] See the poem, 'The Power of Music', where the enthralled group about the street musician ignore the 'coaches and chariots' which rush past them: 'they care not for you, Nor what ye are flying nor what ye pursue'.

morning calls, hurry from door to door, from street to street, on
foot or on carriage; with Mr Pitt or Mr Paul or Sir Francis
Burdett, the Westminster election or the Borough of Honiton?'
He is not concerned with forwarding any cause that the 'World'
will recognize. He plainly limits the wider sphere of influence
to which he aspired in the Advertisement and Preface of the
Lyrical Ballads, and, abandoning his desire to reclaim the prejudiced, he now hopes for his poems another destiny: 'to console
the afflicted, to add sunshine to daylight by making the happy
happier, to teach the young and the gracious of every age, to see,
to think and feel and therefore to become more actively and
securely virtuous'. It was to this more orthodox moral purpose,
limited as it was, that he firmly adhered for the remainder of his
poetic career. As an American visitor Ellis Yarnall later testified:
'to him a deep sense of responsibility had ever been present: to
purify and elevate has been the purpose of all his writings'.[1]

.   .   .   .   .   .

During the remainder of the Napoleonic War, the poet's
abandonment of all sympathy for the Whig party, and the gradual
strengthening of his allegiance to the Tories became more
pronounced. The basis of this reorientation was, of course, freely
acknowledged by Wordsworth himself; in 1816 he wrote to
Crabb Robinson: 'My whole soul was with those who were
resolved to fight it out with Bonaparte; and my heart of hearts
set against those who had so little confidence in the power of
justice or so small discernment concerning its nature, as to be
ready at any moment to accept of such a truce as under the name
of peace he might condescend to bestow.'

After that period of disinterest which followed the death of
his brother, he was gradually drawn back to political interests
by the compelling spectacle of the great European struggle whose
advent he had heralded, and on whose outcome so much of his
hope for human liberty now depended. Sara Coleridge later
recalled 'how gravely and earnestly used Coleridge and Wordsworth and my uncle Southey also to discuss the affairs of the
nation, as if it all came home to their business and bosoms, as if

[1] q. Grosart, *Prose Works of Wordsworth* (1876), Vol. III.

it were their private concern'. The Napoleonic War was even more to Wordsworth than a conflict of ideals, a struggle of freedom against tyranny; it was also a trial by ordeal of England, a testing time in which she was to prove her virtue or her degradation. He believed indeed that the war might help to effect the needed regeneration. 'I hope and pray', he wrote to Scott in 1806, 'that the struggle we shall have will invigorate us as it ought to do; then all will be well; and it will be a blessing: if otherwise we shall fall, a thing that would break my heart, but for this, that we shall deserve it.'

Such a preoccupation with England's role and responsibilities in the world conflict involved, as we have seen, a relegation in Wordsworth's mind of the question of domestic reform. This tendency was strengthened by the perverse and short-sighted war policy of the party which was still the generally accepted parliamentary champion of liberal reform. By ingrafting upon their liberalism a treasonable disloyalty completely repulsive to a patriot of any political creed, the Whigs and the radicals drove Wordsworth to the arms of conservatism as surely as the extremism of Pitt's administration and Burke's calumny had earlier driven him and his fellows to an intransigent republicanism.

The Whig war record was dismal in the extreme: the uninspiring Ministry of All the Talents had been driven from office under the all too justifiable suspicion of having attempted to get Catholic Emancipation past George III by something very akin to sharp practice. Their efforts at peace had met with French scorn, yet they refused, in opposition, to act on the lesson which they had been so dishonourably taught on the Treasury benches. In the face of the commonest knowledge and of their own experience, they insisted right up to Waterloo that peace might be had for the asking.

This conviction took various and strange forms. It led to the adulation of Napoleon, and to an almost religious faith in the invincibility of the Imperial armies; a persistent tendency to emphasize the benefits of French rule on the Continent, allied with a blindness to its vices; a suspicion of English propaganda, matched by an ingenuous faith in the reports of the *Moniteur*. It carried them to lengths which were quite frankly treasonable, and if they revolted the good sense of the nation, far more did they repel the poet who saw in the war, more clearly than most of his contemporaries, a clash of fundamental principles whose outcome would decide the future of the world. If his appeals of 1802 had fallen on deaf ears, they are not lost on later generations whose experience has placed them in much closer sympathy with his conception of total war and its implications; and he could no more tolerate the Whig policy from 1807 to 1815 than we could have tolerated its faintest shadow in the years from 1939 to 1945.

It was quite clearly this disgust with the war policy of the Whig-Radical opposition that drove Wordsworth from their camp and into that of their political rivals. Even while he still agreed with them on the necessity for immediate parliamentary reform he could not support their hopes for political power as long as the war lasted.

Conversely, the fact that he heard his own opinions on the great question of the defeat of France voiced in Parliament by the Government, made him loth to emphasize his disagreement with the Tories upon other questions. The only alternative to the rule of Liverpool was that of a notoriously heterogeneous and self-seeking clique, anxious above all for power even at the hands of the Regent, and whose first step after taking power would have been the conclusion of peace with France, professedly upon any terms. Wordsworth's move to a support of the Tories was therefore the result of a logical desire to associate with that political group—certainly more of a united party than the querulous Whigs—with which he felt more closely allied on the major issue. He was long critical of the war policy of the Tories, of their limitations, of their unworthiness of the cause they were called on to champion, and of their stubborn opposition to reform: the fact remained that they were determined to beat the French.

However limited this initial allegiance, it held the seeds of a much closer identification. Writing of Pitt's war policy, a modern historian has pointed out that he was forced, in the interests of victory, to rely on just those vested interests which he had tried earlier, and in vain, to reform: '... and when a man, in defending his country from foreign conquest, has to rely on certain forces, he ceases to be capable of criticizing them. He becomes subdued to the material in which he works.'[1] This was largely the consequence of a similar association in Wordsworth's case; the Opposition itself made it increasingly difficult to distinguish between the cause of domestic reform and national submission to foreign tyranny,[2] while the Tories were able to put themselves forward as the champions of liberty and national independence, carrying on the struggle in the face of a travesty of parliamentary opposition.

．　　　．　　　．　　　．　　　．

In 1808 he was still in that state of political indifference which had followed the death of his brother, and he was certainly not a positive supporter of the Ministry. More than ever did he feel, in the Government, a want of talents equal to the task before it. To a letter from Wrangham on the question of national education, he replied: 'What can you expect of national education conducted by a government which for twenty years resisted the abolition of the slave trade; and annually debauches the morals of the people by every possible device, holding out the temptation with one hand and scourging with the other. The distilleries and lotteries are standing examples that the government cares nothing for the morals of the people, and that all they want is their money.' It was the governors and not the governed who needed educating.

Abroad, while the progress of the war had given to Great Britain, by the defection of her allies, the exalted status of liberty's unique defender, it gave her little else. With no prospect of a successful Continental venture, British military policy was driven again to that dissipation of its forces about the globe which had been so mournfully typical of the strategy of the Revolutionary war.

In this vacuum exploded the Spanish Revolution. A conservative England fighting in defence of King and Constitution

---

[1] G. M. Trevelyan, *History of England* (1945), p. 559.

[2] Whitbread, the leader of both the peace and the reform groups, was typical of the alliance.

was suddenly given as ally a nation in arms rising in enthusiastic
fury against domestic tyranny and foreign invasion. To Wordsworth and his fellows who had been forced, in accordance with
those very principles of liberalism which had earlier made them
supporters of the French Revolution, to reject the French and
espouse the English cause, the Spanish revolt was heaven-sent.
As compensation for their misgivings about this earlier transfer
of allegiance,[1] the whole contest now took on an entirely new
complexion. When the Spanish people placed themselves at the
side of Britain they rendered a service to British liberals greater
than they knew. At a time when such renovation was sorely
needed, the whole conflict received a revivifying inspiration,
and the whole issue was made indisputably clear. The English
opponents of Napoleon regained the fervour of those days of
threatened invasion for in Spain the struggle, as Southey saw
it, was once more that of 'a nation against a foreign usurper, a
business of natural life and death, a war of virtue against vice,
light against darkness, the good principle against the evil one'.
It was, he said, 'the first instance in which Buonaparte unequivoc-
ally displayed himself in his true character of pure devil'.[2]

The liberal aspect of the Spanish rising was a fundamental one
to Wordsworth; here again was that precious and rare national
unanimity which had thrilled him in the early days of the French
Revolution; indeed, here again was another great revolution
breaking out in another notoriously despotic nation, which
promised even more than its subverted precursor—promised
more because it could be guided by the lesson of that subversion.
The appeal of the rising for Wordsworth lay not so much in the
fact that it was one for national independence against a foreign
invader, but in the fact that it was raised 'against a ruler over
whom they have no control, and for one whom they have told us
they will establish as the sovereign of a free people, and who therefore must himself be a limited monarch'. It was the old promise
again, and, disheartened and disillusioned as he had been, he
could not withhold his response. 'His first and his last thoughts

---

[1] Wordsworth admitted that the change was an 'afflicting alternative' and a
'melancholy' necessity. See *Cintra*, Knight, I, 117-18

[2] *Selections from the Letters*, ed. J. W. Warter (1856), II, 299.

are of Spain and Portugal', wrote Dorothy. The glorious rhetoric of the insurgent Spaniards swept him away on a wave of enthusiasm as completely as that of the French National Assembly had ever done; again he saw 'a country in romance', justifying by its actions his own mature attitude to the international position, his own interpretation of the military contest as essentially one between the spirits of liberty and tyranny.

The event which clarified the international cleavage and its moral basis also applied the acid test to the liberal professions of the Whigs. Their complete inability to grasp the significance and possibilities of the Spanish rising was for Wordsworth proof positive of their degradation; still seduced by their conviction of French invincibility, still intrigued by the benefits which French rule might entail for the degraded nations of the Continent, they saw at best, even in allied victories in the Peninsula, merely an opportunity to make an easier peace with Napoleon. Their initial short-lived enthusiasm only served to point more conclusively their later despicable abandonment.

At first news of the outbreak, even the *Edinburgh Review* joined in the exultation; the whole nation felt the transformation effected in the struggle which had pressed so heavily on them for five weary years. Then, unfortunately from the lips of panic-stricken Portuguese emissaries, came the first news of the Convention of Cintra. The great mass of the people, knowing precious little of the military dispositions on the Peninsula, knew only that they had won a victory, and had then most unaccountably permitted the French criminally generous terms of truce. Their reaction was immediate. From Grasmere Wordsworth wrote: 'For myself, I have not suffered so much upon any public occasion these many years.' There was at first talk of organizing a formal petition of protest among the liberal-minded residents of the Lakes—Calvert, Curwen, Wordsworth and Southey. Southey was certain that 'if anything is done in Cumberland, here it will originate with Wordsworth'. But although no concerted action was taken, perhaps as a result of Lonsdale's opposition, Wordsworth turned once more to the composition of a political pamphlet.[1]

[1] See A. V. Dicey, *The Convention of Cintra*, 1915. J. E. Wells, 'The Story of Wordsworth's Cintra', *Studies in Philology*, January, 1921.

The title of this pamphlet, he wrote to Wrangham, was to be 'The Convention of Cintra Brought to the Test of Principles; and the People of Great Britain vindicated from the Charge of Having Prejudged it'. Now although the published title omitted the reference to the vindication of the popular judgment, such a purpose is of major importance in the text as we have it. The indignation of the whole body of the nation which followed the disappointing of their renewed hopes had been something in which Wordsworth had wholeheartedly shared; had, further, been one of those spontaneous expressions of unanimity which always inspired him as proof of man's sentimental fraternity and equality. When the expression of this indignation, even in its most legitimate forms, received only stern rebukes from the Government, Wordsworth eagerly rose to the defence. In his pamphlet he was concerned with justifying and defending the natural sympathies of the people of England for the people of Spain, and their natural indignation at official trifling with the bases of those sympathies. In the ministerial attempts to silence this indignation he saw the ominous probability that 'a league has been formed for the purpose of laying further restraints upon freedom of speech and of the press'; for such a policy would 'tear, out of the venerable crown of the sovereign of Great Britain, a gem which is in the very front of the turban of the emperor of Morocco'.

The essentially liberal tone of the whole tract deserves especial emphasis. It was the Spanish revolt against foreign and domestic tyranny rather than the Spanish war against Napoleon's armies that appealed to Wordsworth. His patriotic nationalism, which had been growing ever since his return from Germany nine years before, obliged him to see that the immediate aim in Spain, as in England, must be the ejection of the foreign tyrant, the removal of the danger of that French domination which would completely stultify Spanish aspirations in every direction; but only the prospect of a subsequent reform of that domestic tyranny which had laid Spain at the feet of the conqueror could give point to the war of liberation. 'The first end to be secured by Spain is riddance of the enemy: the second permanent independence: the third a free constitution of government, which will give their main (though far from sole) value to the other two, and without which little more than a formal independence, and perhaps scarcely that, can be secured.'

The crime of the politicians and soldiers was that they were completely unable to place themselves in sympathy with this liberal movement, this spiritual and democratic enthusiasm of the Spanish people. Echoing his Letter to Llandaff, Wordsworth found the reason for this limitation in the inevitable ignorance of human nature existing in the 'minds of courtiers and statesmen' who live 'in a situation exclusive and artificial', and are subjected to 'the kindred and usually accompanying influence of birth in a certain rank—and, where education has been predefined from childhood for the express purpose of future political power, the tendency of such education to warp (and therefore weaken) the intellect'. Thus born and bred, they inevitably scorn 'the instincts of natural and social man; the deeper emotions; the simpler feelings'.[1]

In Spain it was the lower classes who had shown the way, and whom Wordsworth championed against 'those who stood higher in the scale'. His hopes of the success of the rising were based on the conviction that 'the cause of the people . . . is safe while it remains not only in the bosom, but in the hands of the People; or (what amounts to the same thing) in those of a Government which, being truly *from* the people, is faithfully *for* them'. Promise for the future he could already detect in the measures taken by the provincial juntas, especially in their encouragement of 'liberal opinions'. The Supreme Junta he attacked as too restrictive and exclusive, too reminiscent of those undemocratic assemblies he had reprobated in the Letter to Llandaff, for it was so organized that 'gratitude, habit, and numerous other causes must have given an undue preponderance to birth, station, rank, and fortune; and have fixed the election, more than was reasonable, upon those who were most conspicuous for these distinctions;—men whose very virtue would incline them superstitiously to respect established things, and to mistrust the people'.

[1] Knight, *op. cit.*, I, 226-7. There is an echo of Godwinism too in Words-worth's justification of the publication as a contribution to Truth's war against falsehood: 'Men will and ought to speak upon things in which they are so deeply interested; how else are right notions to spread or is error to be destroyed?' (Knight, I, 168-9.)

It is no wonder, therefore, that Wordsworth feared lest the pamphlet would 'call forth the old yell of Jacobinism' and even that it might be 'made a handle for exercising upon my person a like act of injustice' to that inflicted upon the publisher Flower for a libel against the Bishop of Llandaff in 1799. Catherine Clarkson agreed at least that 'it is not English; there is no English feeling in it'. Yet, 'for truth's sake and liberty's' Wordsworth carried the tract through to belated publication.

In a letter to Daniel Stuart, the editor of *The Courier*, he admitted that the official handling of the Peninsula question had revived his conviction that 'two things are absolutely wanted in this country; a thorough reform in Parliament, and a new course of education'. It was in 1809 that Beaumont still felt it necessary to caution his guests, Wilkie and Haydon the painter, against Wordsworth's 'democratic principles'.[1] The Tory Ministry had profoundly shocked him by its conduct, and he felt obliged to remind the readers of his tract that the government under which Britain was now waging a just and most necessary war was guilty of 'having first involved [the country] in a war with a people then struggling for its own liberties under a twofold infliction—confounded by inbred faction, and beleaguered by a cruel and imperious external foe'; and that 'the same presumptuous irreverence of the principles of justice, and blank insensibility to the affections of human nature, which determined the conduct of our government in those two wars *against* liberty[2] have contrived to accompany its exertions in the present struggle *for* liberty'. Despite all this, 'of the thoughts and feelings' expressed in the parliamentary debates on Spain, Wordsworth was obliged to admit that 'such an approach towards truth which has any dignity in it comes from the side of His Majesty's ministers'.

There was plainly no rational alternative to the existing Tory Ministry, and a parliamentary reform aimed merely at their removal would not come to grips with the real problem. 'They err', he wrote, 'who suppose that venality and corruption (though now spreading more and more) are the master evils of this day: neither these nor immoderate craving for power are so much to

---

[1] Haydon, *Autobiography and Memoirs*, ed. T. Taylor (1926), II, 786.

[2] i.e. the American and the French Revolutionary wars.

be deprecated, as the non-existence of a widely-ranging intellect.'
Wordsworth was in fact seeking not men who were to be more
democratically elected, but better men, and bigger men at the
head of affairs. At least the deficiency would in some way be
made good if legislators would take advantage of that almost
divine guidance occasionally vouchsafed them when the mass of
the people spoke with the single voice of unanimous sentiment; in
its untainted natural wisdom they would at least find a corrective
to their own prejudices and limitations. 'If the people would
constitutionally and resolutely assert their rights, their Representatives would be taught another lesson; and for their own
profit. Their understandings would be enriched accordingly:
for it is there . . . that the want, from which this country suffers,
chiefly lies.'

So *The Eclectic Review* was in fact accurate when it described
the tract as 'self-evidently the work of a retired man, of deep,
enlarged, and patient thought, connected with no political
party, warped by no vulgar prejudices'. His criticism was
modelled rather on Burke's *Policy of the Allies* than on the
strictures of the *Edinburgh Review*, on the Burke who had so
early and so clearly recognized the essential energy of England's
new enemy, and who had entreated his countrymen to match it
with their own: 'If we meet his energy with poor commonplace
proceedings, with trivial maxims, paltry old saws, with doubts,
fears, and suspicions, with a languid, uncertain hesitation, with a
formal, official spirit, which is turned aside by every obstacle
from its purpose, and which never sees a difficulty but to yield
to it; down we go to the bottom of the abyss. We must meet a
vicious and distempered energy with a manly and rational vigour.'
Such a passage from Burke expresses the central theme of Wordsworth's tract. But the Burke who had called for energy and
heightened inspiration had, like Wordsworth, received little
comfort from narrow-minded politicians and hidebound soldiers.

Wordsworth realized too that the Spanish revolt had a traditional, a conservative, as well as a liberal aspect. Napoleon was
outraging the traditional independence and the historical institutions of a sovereign nation, wantonly cutting off Spain 'from its
inheritance in past ages'. In the force of the Spaniards' veneration

for their ancestral traditions, however vitiated by superstition and servility, he found another basis for his hopes of victory. The French fought as an invading army, the Spanish as patriots defending the land of their fathers, the noble living defending the legacy entrusted them by the noble dead, defending, in the spirit of Burke, their national heritage against the brutal innovations of a foreign creed.

.   .   .   .   .

He had not forgotten the lesson of earlier disappointments, and he had learned by now that 'there is danger in being a zealot in any cause—not excepting that of humanity'. Still, his hopes were again somewhat too high, and it was hardly possible that events should keep pace with his enthusiasm. It is regrettable that he should have pinned so much faith on a conflict taking place under conditions of which he had no real knowledge; it was perhaps inevitable that he should go astray. Not only his ignorance of Iberian conditions, but even his idealism helped to mislead him. As a correspondent of Crabb Robinson's wrote: 'in general he estimates the moral motives which impel man, in these degenerate days, too highly'.

Again disappointment followed enthusiasm. By May, 1809, he was writing to De Quincey that 'in fact, as far as relates to this country, as connected with the cause, my zeal is much abated, as are my hopes.' So much so indeed, that he was no longer 'willing to incur any risks in directing the indignation of the public'. Spain was not long a major interest with him, except as a mere field of battle against Napoleon, and in an unpublished sonnet he was soon lamenting his disillusionment with 'that degenerate land'. But once again the fault was not attributable to the immediate agents; as in the case of the revolutionary excesses in France, he placed the guilt of failure at the door of the despotism of the past; Spain had failed not because of her patriots, but because—

Full long relinquishing a precious dower
By Gothic virtue won . . .
The Spaniard hath approached on servile knee
The native ruler all too willingly.

CHAPTER VIII

The Confirmed Tory

Although Whig pessimism was given considerable colour by the discouraging succession of events on the Peninsula, Wordsworth's heart-felt disappointment was a far cry from the jubilant 'I-told-you-so' of Brougham and the Edinburgh Reviewers. British reverses were Whig triumphs[1] and the *Edinburgh Review* by October, 1809, had settled in the conviction that 'there was at no time any reasonable chance of driving the French out of the Peninsula, and . . . consequently, no British army should ever have been sent there at all'. Agitation for reform was renewed but even the *Edinburgh Review* found difficulty in stomaching the proposals put forward by the radical Wardle in July, 1809; as an essential part of his policy of economic retrenchment, he advocated a reduction of the military forces involving the discharge of all foreign troops and volunteers, the cancelling of all military construction, the reduction of allowances to the militia, and the withdrawal of a third of the naval grant. This was the sort of thing that made Dorothy Wordsworth write to her brother: 'It is my opinion that Mr Whitbread and a few others deserve hanging.' For Whitbread and his associates gradually made the obtaining of peace the prime motive of their reform agitation.[2]

Tory proposals for coalition were rejected out of hand. In September, 1809, Perceval (on Lonsdale's insistence, it might be noted) obtained royal permission to discuss with Grey and Grenville the forming of a national ministry. The proud Whig magnates, insulted by this indirect approach, declined the offer. It was

[1] See Creevey (ed. Gore), pp. 78 *et passim*.

[2] See *Parliamentary Debates* (pub. T. C. Hansard) for 1810, Vol. XVII, pp. 115, 149-50, etc.

repeated on Perceval's death, but the proposals put forward by
Wellesley were again rejected, this time because the Whigs
frankly admitted that they could not countenance the con-
tinuation of the war in the Peninsula: 'no person feels more
strongly than we do', they replied, 'the advantages that would
result from a successful termination to the present contest in
Spain. But we are of the opinion that the direction of military
operations are questions not of principles but of policy, to be
regulated by circumstances. . . . On such questions therefore no
public men . . . can undertake for more than a deliberate and dispassionate consideration according to the circumstances of the
case. In the present state of the finances we entertain the strongest
doubts of the practicability of an increase in any branch of the
public expenditure.'[1]

In the Peninsula itself, Wellington found cause to complain
of the spread of Whig defeatism among his officers, 'which', he
wrote, 'I must devise some means of putting an end to, or it will
put an end to us'. At home even Leigh Hunt recoiled, with the
rest of England, from the possibility of a Whig ministry, with or
without reform: what could the country expect, he asked, from
a government led by Grenville, 'the prince of sinecurists', and
by Grey the apostate, 'whose first proceeding, after the Duke of
York's expulsion from office, was to go and take a pathetic chop
with him'. Even military calamity was insufficient to rehabilitate
such a party in the national esteem, and the Parliamentary vote for
the Government upon the Walcheren expedition indicated a
want of confidence in the Opposition far more than a positive
support of Tory policy.

Wordsworth's progress from this same comparative preference
of Tory war policy to a complete opposition to liberal reform can
be plotted in considerable detail from 1809 on. In 1810 he
recorded his approval of Coleridge's essay in the tenth number of
The Friend as the soundest expression of political principles which
that short-lived periodical contained. Now, this essay, 'On the
Errors of Party Spirit: or Extremes Meet', was certainly not
restrained in its condemnation of Ministerial shortcomings. If
the Whigs and radicals had culpably prejudiced the cause of

[1] Roberts, *Whig Party*, p. 386.

reform, 'the errors of the aristocratic party were full as gross, and far less excusable. Instead of contenting themselves with opposing the real blessings of English law to splendid promises of untried theory, too large a part of those, who call themselves Anti-Jacobins, did all in their power to suspend those blessings; and thus furnished new arguments to the advocates of innovation.' Wordsworth still resented at this stage any tendency to whitewash the whole administration merely because it voiced sound opinions on the major issue, or any attempt to discredit the whole reform movement merely because of the pacificism or extremism of its more articulate representatives. In May he wrote to Stuart, the editor of *The Courier*, in which he had originally published 'Cintra': 'I cannot say that I have been so well pleased with the course of *The Courier* lately; neither in the instance of Castlereagh, whom it has endeavoured to screen, nor with respect to the extreme bitterness with which it has declared against all those who have countenanced, in connection with Burdett, the attempt at Reform. As for Burdett himself, I have as little respect for him as for any man, but I do not think the welfare of the country can be promoted by accusations tending to involve all those who might have attended at that meeting, in direct and deliberate participation in such bad views as *The Courier* has attributed to him. If we, who work for a temperate reform, are utterly to reject all assistance from all those who do not think exactly as we do, how is it to be attained? For my part, I see no party with whom in regard to this measure I could act with entire approbation of their views, but I should be glad to receive assistance from any . . . it is natural that in meetings of this kind the most violent men should be the most applauded, but I do not see that it necessarily follows that their words will be realized in action. The misfortune of this question of reform is that one party sees nothing in it but dangers, the other nothing but hopes and promises. For my part, I think the dangers and difficulties great, but not insurmountable, whereas, if there be not a reform the destruction of the liberties of this country is inevitable.'

Now the significant passages of this letter are that in which he admits that he is still unable to give his entire approbation to any of the political parties, and that in which he depreciates the possibility of action corresponding in violence to the language of the reformers and agitators. We remember that, in the sphere of domestic politics, the lesson he had learned from the Convention of Cintra was the desirability of some measure of political reform, and it was because of their refusal to countenance any such measure that he still found himself debarred from complete allegiance to the Tories, just as it was the liberal opposition to the war that prevented him from associating with their opponents, Whig or radical. For some time the influence of these two convictions was balanced: in 1809 he not only composed his war sonnets on Hofer, 'brave Schill', and the Tyrolean revolt, panegyrics as they were of the slighted defenders of liberty, but he saw fit at the same time to publish in *The Friend* his noble poetic tribute from *The Prelude* to the pristine glory of the French Revolution. When Cintra drew him back to political reform, and decided him to follow his tract with further polemical contributions to *The Courier*, it was as a 'patriot' that he took his stand. As he wrote in the published letter to 'Mathetes', his faith in the old liberal tenet of perfectibility was still strong, despite the 'apparent stagnation or . . . retrograde movement of the last few years'.

Nevertheless, it has already been noticed that several elements in Wordsworth's environment, and even certain implications of his poetic inspiration, supplemented the influence of his agreement with Tory war policy in impelling him to conservatism, and in tempering his anxiety for constitutional reform. For example, his suspicions of the aristocracy were gradually allayed by his friendship with another Lord Lonsdale, and with Sir George Beaumont. Their culture and magnanimity wore down his resentment of social distinctions, as similar associations had done in the case of Rousseau.

The world in which he lived and of which he wrote also had its influence. We can see in the 1801 letter to Fox the nature of his affection for the rural community of the North, men 'placed above poverty' . . . 'small independent proprietors of land . . . men of respectable education . . . who live in a country not crowded with population'. His admiration of the unique virtue of their domestic life was bound to lead him to an even closer identification with their interests and outlook. Politically, in the North as elsewhere, this landed interest was solidly conservative, and was to become increasingly so in face of the liberal-commercial alliance of early nineteenth-century Whiggism. In the same way their piety, their strong feeling for the traditions of the past, the strength of their local attachments—all these traits Wordsworth cherished as sources of their felicity and potential sources of his own. Inevitably they stimulated his own religious sentiment, his patriotism and his historical sense.

But, more important, ever since the *Lyrical Ballads*, he had been concerned not with those aspects of human existence which call for modification, but with the sources of joy and consolation inherent in the unchangeable elements of man's environment: the permanent forms of nature, the fundamental domestic affections and sympathies. He wished attention drawn not to the existing imperfections of social or political organization, but to those unalterable and inalienable springs of pleasure which even an 'unjust state of society' could not endanger. As John Stuart Mill saw, the fundamental implication of his poetry was its rejection of 'struggle or imperfection'.[1]

Now, whatever the limitations of the Tories, they were inevitably the party of 'repose', inspired by principles of permanence and stability on which they based their opposition to Whigs and Frenchmen alike. The Whigs were necessarily the party of discontent. The direction of Wordsworth's political drift was inevitable, and it was confirmed by the fact that his mature approach to the question of human happiness convinced him in time that nothing was radically amiss. The great sources of real happiness were open to all:

> Throughout the world of sense,
> Even as an object is sublime or fair,
> That object is laid open to the view
> Without reserve or veil; and as a power
> Is salutary, or an influence sweet,

[1] q. Myers, *op. cit.*, p. 136. Lowes Dickinson might have been talking of Wordsworth's poetry and not of his own 'Modern Symposium' when he said: 'Practical politics involves fighting, and the object of such a book as mine . . . is to raise the mind above the fighting attitude.'

Are each and all enabled to perceive
That power, that influence, by impartial law.
> (*Exc.*, IX, 214.)

All mankind had the solution of its problems, of its doubts, and
of its sufferings within its reach:

The primal duties shine aloft—like stars;
The charities that soothe, and heal, and bless,
Are scattered at the feet of man.
The generous inclination, the just rule,
Kind wishes and good actions, and pure thoughts—
No mystery is here! Here is no boon
For high—yet not for low; for proudly graced—
Yet not for meek of heart.
> (*Exc.*, IX, 238.)

This was the core of Wordsworth's new egalitarianism, and it
inevitably drove him from a concern with legal or political
reform. Turning from a lamentation of the social handicaps of
the lower classes, he became the poet of their virtues and, more,
of the lesson which these virtues could teach to the rest of mankind; he no longer complained of their oppression or pleaded
for their emancipation to political and social equality, but
proclaimed the moral, emotional and spiritual equality of all men
as actual and visible.

Political and social reform was thus replaced by a faith in
the more real reform, the leading man back to the natural
sources of never-failing joy and consolation, which he hoped his
own poetry would effect. In face of the central problem of
human happiness, the question as to whether its significant
sources are fundamentally internal or external, Wordsworth, in
the light of his own dramatic experience, had decided in favour of
the personal, the internal source. Although the implications were
only later to be made plain, we can see in such a decision the
seeds of that apathy and eventual violent antipathy towards
nearly all political schemes which attempted to solve the problem
in the other way. There was an inherent contradiction between his
worship of Nature's calm permanence, its benignant restraint of
passion and enthusiasm and any passionate political fervour which

aimed at change. He could not see in Nature an independent and a supreme source of the only real joy and substantial consolation, a source distinguished above all by its universal accessibility, and at the same time persist in a demand for political reform as an essential prerequisite of human happiness and progress.

Furthermore, as far as the war itself was concerned, it was not only being waged by the conservative party, but was being fought in defence of the British Constitution as it existed. To some extent the Whigs and radicals were honest in refusing to defend a political system which they condemned as fundamentally perverted: in the same way it became increasingly difficult for Wordsworth, having apotheosized his country as the defender of liberty, as the shining example to the world, to continue to find fault with that very constitution by virtue of which his country seemed to maintain her supremacy. If the Tories shone by comparison with the Whigs, how much more did England shine by comparison with her tyrant-ridden enemy and the effete despotism of her faithless allies. The very military power of his country, her obvious strength, of itself made it increasingly difficult for him to question the basis of her supremacy and the political organization in which the domestic sources of that strength were expressed.

The influence of the spectacle of Britain's armed might is plain in the important letter written in 1811 to Sir C. W. Pasley, an officer in the Royal Engineers and a writer on military affairs. 'How comes it', Wordsworth asks, 'that we are enabled to keep, by sea and land, so many men in arms? Not by our foreign commerce, but by our domestic ingenuity, by our home labour, which, with the aid of capital and the mechanic arts and establishments, has enabled a few to produce so much as will maintain themselves and the hundreds of thousands of their countrymen whom they support in arms.' It was in England's strength that he found hope, and in the peculiar sources of that strength which distinguished her from her enemy: '. . . when I look at the condition of our country and compare it with that of France, and reflect upon the length of time, and the infinite combination of favourable circumstances which have been necessary to produce the laws, the regulations, the customs, the moral character, and the physical enginery of all sorts, through means and by

aid of which labour is carried on in this happy land; and when
I think of the wealth and population . . . which we must have at
command for military purposes, I confess I have not much dread,
looking either at war or peace, of any power which France . . .
is likely to attain for years'. In the face of the impressive proof of
Britain's greatness which the war called forth, Wordsworth
became inevitably and increasingly loth, finally unable, to find
radical fault with any of the elements of her polity, whose very
anomalies eventually appeared too sacred to be meddled with,
lest they prove unsuspected sources of that same greatness: he
was increasingly afraid that the rash removal of the spots on the
sun might in some way diminish its brightness.

The war was fought by, if not essentially for, an 'unreformed'
England, the product of the past and of slow-maturing development; as Wordsworth saw so clearly in Spain, it was a struggle of
tradition against innovation, of the wise past against the rash and
frantic present, a contest between the real freedom produced by
gradual progress, and that heady passion for a spurious liberty
in whose name armies were led to conquest. And it was the
British Constitution, with the course of political development that
it implied, which embodied the 'national liberty' in whose
name the war was fought and won.

As we noticed above, Wordsworth was, in 1809, willing to
tolerate the demagogy of reform agitators because he did not
believe that their violence would be translated into action. In
the very next year the notorious Burdett riots[1] seemed to correct
this delusion. They were enough to convince Southey, who
announced that 'the Burdettites have cured me of all wish for
parliamentary reform, at least for any reform of their making, or
after their fashion', and Wordsworth's reaction was substantially
the same. Liberalism which found its main expression in an un-
timely pacifism was *de facto* discredited for Wordsworth the
champion of war: liberalism expressed in physical violence con-
flicted with an even more fundamental conviction. Even in
1794 his condemnation of violence had been so strong that the
averting of all danger of an outbreak had been as much a motive

[1] 'The very first instance, within our recollection, in which our English
mob ever fired on the troops.' (*Anti-Jacobin Review*, April, 1810.)

of his projected political activity as the effecting reform.

Today we tend to depreciate the significance if not the extent of the Luddite outbreaks and related incidents of social violence which occurred during the later years of the Napoleonic War and afterwards. It is fatally easy for posterity, in full possession of the facts, and experienced in social disorder of every kind and extent, to smile at the melodramatic fears of Wordsworth, Southey and Scott. In the age of the Cato Street Conspiracy and the Spa Fields Riots, these fears were so widely shared that we cannot dismiss them as reactionary panic. The Committee of Secrecy set up by the Government announced itself convinced of the revolutionary aims of the Spenceans and even of the Hampden Clubs. In 1816 even Shelley, remarking on 'the strength which the popular party have suddenly acquired, and the importance which the violence of demagogues has assumed', admitted that 'the whole fabric of society presents a most threatening aspect', and only hoped that 'reform may come without revolution'. A year later Mary Shelley 'shuddered' at reading Cobbett, who appeared 'to be making out a list for a proscription'; it was enough to convince her that 'a revolution in this country would not be bloodless if that man has any power in it'.

It must be remembered in justification of contemporary panic that it was the unique misfortune of Wordsworth's generation and the one that followed to be witnesses of the first stirrings in England of proletarian discontent in the modern sense, of an organized violence which was strangely and terrifyingly novel. Nor must the extent of the Luddite disturbances, for example, be minimized,[1] nor their effect depreciated. In an era before the inauguration of a non-military police system, the temper of movements of that nature and the fears consequent upon them, were heightened and sharpened much more than would have been the case at a time when social discontent called forth other defensive weapons than musket and bayonet. It is not difficult to sympathize with the fears of men who knew that society's only defence against anarchy was an army never large and now weakened by a major continental war.

[1] See Home Office Papers, reports, etc., in P.R.O., H.O. 40/1; H.O. 40/2, etc.

The Luddite riots possessed every element needed to provoke the fears of many who cannot all be dubbed mere timid fools. The military organization of the rioters, their presumed nation-wide connections, the very rumours to which the outbreak gave so much colour—all these must find their place in our endeavour to reconstruct the contemporary background. Nor should we fall into the error of seeing in the clamour provoked by the isolated assassinations perpetrated by the rioters merely proof of the infrequency of such events in current outbreaks: the significant fact is, of course, that just because England was not accustomed to violence on a serious scale, she was all the more terrified by such single outrages as the murder of Horsfall, and the totally unrelated assassination of Perceval. The Prime Minister was shot by a maniac, but the assassination occurred in 1812, immediately after the Luddite riots, and the popular acclamation which greeted the event seemed particularly significant to Wordsworth. To him the cheers of the mob over Perceval's coffin, the rioting of Burdett's supporters, and the lawless banditry of the Luddites were all related indications of a real danger of revolution.

Certainly violence was far more typical of the post-war disaffection than had earlier been the case. As Hazlitt saw, the rage of speculation had been replaced by a new rage of hunger. Coleridge thought that the damage had been done by the declension of Jacobinism from the upper and middle classes to the lower. In any case Wordsworth found little in its new ex-pression to remind him of the speculative republicanism of his youth. As Godwin had said, the aim of the reform 'movement' (insofar as it can be called such) of the 1790s had been 'to prepare the enlightened to sympathize with the just claims of the oppressed and humble'; it was essentially an appeal *to* the enlightened *for* the lower classes, and the fear of anything approaching demagogy, even in organizations like the Corresponding Societies, often made the reformers ludicrously timid. But with Priestley, Wake-field and Godwin out of the picture, the new Jacobinism found its champions in Burdett, Cobbett and Hunt: they appealed not *for* the people, but *to* the newly created industrial proletariat; they wanted not sympathy, but political power, and Wordsworth condemned them in 1820 as he would have done in 1794, when he

had written, in the course of an avowal of his republicanism:
'I severely condemn all inflammatory addresses to the passions
of men even when it is intended to direct those passions to a good
purpose.' The democrat who had then proclaimed his determined
enmity 'to every species of violence', to whom the averting
of rebellion was almost as important as the furthering of reform, saw
now that the same danger was considerably greater, and that the
prime aim of government policy must be the repression of the
violence of discontent as an essential prerequisite to any measures
of amelioration.

The influence of this violence, or rather of Wordsworth's
reaction to and interpretation of it, upon his liberal sympathies
is obvious. However indirectly, the movement for political
reform became associated with rioting, lawlessness, and even
murder, and such an association did almost as much to temper his
anxiety for political reform as its association with the 'peace-
mongering Whigs'. In the face of a threat of anarchy, he reacted
typically and inevitably into the championing of order. He was
genuinely afraid of revolution, and could not agree that, in view
of the political and the moral temper now demonstrated by the
lower classes, concessions to them in the shape of increased
political influence were either advisable, or would be efficient
in removing the danger. Events very quickly gave the lie to that
complacency with which he had earlier been able to tolerate the
fiery incitements of Burdett and the violence of the radical
press. A Wordsworth who knew something of the ferocity of the
mob had his memories renewed and his old fears strengthened; he
was hardly likely to underestimate the danger, nor to be behindhand in his denunciation of all whom he suspected of stimulating
the tendency.

But if he agreed with Southey, that the immediate danger was
'an insurrection of the Yahoos', and that 'till the breed can be
mended it must be curbed', he also concurred with the rider that
'it is the fault of the Government that such a caste should exist
in the midst of a civilized society'. He was indeed more scrupulous
than Southey and complained of him that 'in his vivid perception
of the danger to be apprehended from the disaffected urging on
the rabble, and the consequent necessity of Government being

empowered to keep them down, he does not seem sufficiently jealous of the power whose protection we all feel to be necessary'. Repression was at best but a regrettable necessity for Wordsworth, and he was certain that wiser administration of existing laws would answer better than the curtailment of freedom by new official powers or by such measures as the suspension of Habeas Corpus, on which his sister commented: 'if it be necessary, I can only think that the feeble execution of the laws which we have already is the cause of that necessity, and it is greatly to be lamented. Nothing can so much tend to irritate the minds of the people.' Such an attitude displays the other and more agreeable side of Wordsworth's conviction that the new problems could be solved by the traditional methods. In 1816 he still could not acquiesce in restrictions upon the liberty of the Press; Crabb Robinson noted the question as the one 'on which Southey and Wordsworth differed most', for whereas 'Southey would have punished a second political libel with transportation, Wordsworth was unwilling to restrain the press'. His detestation of hysterical reformers was balanced by his contempt for Tory libel: 'I know little of *Blackwood's Magazine*', he wrote to Wrangham in 1819, 'and wish to know less. I have seen in it articles so infamous that I do not choose to let it enter my doors.' In 1821 he was reading both *The Morning Chronicle* and *The Courier*, and so, as he told Catherine Clarkson, stood 'a chance of coming to something like impartial judgment between the two'.

. . . . . .

Before the end of the war, Wordsworth had dropped his insistence on the need for political reform, and was preaching instead, in verse and prose, the need for moral regeneration, for that spiritual reform which had, in fact, always been closer to his heart and more essentially in keeping with the implications of his poetic inspiration. By 1811, although he was still anxious for a 'new course of education', a desire for reform was significantly replaced by one for that 'higher tone of moral feeling' which had been the burden of the 1802 sonnets.

The letter to Pasley in which this interesting substitution is so pointed, and to which reference has already been made, is a valuable document in many ways. Pasley's book, *An Essay upon the Military Policy and Institutions of the British Empire* (1810),[1] was not, on the surface, calculated to appeal to Wordsworth's views on the war. The author was all too aware of France's power and Britain's limitations, and while he advocated a policy of vigour and daring, his hopes ultimately rested on the belief that a just God would work 'some unexpected change in our favour'. Still, he was not blinded by French material supremacy, and was all for carrying on the struggle on the grandest scale, if only to prove worthy of divine intervention.

It was to correct his underestimation of Britain's position, and to point out the bases of his own faith that Wordsworth wrote to him. It is plain that this faith was now intimately bound up with his conception of England as the embodiment of tradition, as the product of the past matched against the rootless and new-born polity of her enemy. It was in this England, the fruit of steady growth matured into greatness by the slow passage of time, that land whose very countryside exemplified its 'calm felicity and power', the England of Burke, that he gloried and trusted. It was this England that he held out as a living and shining example to the countries of Europe.

The letter proclaims the mature Wordsworth's faith in his country, and it was now rather a positive faith in what she had become, no longer a conditional one in what she might become. Subject only to that regeneration which he still demanded, and which he thought the war itself might well be effecting, he declares his entire satisfaction, his willingness to give his country that entire approbation which he had felt forced so long to deny her.

Yet as far as party allegiance was concerned he still preserved his independence. It was also in 1811 that, in some perturbation, he wrote, evidently to his Whig friend, Sharp, reprobating the reported intentions of the opposition to recall the Peninsula army in the event of their accession to power. He still admits that 'the transgressions of the present ministry are grievous', but as long as they refrain from 'a deliberate and

[1] Which Jane Austen found 'delightfully written and highly entertaining'. See *Letters*, ed. Chapman (2nd ed.), p. 292.

direct attack upon the civil liberties of our own country' they must be preferred to those who show 'a desponding spirit and the lack of confidence in a good cause'. In his condemnation of the Whigs he was not yet prepared to accept Coleridge's 'servile adulation of the Wellesleys', and he no doubt shared his sister's opinion that his friend's writings in *The Courier* 'in general evidenced (*a*) sad weakness of moral constitution. . . . They are as much the work of a party spirit, as if he were writing for a place.' He still retained his friendship with the liberal coterie in the Lakes, with Sharp and Calvert, and, no doubt relying upon the opinion of the latter, Shelley reported of him in 1811 that, as compared with Southey, he still retained 'the integrity of his independence'.

These testimonies should be remembered when we learn that early in the following year the indigent father of a family found himself obliged, in view of the 'unexpected pressure of the times, falling most heavily upon men who have no regular means of increasing their income in proportion', to apply to Lord Lonsdale for a place. Six years earlier Lonsdale had made to him an unsolicited offer of a property worth £1,000, which the poet, with some embarrassment, felt obliged to refuse. But by 1812 his position had worsened, and the spontaneous generosity of the earlier gift no doubt suggested that his petition need not involve dependence. He did not ask for a reward for services rendered in the past, and made no mention of any intention to give literary proof of his indebtedness in the future. His last appearance in print had been as the author of a pamphlet whose avowed intention was to attack 'the opposition which was made by His Majesty's ministers to the expression . . . of the opinions and feelings of the people',[1] upon a subject on which he knew Lonsdale's opinions were contrary to his own. The letter was a frank request for assistance, not an endeavour to conclude a bargain. He was at pains to point out his 'utter inability . . . to associate with any class or body of literary men, and thus subject myself to the necessity of sacrificing my own judgment, and of lending even indirectly countenance or support to principles— either of taste, politics, morals or religion—which I disapprove'.

[1] Advertisement to 'Cintra'.

It was perhaps inevitable that, in thus placing himself under an obligation to the great Tory peer, he should at least modify the future expression of his political sympathies; it is hardly likely, for example, that he would have taken such an active and public part in the 1818 election, had he not felt obliged to assist his benefactor; nor can there be much doubt that his subsequent letters to Lonsdale exemplify, on some occasions at least, that 'courteous, yet often innocent, compliance—to gratify the several tastes of correspondents' which he defended in Burns. But there can be no doubt at all that his opinions on major issues such as Catholic emancipation and parliamentary reform would have been substantially the same whatever the politics of his patron.

The request itself was made in good faith, and Wordsworth, whose poverty was such that Shelley reported that he was 'frequently obliged to beg for a shirt to his back', was not appealing merely for himself. He was not disappointed, and in the following year the erstwhile republican became a Distributor of Stamps.

Shortly afterwards the author of 'Joan of Arc' became Poet Laureate, and the Wordsworths hoped that Southey's good fortune might be as free from galling obligations as their own. Even if their neighbour were obliged to panegyrize his royal patron, 'surely', wrote Dorothy, 'there will be something to praise without falsehood or bad indeed he must be'. The British monarchy, to whom De Quincey reported Wordsworth to have been so treasonably indifferent in 1807, was by 1812 rehabilitated in his esteem, as was the British Constitution as a whole, largely because it was British, and because it was at war with France. Yet in his intervals of sanity George III did display a determination which expressed, within the limits of his position, the military resolution of his people, earned their esteem and affection, and presented a notable contrast to the behaviour of his royal continental associates.

Something of the same reactive defence of an English institution, whose merit and significance had been considerably enhanced for Wordsworth by England's war against tyranny, was at work in his revised attitude to the English Church. As the English Constitution had become his ideal because it was freedom's bulwark against the forces of oppression, so the English Church came to symbolize that spiritual and religious faith which freedom's sanctuary opposed to the frank materialism of her enemy. Despite his persistent criticism of details of religious polity, he was convinced that the English Church 'must' be prized, if rather for what it represented than what it was.

During the latter years of the war his own religious convictions had been strengthened considerably. His faith in victory owed much to his belief that England's cause was the just one which God must favour. Prayers for national triumph could no longer leave him unmoved, and by 1811 he and Dorothy were regular in attendance at divine service, though certainly not from the very highest of motives. 'I assure you', wrote Dorothy, 'we are become regular church-goers . . . for the sake of the children, and indeed Mr Johnson, our present curate, appears to be so much in earnest and is so unassuming and amiable a man that I think we should often go even if we had not the children.' Double bereavement in the death of two of his children in 1812 strengthened his religious sentiment, as the death of John had done seven years before, and again drove him for consolation, not to the vernal woods, but to direct supplication of God, whom he prayed to lead him, not to elevation above human grief, but to 'calm submission to Thy wish'. He came to fear for the religious establishment of England beset by its opponents as he feared for its political constitution subjected to military onslaught.

In 1807 he was still undecided on the question of Catholic emancipation. He confessed to Wrangham: 'I am not prepared to see the Catholic religion as the Established Church of Ireland; and how that can be consistently refused to them if other things are granted on the plea of their being a majority, I do not see.' Southey complained in the same year that Coleridge was the only one of his friends who agreed with him in opposing Catholic claims. But by 1809, guided more by patriotic motives, Wordsworth had become increasingly solicitous of the fate of the English Church subjected to attack on two fronts. 'With the Methodists on one side, and the Catholics on the other, what is to become of the poor Church and people of England, to both of which I am most tenderly attached?'

The other bases of his opposition to emancipation we shall

L

discuss later, but by 1813 he found his allegiance to the Tory ministry cemented by his agreement with them on the religious issue as well as upon the military one. In August he wrote to Wrangham: 'As to what you say about the ministry—I very much prefer the course of their policy to that of the Opposition, especially on two points most near to my heart, resistance of Buonaparte by force of arms, and their adherence to the principles of the British Constitution in witholding political power from the Roman Catholics. . . . I cannot act with those who see no danger to the Constitution in introducing papists into parliament.'

CHAPTER IX

Post-war

In 1814 came long-awaited victory. 'I congratulate you', wrote Wordsworth to Wrangham, 'on the overthrow of the execrable despot and the complete triumph of the war (party) of which noble body I had the honour to be as active a member as my abilities and industry would allow.' It was something in the nature of a personal triumph for Wordsworth, as we can see, and, as he points out, a triumph also for that political party which had championed his cause. Professor Trevelyan makes an enlightening comparison with an earlier war in pointing out that 'the honour of beating Napoleon fell as clearly to the Tories, as the honour of beating Louis XIV had fallen to the Whigs';[1] a fact which Byron somewhat lamented in *Beppo* (XLIX): '(I) greatly venerate our recent glories, And wish they were not owing to the Tories.'

The opposition ran true to form to the very end, with Grey, in the interests of a quicker peace, hoping for an allied defeat during the advance of 1814 and opposing the renewal of hostilities after Napoleon's escape from Elba. In the light of these justifications of his fears it is small wonder that Wordsworth was so vehement in his exhortations for the maintenance of Allied determination and for a clear decision.

The attempted restoration of the *status quo* in Europe aroused his open condemnation, particularly the Italian settlement. 'The Italians have been abominably used', he wrote, 'in being transferred to Austria, to the king of Sardinia, and the rest of those vile tyrants.' He had hoped for Britain's triumph, not only as an end in itself, but also because he imagined that her success would inevitably stimulate the liberalization of the Continent upon her

[1] *British History in the Nineteenth Century and After* (1937), p. 108.

example. But while he expected some reaction, and indeed blamed the Jacobins and their successors for driving the monarchs back into the arms of absolutism, he lamented that so little seemed to have been learned. He hoped that in time at least the balance would be righted: 'the fate, the undeserved fate of Louis XVI, who lost his throne and his life because his people erroneously thought that he deserved to lose them, will . . . operate beneficially as a warning, and be fully adequate, as far as example goes, to counteract any encouragement to misconduct which might be derived from the restoration'. There was another lesson that kings must learn from the war which had saved them: they must remember

> . . . that the nerve
> Of popular reason, long mistrusted, freed
> Your thrones . . . ;

and so he implored them:

> . . . from duty fear to swerve!
> Be just, be grateful; nor, the oppressor's creed
> Reviving, heavier chastisement deserve
> Than ever forced unpitied hearts to bleed.
>   ('Emperors and Kings.')

Nevertheless, victory was for Wordsworth, in a very real sense, the culmination of more than ten years political anxiety; he had been completely preoccupied with the military struggle by which the cause of human freedom was being defended. When the supreme ambition of his mature political life was fulfilled, he was somewhat exhausted, and there was an inevitable decline in his fervour. He was only too glad to find in victory a 'lasting resting place' for his liberal aspirations.

Further, it had always been the dramatic conflict, more usually the unequal conflict, of the champions of liberty against the massed forces of tyranny, the forlorn struggle of the patriot which had stimulated him, rather than the spectacle of the good cause triumphant. When Schill and Hofer and Toussaint were replaced by Wellington and Castlereagh and Metternich, when the field of battle moved from the Swiss mountains to the conference tables of Paris and Vienna, Wordsworth turned away. He was content that his country, by her persistence in the good cause, by her energy and valour, had proved the soundness of her polity and the principles upon which it was based; had given, by meriting the Divine reward of victory, the final confirmation of his hopes and his confidence.

This conviction that England's success was due more than anything else to Divine favour was no merely rhetorical pietism; Wordsworth's belief that the palm of victory was the seal of approval vouchsafed to England by a benignant Deity was sincere and profound enough to modify the whole body of his subsequent opinions—and not only his religious opinions. In the Essay Supplementary to the Preface of 1815 he gave striking critical expression to his new and essentially religious inspiration in claiming that 'poetry is most just to its own divine origin when it administers the comforts and breathes the spirit of religion'. It is indeed essential to remember that for the last forty years of his life Wordsworth was above all a religious poet, often in the very narrowest sense of the term. His religious convictions had been maturing and crystallizing ever since the death of his brother, and there can be no doubt of the influence upon them of his conception of the spiritual and religious implications of the struggle against and final victory over Napoleon.

It was under the strong influence of these convictions that he wrote the bulk of *The Excursion*, whose theme is the strength of religious sentiment as that of *The Prelude* had been the re-generative power of nature. The Solitary is told to turn to God, to the supreme judge whose promise of immortality can alone balance temporal evil and suffering, as the poet of *The Prelude* had turned to nature to find solace in its lesson of peace and joy. And the religion which Wordsworth preached was based on the orthodox doctrine of the Church of England, the national institution in whose formal certainty he had found repose in time of bereavement and doubt, and whose merit, along with that of all things English, had been enormously enhanced for him by the events of the last few years.

It was therefore an essentially religious turn which he now gave to his persistent endeavour to counter the materialism of his age. For the regeneration of

> . . . busy men
> Depraved, and ever prone to fill the mind
> Exclusively with transitory things[1]

he advocated, not a 'wise passiveness', not impulses from vernal woods, but, briefly, more churches—and more 'Pastors'. He was fully aware of the shortcomings of that Established Church the increase of whose influence he henceforth so earnestly promoted, and, personally experienced in the matter of 'vile' priests, he knew that his Pastor was an idealization, one

> . . . the like of whom
> If multiplied, and in their stations set,
> Would o'er the bosom of a joyful land
> Spread true religion and her genuine fruits.[2]

It was of course because his Pastor was not typical that Wordsworth later welcomed the stimulation afforded to clerical piety by the Oxford Movement.

It should also be noted that, to the poet who ten years later was still subject to 'Misgivings hard to vanquish or control',[3] who could never resolve to his own satisfaction the contradiction between Divine foreknowledge and accountability in man, the unswerving faith of the Wanderer was similarly ideal. *The Excursion* is a dramatic poem, and if the Solitary depicts Wordsworth as he might have become, the Wanderer possesses that faith and certainty for which Wordsworth longed, but which he seems never to have attained.

The tales which form so large a portion of the poem are not concerned with questions social or political, and indeed they studiously avoid the remotest hint at distress or dissatisfaction due to oppression or injustice. The widower who finds that—

> . . . all his rights
> In his paternal lands were undermined,

is taught not of human injustice, but of human benevolence:

> For he who now possessed the joyless right
> To force the Bondsman from his house and lands,

[1] *Excursion*, VI, 37.   [2] *Excursion*, VI, 77.
[3] 'O dearer far than light and life are dear.'

> In pity, and by admiration urged
> Of his unmurmuring and considerate mind
> Meekly submissive to the law's decree,
> Lightened the penalty with liberal hand.[1]

The dalesmen watch the rising castle of Sir Alfred Erthing 'free from touch of envious discontent'.[2] It is clear that in an age of frame-breakers and Burdettites, Wordsworth was more anxious than ever to calm the 'morbid passions'.

If the author of *The Excursion* steered clear of the inflammable topic of political disaffection and social animosity, he was not blind to actual distress nor behindhand in his advocacy of relief. The notorious rural and urban degradation of England ill became the champion of freedom, and its remedy must no longer be delayed. He proposed educational reform and, with refreshing realism, large-scale emigration. The policy was to be put into immediate operation:

> . . . Begin even now,
> Now, when oppression, like the Egyptian plague
> Of darkness, stretched o'er guilty Europe, makes
> The brightness more conspicuous that invests
> The happy Island . . .
> Now, when destruction is a prime pursuit,
> Show to the wretched nations for what end
> The powers of civil polity were given.
>   (*Exc.*, IX, 408.)

It is evident that if by now Wordsworth had abandoned the cause of parliamentary reform, if he could not bring himself to lay the knife to any branch of the polity of the victor of Waterloo, he had not abandoned the humanitarianism fundamental to his personal creed. In the Essay Supplementary to the Preface of 1815, he is still at war with intellectual snobbery and pride, with an artificial preoccupation with 'those points wherein men differ from each other, to the exclusion of those in which all men are alike, or the same'. Still combatting the whole tradition of an exclusive 'taste', he appeals still to the 'people' over the

---

[1] *Excursion*, VI, 1233—in 1814 and 1820 eds. only; cf. 'Guilt and Sorrow'.
[2] *Excursion*, VII, 952.

heads of the 'public', and to fundamental sympathies cutting across the strata of class and education.

It is nevertheless significant that in reprobating the vanity and pride of the aristocratic literary tradition, he now sees the compensating advantages which nature 'illimitable in her bounty' has conferred upon those low in the social scale as of such value that they render the 'civil arrangements' which are responsible for the social distinction 'less unjust than might appear'. The conclusion that the very social inferiority of his favoured classes protected them from the tainting sophistication of their superiors was of course inherent in the earliest expositions of his doctrines; but not until 1815 did he recognize this condition as to some extent compensating the lower classes, as specifically justifying the existing social distinctions.

Any account of Wordsworth's position in 1815 would perhaps be incomplete if it failed to draw attention to the fact that, in this year, acting upon information given him by Brougham, he dispatched to Leigh Hunt, then serving a prison sentence for a libel on the Regent, a copy of his works. Three of his sonnets appeared in Hunt's reforming *Examiner* in 1816, and one in Scott's equally advanced *Champion*. In the following year he admitted to Haydon that he did not approve 'the tone of [*The Champion's*] politics' although he had been reading it until a few months before; yet, he went on, he still had affection and respect for its editor.

·   ·   ·   ·   ·

As we have already noted, the final event of military victory, the attainment of the great ambition of Wordsworth's mature years, inevitably led to something of a decline in his interest in political affairs. Describing his reaction, he wrote: 'After the Battle of Waterloo, the course of public events, however interesting to an observing and thoughtful mind, was of a less exciting and therefore of a less poetic character, and he [the poet] confined himself to subjects less discordant in their elements.'[1] His political position had been finalized in the course of the war, and the

[1] MS. of 1835 Postscript. See *Poems*, ed. de Selincourt and Darbishire, IV, p. 426-7.

allegiances and sympathies formed during that vital period from his thirty-fifth to his forty-fifth year directed and moulded his opinions upon all subsequent political questions. All the major issues of the post-war era had been first raised during the war, and Wordsworth's attitude to them had been substantially decided upon before Waterloo.

Even at the lowest level he could never forget that the Tories had been the architects of victory, and their opponents, Whig and radical, were always for him those who had gazed 'on prosperous tyrants with a dazzled eye'. He felt indebted in no superficial way to the politicians who had championed a cause he had made so peculiarly his own. When his friend Haydon asked him in 1831: 'Do we not owe something to the fortitude of that party which preserved our laws and institutions from Napoleon's grip, and from French infection?' his correspondent could have replied with genuine conviction.

Nor must the continuity and extension given to Wordsworth's wartime position by the influence of personality be overlooked. He could not forget that the reformers of the post-war era were the Broughams, Greys and Burdetts who had done their utmost to prevent the downfall of the Napoleonic tyranny. As late as 1846, on meeting a Whig neighbour, he was genuinely surprised to learn that he was nevertheless 'not a gallican, that he never loved Sir Francis Burdett, never was a worshipper of Henry Brougham; (and) disapproved of the Whig apologies for Bonaparte in the days of his glory'.

Perhaps the essential point to make is that the war years had not left Wordsworth unaltered. Despite 'The Happy Warrior', war is not a good training ground for humanitarian benevolence, particularly in civilians. In supporting the long conflict he had been forced to vindicate the policy of reprisal and superior violence which the war demanded, and Wordsworth the sentimentalist, Wordsworth the poet of the domestic affections and the mild sympathies of common humanity had lost ground before Wordsworth the patriot, the champion of righteous war, the advocate of unconditional surrender.

Nor must we leave out of account the obvious fact that the Revolution, to whose golden promise he had so completely entrusted his hopes, the movement which was to bring about the triumph of reason, had ended in a welter of despotism and war. Even its earlier excesses, excused at the time as mere transitory incidentals, could no longer benefit from such an explanation. Nor was his maturer interpretation of its course unaffected by the sight of the very people of France, in whose virtues he had so firmly trusted, not only acquiescing but glorying in their return to despotism. The French he regarded as proved to be 'less fitted than any other (people) to be governed by moderation', and so incapable, as yet, of rational liberty. But the spectacle had a general consequence, and liberal pleas for the rights of the virtuous unfranchised to political power could never again evoke in him the old ingenuous reaction. If the initial glories of the Revolution had seemed to give new validity to speculation in every sphere, its final catastrophe provoked an inevitable reaction, and the enthusiast who had proclaimed his own poetic theory in 1798, who had preached his own pantheistic religion, had, by the year of Waterloo, turned to classical history and mythology for the subjects of his poetry, and to the Church of England for his religious consolation.

The very tragedies of his personal experience were similarly influential in leading him to distrust his former spontaneous emotional sympathies, to substitute sober realism for enthusiasm as the basis of his practical opinions. The outcome of his affair with Annette, the stoic submission which he found necessary in his bereavements, the catastrophe which the culmination of the French Revolution wrought in his political idealism, his very acquaintance with Coleridge—all worked to the same end. In 1812 Crabb Robinson records that a mention of Coleridge's facile emotionalism 'led Wordsworth to observe on the false sensibility and tendency to tears in the present age'. Such a remark foreshadows the stern politician who thirteen years later wrote: 'We must have in our rulers no luxuries of sentiment, none of those persuasions which flatter the feelings at the expense of the understanding—no self-applauding spirit of unreflecting liberality—we must look sternly at the case, and we shall find that it is vigour, and not self-indulgence that must save us.' The war years had clearly trained Wordsworth, not to the milder virtues of forbearance and benevolence, but inevitably to a sterner self-discipline and determination, to resolution and inflexibility. In the years that followed he was little prepared for that policy of compromise and concession which, as he never realized, was alone able to prevent revolution.

He felt too, by 1820, that he had a far larger body of personal experience to guide him than had been the case in the 1790s. His ardent hopes of the greatest reforming movement of his age had since been completely dashed by the advent of a military despot whose inevitability had been, apparently, so inherent in that very phase of the Revolution which had aroused Wordsworth's fondest enthusiasm, that a more mature political observer had been able to prophesy almost every step of his advance to power.

The heightened respect which Wordsworth at this stage began to pay to Burke the conservative in the light of the proven accuracy of Burke the prophet[1] did much to confirm the tendency we are tracing. Even in his republican days he had, of course, a considerable respect for Burke.

In 1797 Hazlitt and Coleridge agreed that a just appreciation of the great anti-Jacobin was the test of a sound liberal mind[2] and there is no evidence that Wordsworth would ever have failed such a test. Despite a backhanded reference in the 1793 Letter to Llandaff, we know that his admiration for the great orator whom he heard in the Commons that year was considerable. 'You always went away from Burke', he later wrote in retrospect, 'with your mind filled.' The earliest version of The Prelude contains a frank avowal of this admiration, even for the author of the Reflections: 'no trifler, no short-flighted wit', but one who pursued '. . . a track That kindles with . . . glory'. At no time did he class Burke with Pitt, and Hazlitt was not the only Jacobin to pay tribute to 'the profound legislative wisdom, piercing sagacity, or rich impetuous, high-wrought imagination' of the most famous of the anti-Gallicans. Yet actual agreement with him was a rather later growth. In 1804 he wrote, in criticism of Reynolds,

[1] A process with which we are all, of course, directly familiar from our contemporary political experience.

[2] Hazlitt, 'My First Acquaintance with Poets'.

that 'he appears to me to have lived too much for the age in which he lived, and the people among whom he lived, though this in an infinitely less degree than his friend Burke, of whom Goldsmith said, with such truth, long ago, that—

> "Born for the universe, he narrowed his mind,
> And to party gave up what was meant for mankind";'

and this qualification he no doubt would have retained until a considerably later date.

It does in fact seem that many of the principles and opinions which the later Wordsworth held and which are so similar to Burke's were arrived at more as a consequence of his own experience than as the result of his study of the politician's writings.[1] He drew conclusions from the course of the French Revolution almost identical with those which Burke had prophetically drawn; his attitude to nature and his life among the statesmen of the Lake District led him to opinions about the role of tradition, permanence and gradualism in national life which were again almost identical with Burke's. It seems as though it were only when he realized the large area of agreement which had been unconsciously established between them that he turned to Burke's writings for confirmation.

It was however under Burke's more direct influence that Wordsworth and Southey feared that a rash outbreak of reforming violence must inevitably lead to the establishment of a Napoleonic tyranny in England, with all that it implied for the progress of the cause of rational freedom. It was as liberticides that Wordsworth condemned the agitators of the post-war era, and their rash prematurity made them 'the worst enemies of mankind; because it is mainly through them that rational liberty has made such little progress in the world'.

In this light must we approach the question of his opposition to the post-war liberal movement. Hard upon the heels of glorious victory came social ferment upon a scale and of an intensity which Wordsworth, at least in England, had never known before. The country which had triumphed by virtue of her unanimity and unity was almost at once split by dissension. But

[1] See on the 1802 Sonnets, pp. 115ff, above.

he was so convinced of the essential reality of this war-winning
spirit that he could only conclude that the disillusioning conflicts
of peace were factitious, and provoked by that same political
faction which had already given proof of its small concern for the
country and her institutions, of its complete lack of sympathy for
the harmony with which time and tradition had endowed
England. In 1816 Southey summed up his own and Wordsworth's attitude by pointing out that 'at this time, when the
plans of Government have been successful beyond all former
example ... when the object of a twenty years war ... has been
obtained, and England, enjoying the peace which she has thus
bravely won, should be left at leisure to pursue with undistracted
attention those measures which, by mitigating present evils and
preventing crimes in future may, as far as human means can be
effectual, provide for an increasing and stable prosperity; ...
at this time a cry of discontent is gone forth, the apostles of
of anarchy take advantage of a temporary and partial distress'.

The existence of distress Wordsworth did not deny, and to
him it was more than temporary and partial; he knew that it was
the inevitable outcome of an industrial system whose vile and
uncontrolled spread he had consistently opposed. Yet we must
take into account his relative ignorance of the precise nature of the
new England which was rapidly taking shape about him, and of
the actual extent and intensity of the human suffering which it
involved. The changes were rapid and dramatic enough to
explain a great deal of notorious ignorance among the most
sympathetic of contemporaries. During the reign of George III
England's population had doubled;[1] whereas at the time of the
Lyrical Ballads the number of country labourers was double that
of the town labourers, the position had been exactly reversed
shortly after the passing of the Reform Bill;[2] in the first thirty
years of the century towns like Manchester and Leeds almost
tripled their population. With so much of this development taking
place in time of war, it is no wonder that the implications escaped
the attention even of politicians and economists; and if they
displayed an ignorance at times alarming, what should we expect

[1] Trevelyan, *History of England* (1945), p. 602.
[2] Cole and Postgate, *The Common People* (1938), pp. 299 *et seq.*

of the recluse of the Lakes, living in a district where the passing
of a chaise was an event singular enough to be noted in Dorothy's
Journal? On Windermere in 1818 Keats found that the mere 'views
of the lake . . . make one forget the divisions of life, age, youth,
poverty and riches'. The society of the 'statesmen' was something
unique even in rural England, and Coleridge thought them
'gods' 'compared to our peasants and small farmers in the south'.
A district populated thinly with independent freeholders living
in a state of traditional equality, knew little of the social distress
that the new industrialism was bringing to England. It was a
physical and spiritual environment which was all too likely to
lull a person of Wordsworth's opinions into something danger-
ously akin to complacency.

His own habit of life predisposed him in the same way.
However she overstated the case, one of the friends of the poet's
later years was substantially correct in lamenting 'that his habits of
seclusion keep him ignorant of the real wants of England and the
World. Living in this region, which is cultivated by small
proprietors, where there is little poverty, vice or misery, he
hears not the voice which cries so loudly from other parts of
England, and will not be stilled by sweet, poetic suasion, or
philosophy, for it is the cry of men in the jaws of destruction.'[1]
Amid the tumult of the birth labour of an industrial nation,
Grasmere was, as Thomas Arnold found it, 'another world,
for the quietness of the valleys and the comparative independence
of this population are a delightful contrast to what one finds
almost everywhere else'. So even if Wordsworth did admit the
existence of suffering, he could not, in such an environment, be
fully aware of its real extent, of its detailed nature.

But while he admitted that there was suffering, and that it
was remediable, what exasperated him was that the reformers
placed all their hopes of amelioration in the efficacy of legislative
enactment, in a mechanical rearrangement of the superficialities
of political organization.

He saw, and I believe we are now in a position to agree with
him, that however obvious was the material, the physical effect
of the new industrial system upon its victims, the real evil lay

[1] *Memoirs of Margaret Fuller Ossoli* (1852), II, 175.

deeper; physical degradation was only an outward expression of a causative degradation of the spirit which the new development of the social and economic system wrought upon master and servant alike. He rejected the political demands of the reformers for they were to him as indicative of spiritual blindness, of a preoccupation with the material superficialities of human existence and human relationships as was the physical distress which a heartless industrial system made inevitable. Combinations and societies of working men were to him as reprehensible as the factory system, for they both implied, in their unnatural 'crowding of men together' in masses and classes, the subversion of the individual personality. He was as bitterly opposed to 'The Thing' as Cobbett was, but he saw the influence of its inhumanity and its materialism in just those political projects which Cobbett championed.

He was aware that a new class had been produced which was not provided for in the existing social structure. That this class was not possessed of political power did not concern him, for he could not admit that it was, in view of its admitted degradation, either worthy or capable of wielding that power responsibly; demands for its immediate enfranchisement were both irrelevant and irresponsible.

Although we might blush to say so, this was a belief founded on a sincere humanitarianism. He felt justified in denying political power to the unfranchised only because he was convinced that their interests would be best cared for not by their own elected representatives, but by their existing governors. He was convinced that existing institutions of proven efficacy could cope with the task of carrying out the necessary incorporation of the new proletariat into the social framework, and he knew that this must be a gradual process. With firm government the rash demands of misguided labour, however stimulated by demagogues, would prove transitory,[1] and the traditional process of slow modification would go forward.

[1] It was perhaps unfortunate that the periodic decrease of social disturbance, actually the result of economic improvement, only served to convince him, along with most of his contemporaries, of the essentially transitory nature of the political agitation, and of the efficacy of the repressive measures taken against it.

The fallacies at the root of such an assessment of the problem are obvious enough to a cynical posterity, but they are not such as to discredit its author. They only make plain to us that his Lakeland retirement had also kept him from contact with what are euphemistically called, I believe, political realities. What he did not realize was that an eighteenth-century social organization could not in any sense cope with a nineteenth-century society, and that the new classes would not tolerate, without revolution, exclusion from political power.

Nevertheless, he was being as wise as he knew; his judgment was based on sound principles logically drawn from intimate if incomplete experience, and events did not entirely prove him in error. The franchise was extended, religious emancipation was effected, but history also proves the wisdom of the political thinker who saw these legislative measures as experiments dangerous in execution, and destined to prove eventually mere scratches on the surface of the great problem of human happiness and human relations in a modern industrial society. An age when government seemed all too likely to do nothing at all was perhaps an ill season for Wordsworth to proclaim the ultimate inefficacy of political action; but a posterity which sees so much yet unaccomplished after four generations of legislation should be able to appreciate his attitude.

On the exact nature of the reforming measures which he imagined might finally be applied he was far from specific, but it is doubtful whether he intended them to be legislative in any exact sense of the term at all. The extension of education, the modification of the Poor and Corn Laws, control of factory conditions, stimulation of emigration—these reforms he did support, but his real interests lay in other directions, unembodied by any programme merely political. His main aim was to bring about the rule of the wise and the virtuous, and to prevent the accession of the O'Connells, the Hunts and the Broughams. Unfortunately, in our efforts to secure the same ends, we see our way no more clearly than did Wordsworth.

There can be no doubt of the sincerity of his desire for a real improvement in the condition of the people. If he was reading Burke with closer attention after the war, he was not neglecting the philosophers of the new society; and if a brief visit by Godwin led to disagreement and hurried departure, a subsequent one made by Robert Owen of Lanark was apparently more cordially welcomed. Owen's plans for the betterment of industrial conditions and the humanizing of the factory were just the type of reforms which appealed to Wordsworth, however unacceptable the religious views of their advocate. Owen was at least in agreement with Wordsworth and Southey on the superficiality of political reform unaccompanied by that economic and social reorganization which the age, deaf to the voices of all three, left for posterity so painfully to attempt. To the Whigs and radicals, of course, who were not to be deceived by obscurantism, Owen was but another reactionary opponent of that grand panacea, parliamentary reform.

.   .   .   .   .

As we have seen, Wordsworth had hoped that the successful conclusion of the war against Napoleon was to mark the conclusion of his long preoccupation with political affairs. For the sake of his reputation it is perhaps unfortunate that it did not. To exhort a nation to defence and victory was a political aim on the highest level, to which posterity can at all times respond; but to champion any cause in the smaller sphere of domestic politics, no matter how noble the principles involved, is a course of action inevitably less inspiring, inevitably contaminated by the petty temper of party. Commenting upon his father's much-abused 'Vision of Judgment', the solemn Cuthbert Southey wrote with unconscious humour: '. . . to speculate upon the condition of the departed, especially when under the influence of strong political feelings, is a bold, if not a presumptuous undertaking'. Wordsworth, with a somewhat surer taste, was never guilty of such boldness nor such presumption, but the perils of this same influence are unfortunately not confined to such speculation.

His share in the Westmorland election of 1818 is the most unsatisfactory incident in his political life. Election pamphlets in the Tory cause we can surely tolerate, but it is difficult to reconcile something which looks like an attempt to 'rig' an

M

election[1] with the authorship of the last lines of 'Dion'.[2] The story of the whole affair perhaps does little more than point the wisdom of Wordsworth's early suspicion of and abstention from the dubious arena of contemporary and local politics.

There are, however, certain aspects of the event which deserve consideration, and prominent among them is the often slighted one of the personalities involved. The election was not, for the poet, a mere contest between Tory and Whig so much as a trial of strength between his benefactor, Lord Lonsdale, and Brougham, an outsider, and a peace-monger and Edinburgh Reviewer to boot. There appears to have been every justification for Wordsworth's admiration for Lonsdale. 'I do not think', he wrote, 'that there exists in England a man of any rank more anxiously desirous to discharge his duty in that station of life to which it has pleased God to call him. ... The more he is known, the more is he beloved, and respected and admired.' In an era which he was convinced needed good government rather than reformed government, Lonsdale was a type of those whose influence he wished to increase. It was not merely a question of birth or wealth, for he admitted that 'pride, hardness of heart, grasping avarice, and other selfish passions (were) the not infrequent concomitants of affluence and worldly prosperity'. But in Lonsdale's case 'opulence, rank, station, privilege, distinction, intellectual culture' implied 'protection, succour, guidance, example, dissemination of knowledge, introduction of improvements'. It was this personal esteem which was the basis of his part in the campaign; as his sister wrote: 'For my part, I wish not success to any opposers of the House of Lonsdale: for the side that house takes is the good side.' Furthermore, the right of his friend and benefactor to a preponderant political influence in the country by virtue of his tremendous holdings, had already been conceded by his traditional local opponent, Curwen, and even by Brougham himself.[3]

[1] See Letter 601. Wordsworth's proposal to Lonsdale was to acquire an estate and to settle on it twelve Tory freeholders, i.e. voters.

[2]   'Him, only him the shield of Jove defends,
          Whose means are fair and spotless as his ends.'

[3] See the reference to Brougham's endeavour to come to an understanding with Lonsdale in 1806, in Wordsworth's unpublished squib, 'The Scottish Broom' (de Selincourt, IV, p. 377).

It is plain that his part in the campaign did not indicate Wordsworth's permanent reconciliation to any completely partisan
loyalty; six years later, although he still looked upon the Opposition as 'the contumelious and vacillating Whigs', he found little
enough to praise among the 'prostrate Tories'. Lonsdale was to
Wordsworth no ordinary Tory, as Brougham was no ordinary
Whig. The freeholder of Rydal Mount resented the intrusion of
the outsider, the emissary of the forces of radical discontent
dispatched to disrupt the placidity of the local political tradition;
an emissary too who was strongly suspected of supporting the
doctrine of annual parliaments and a widely extended suffrage.[1]
He was, further, a peculiarly appropriate representative of a
party damned by a policy of treason which had proved it completely lacking in due respect for 'the religion, the laws, the morals,
the manners, (and) the literature of the country, especially as
contrasted with those of France'.

In his election pamphlets it was the war that was still the acid
test, whose results were still valid: '. . . here we behold them
[Tories and Whigs] in full contrast with each other—To whom
shall the crown be given? On whom has the light fallen? and who
are covered by shade and thick darkness?' The war had proved the
right of the Tories to guide the nation, for they alone had been inspired by the true patriotism: 'While the Opposition were taking
counsel from their fears, and recommending despair—while they
continued to magnify without scruple the strength of the enemy,
and to expose, misrepresent, and therefore increase the weaknesses
of this country, His Majesty's Ministers were not daunted . . .
and for this determination everlasting gratitude will attend them.'

In the same context he uses for the first time another argument
to which he frequently recurred, namely the necessity of balancing
the political forces of his time. His consciousness of his own
youthful seduction by the promises of a 'too credulous day', made
him see himself in his maturity as eminently fitted to be a corrector
of immoderate expectations.

[1] Personally, of course, Wordsworth had considerable respect for Brougham;
see Greville's *Memoirs* (1874) II, p. 120, where Wordsworth is described
(1831) as talking 'a great deal of Brougham, whose talents and domestic virtues
he greatly admires'.

Aubrey de Vere pointed out that 'in siding politically with the Crown and Coronets, (Wordsworth) considered himself to be siding with the weaker party in our democratic days', and, after all, he had displayed the same spirit as early as 1794. The balance called for by the demagogy of 1818 he found not unnaturally in the stable traditions and political power of the land-owning aristocracy: 'What else but the stability and might of a large estate, with proportional influence in the House of Commons, can counter-balance the democratic activity of the wealthy commercial and manufacturing districts?' he asked. And Westmorland he saw as an ideal district in which that countering influence should be favoured; even if the Lowther supremacy were locally resented, '. . . our duty might still be to bear with the local evil, as correcting an opposite extreme in some other quarter of the Island—as a counterpoise of some weight elsewhere pressing injuriously upon the springs of social order'. Even the surviving elements of an older order appealed to the traditionalist as serviceable in this cause: 'I cannot but be of opinion that the feudal power yet surviving in England is eminently serviceable in counteracting the popular tendency to reform. . . . The people are already powerful far beyond the increase of their information and their improvement in morals.'

In any case, at a time when the duty of government was primarily that of avoiding anarchy, Wordsworth remained convinced that Brougham and his party were far too entangled with revolutionary elements, far too indifferent to the value of the institutions which must be protected to be able to control the whirlwind. Dorothy at least 'firmly believed' that 'the majority of the population of Westmorland are ready for revolution . . . and they would be set to work before many years are over, if a majority of county members such as Brougham in political conduct and principles were returned to Parliament'. Even Graham and Curwen, both liberal members for Cumberland, admitted that seditious drilling was going on near Carlisle.

The election addresses likewise give evidence of Burke's growing influence. The Lowther nominees are 'independent in every rational sense of the word; acknowledging, however, that they rest upon a principle, and are incorporated with an interest'; whereas the independence boasted of by their opponent 'despises habit, and time-honoured forms of subordination; it consists in breaking old ties upon new temptations ... (in) sacrificing with Jacobinical infatuation the near to the remote, and preferring, to what has been known and tried, that which has no distinct existence even in imagination; in renouncing ... everything intricate in motive and mixed in quality, in a downright passion for absolute, unapproachable patriotism'.

But we hear not only the voice of Wordsworth the conservative, but that of the 'sorrowful observer' of the Revolutionary promise and its subversion, of Wordsworth the national patriot of a long war waged by the forces of tradition and the past against the innovating zeal of rationalism; the voice too of the enthusiast who had been sobered by a grim acquaintance with '. . . the dominion of the impure . . . That soul of Evil—which, from Hell let loose, Had filled the astonished world with such abuse'. It was the disillusioned idealist who regretfully pointed out that 'good men turn instinctively from inferences unfavourable to human nature. But there are facts which are not to be resisted, where the understanding is sound'. This was the voice of the poet who, as his receptivity to natural beauty declined, as the lesson of natural joy grew less compulsive, inevitably lost much that had formerly balanced his consciousness of human wickedness, his conviction of the power of sin and evil. With a recrudescence in England of a violence which he was not alone in fearing as the precursor of another rule by the Marats, the Robespierres and the Oswalds of earlier days, he was forced to the melancholy conclusion that 'human nature, be it what it may, must be looked at by legislators as it is'.

The emendations made in his poems about the time that he composed his election addresses are similarly indicative of his political position. He dropped from *The Prelude* (though later, as was often the case, to replace it) the line in which he proclaims the persistence of his belief that the Revolution had been led astray only because it had wanted the timely advent of 'one paramount mind'; he emended the reference to his departure from France in 1792 in order to acknowledge his gratitude to 'the gracious providence of heaven' acting in the guise of 'harsh necessity' to withdraw him from danger. It was probably at this time too that he altered the reference to the fête de fédération, in the sonnet 'Jones! as from Calais', to describe it but as 'the pomp of a too credulous day'.

CHAPTER X

Reform

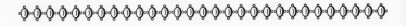

In 1820 Wordsworth returned to Europe, and revisited the scenes of the Revolution for the first time since 1792. The poet who in the same year despatched his volumes to the press with the comment that 'in more than one passage their publication will evince my wish to uphold the cause of Christianity', and who was shortly to insert in *The Prelude* his glowing tribute to the author of *Reflections on the Revolution in France*, had changed considerably since his last visit, and he found that Paris too was not unaltered. 'I miss', he wrote back to Lonsdale, 'many ancient buildings, particularly the Temple, where the poor king and his family were so long confined.'

Perhaps not entirely unconnected with his growing admiration for the political champions of tradition against 'upstart theory', of which the tribute mentioned is but one of many indications, is the omission from the edition of his poems published in this year of 'Alice Fell', which is, significantly, one of the few thorough-going exemplifications of his own rash theory of poetic diction.

Yet he still retained the fundamental liberalism of his literary principles. In an 1823 letter to the anthologist, Allan Cunningham, he faithfully echoes the sentiments of the famous letter to Fox: 'I have endeavoured to dwell with truth upon those points of human nature in which all men resemble each other, rather than on those accidents of manners and character produced by times and circumstances.' On an anthology sent to him three years later, he commented: 'It would be, as you will conjecture, something more to my particular taste, if it were less for that of the *fine* world—if it pressed closer upon common life. . . .' His sympathies were still with the humble and rejected even if his tone had become somewhat parsonical. In the year of the

Westmorland election he wrote the verse tale of 'The Star and the Glow-worm', in which the pilgrim, spurned by the 'haughty warder' from 'a lodging begged beneath a castle's roof,' sees in a dream a celestial cataclysm, after which—

> ... new heavens succeeded ...
> ... And all the happy souls that rode
> Transfigured through that fresh abode
> Had heretofore, in humble trust,
> Shone meekly 'mid their native dust,
> The Glow-worms of the Earth!

The 1820 visit to Switzerland reaffirmed his admiration for its republicanism and he praised the simple dignity of its democracy in terms fully as liberal as those of his youth:

> Let Empires fall; but ne'er shall ye disgrace
> Your noble birthright, ye that occupy
> Your council-seats beneath the open sky.
> On Sarnen's mount, there judge of fit and right,
> In simple democratic majesty:
> Soft breezes fanning your rough brows, the might
> And purity of nature spread before your sight.
> ('Desultory Stanzas, 1822.')

But even the glory of national independence and liberty could not divorce him from his concern for the individual; even in Switzerland, the sight of peasant degradation, especially among the young, provoked him:

> Ah, what avails heroic deed?
> What liberty? If no defence
> Be won for feeble Innocence.

When he returned he wrote to James Losh that long explanation of his political development to which we have already referred and which Losh rather glibly, and somewhat unfairly, dismissed. It was written in the year (1821) when Catherine Clarkson reported him 'thoroughly Torified', and it is a document which modifies that judgment, to the extent that any full consideration of his position must do. Its reference at this late date to the influence of the war policy of the English parties

upon his subsequent attitude to their domestic policy is, of course,
indicative of the profound and persistent importance of that consideration in his mature opinions. On the question of control of
the Press, he had now overcome the doubts of 1816. He was still
of the opinion that, in principle, 'free discussion . . . through the
press (is) . . . the *only* safeguard of liberty; without it I have neither
confidence in Kings, Parliaments, Judges or Divines—they have
all in their turn betrayed their country'. The events of the last
few years, however, had proved that '. . . the Press, so potent for
good, is scarcely less so for evil'; so, although he was plainly
troubled by the necessity, even willing to concede that 'there is
scarcely any abuse that I would not endure, rather than sacrifice,
or even endanger this freedom', a consideration of existing circumstances forced him temporarily to favour 'vigorous restrictions'. The whole tone of the paragraph is indicative of that
struggle between principle and circumstance which can so often
be detected in his later correspondence upon political affairs.

The same awareness of complexity, something of the same
confusion springing from this conflict, is present in his discussion
of reform. Some modification of the existing franchise qualifications he does desire, but he does not see how the evils of the
existing Constitution can be remedied without endangering its
virtues, for both reside in its peculiar complication. 'When I
was young', he wrote, 'giving myself credit for qualities which
I did not possess, and measuring mankind by that standard, I
thought it derogatory to human nature to set up Property in
preference to Person, as a title for legislative power. That notion
has vanished. I now perceive many advantages in our present
complex system of representation, which formerly eluded my
observation; this has tempered my ardour for reform; but if any
plan could be contrived for throwing the representation fairly
into the hands of the Property of the country, and not having it so
much in the hands of the large proprietors as it now is, it should
have my best support—though even in that event there would be
a sacrifice of Personal rights, independent of Property, that are
now frequently exercised for the benefit of the community.'

This same letter to Losh also gives an adequate summary of
Wordsworth's attitude to the Irish question, which was in fact

the question of Catholic emancipation. We have noticed that, as he moved closer to the Established Church between 1807 and 1813, so he became more convinced of the necessity of defending its position by resisting the claims of the Catholics. The problem was, as he saw it, the fact that the possibly desirable emancipation of a politically innocuous minority in England would lead to the fatal supremacy of a hostile majority in Ireland. He could not see any form of political concession to the Irish but as the prelude to the overthrow of the English Established Church in an integral part of the United Kingdom. Even in England itself concession in one direction would establish a precedent of which other dissenters would quickly avail themselves, 'and deeming the Church Establishment not only a fundamental part of our Constitution, but one of the greatest Upholders and Propagators of civilization in our own country, and, lastly, the most effectual and main support of religious toleration, I cannot but look with jealousy upon the Measures which must reduce her relative Influence, unless they be accompanied with arrangements more adequate than any yet adopted for the preservation and increase of that influence, to keep pace with the other powers in the community'.

As we can see in his *Ecclesiastical Sonnets*, he had considerable admiration—even 'love', so he told Gladstone in 1844—for many aspects of Catholicism, but he could not condone the allotting political power within the British constitution to that religion which was of necessity at enmity with the Protestant basis of the kingdom. He could not imagine the Catholics 'with their doctrine of infallibility (and consequent immutability)' being satisfied with anything less 'than the overthrow of the Protestant Church'.

Apart from this political objection, and despite his qualified admiration for Catholic worship, he was also moved by the common liberal's distrust of Catholicism as the religious counterpart of political despotism.[1] 'Papacy', he wrote, 'is founded upon the overthrow of private judgment—it is essentially at enmity with light and knowledge.' He was therefore convinced that in withholding political power from its devotees he was 'working

[1] See the poem, 'Incident at Bruges'.

for the welfare, and supporting the dignity, of human nature'.

The argument of the emancipators that, as the religion of the majority, Catholicism was entitled to occupy in Ireland the place of the Established Church in England troubled Wordsworth for some time, until he realized that it was based upon a separatist attitude which he—and most of the reformers—were unwilling to countenance.[1] He was wiser than his contemporaries in seeing that the effectual disestablishment of the English Church in Ireland must be 'introductory to the separation of the two countries'. He refused to consider Ireland but as a part of the United Kingdom.

He was aware that she was a part of the United Kingdom strategically as well as politically. During the war there had been no doubt of the dangers of giving way to Irish claims. As Southey had said: 'If Ireland were far enough from our own shores to be lost without danger to our own security, I would say establish the Catholic religion there, as the easiest way of civilizing it; but Catholic Ireland would always be at the command of the Pope, and the Pope is now at the command of France.' Even after Waterloo Wordsworth trembled at the prospect of a 'hostile or suspected Ireland at our backs' in the event of a future conflict with the Catholic states of Europe.

With the same perspicacity and something like the same failure to comprehend the strength of the forces at work that he displayed in his attitude to other progressive measures, Wordsworth condemned emancipation because it was superficial and ineffective as a measure of Irish reform. Whatever a misguided peasantry demanded, their real needs were not Catholic representatives but good representatives, good and conscientious resident landlords, education and increased emigration. Of Irish miseries he was not unaware but he was convinced with Southey that they 'were not caused by the laws which exclude the Roman Catholics from legislative power'.

In 1825 he went to the length of organizing an anti-emancipation petition in his neighbourhood, and there can be no doubt

[1] Thomas Arnold was one exception; see his *Life* by Stanley, (1882 ed.) I, p.323: 'I always grounded the right to emancipation on the principle that Ireland was a distinct nation, entitled to govern itself.'

of the sincerity as well as the strength of his convictions on the matter. His writings on the subject indicate no intolerance, no blind opposition to a progressive movement, but a reasoned disagreement based upon principles which he was certain outweighed those of the supporters of the measure: 'Whatever may be the weight of such evidence [produced in Parliament] it cannot overbalance in my mind all that I have read in history, all that I have heard in conversation, and all that I have observed in life.' What distressed him above all was the absence on both sides of what Greville called 'reason, principle or consistency', and the preponderant influence of 'prejudice, subserviency, passion, and interest'.[1] When emancipation did come, it came plainly as a concession forced from a government which was unable to justify its sudden rejection of the arguments which it had used to refuse concessions in the past. This ministerial abdication in the face of popular agitation seemed to many an ominous precedent.[2]

Yet at the conclusion of a long letter on the subject to Sir Robert Inglis in 1825, Wordsworth made an enlightening if rather surprising admission of the possibility of his being in error. This letter gives us a rare, but, as we shall see, not a unique insight into a state of mind far different from that suggested by the usual downrightness of his expression. After explaining the reasons for his opposition he goes on: 'What the contrary course may lead to it is impossible to foresee, but . . . we risk far too much in entering upon it—much of the evil which we forbode may, through the blessings of Providence, be prevented; and concession may possibly after all be the best course to take; but, sure I am that it is not justifiable by the reasons which in parliament have been brought forward in support of it. Providence will prevent evil and deduce good by agency hidden from our limited faculties.'

[1] Greville, *Memoirs* (1874), Vol. I, p. 168.
[2] Greville saw the Tory retreat as the result not of 'calm and deliberate political reasoning, but (of) a fearful sense of necessity and danger'. He went on: 'Who will have any dependence hereafter on the steadiness and consistency of public men, and what credit will be given to professions and declarations?' (I, pp. 164 *et seq.*)

The same moderation is expressed in his impressions of his 1829 visit to Ireland. Although he reported that his 'apprehensions are little abated', he scorned the 'Brunswickers' who 'describe the state of the country as more unquiet than ever, and forebode the very worst from Catholic bigotry and intolerance in alliance with political demagogues'. As at all times he was still open to the persuasion of experience, and admitted: 'I am inclined to think less unfavourably of the disposition of the upper ranks of Catholics to exalt their Church, however much they may wish ours to be depressed.'

It was largely a consideration of the Irish political situation which made Wordsworth nervous of Canning's foreign policy. He realized that England, trying to control a turbulent kingdom, was in no position to flaunt her recognition of the insurgent colonies of other nations: '. . . be assured the liberal policy of being so ready to acknowledge the independence of the revolted South Americans will not easily be forgiven by Spain, or any continental government. . . . This measure will both furnish an impulse and an excuse for the Catholic states interfering to foment the disturbances of Ireland.' In any case the rejoicing of victory had not erased from his memory the prolonged anguish of the earlier struggle, and he was genuinely perturbed at the prospect of another war which such a foreign policy might entail. A new outbreak could have but one effect upon the gradual extension of political liberty so recently resumed: ' . . . France, Prussia, Russia and Austria will probably dismember Poland, and the absolute sovereigns will make a further attack on representative governments.' For England itself war would entail a military system upon an unprecedented scale, and Wordsworth preserved the liberal's hatred of the rule of the army: 'Where then would be the liberties of Great Britain, with a Standing Army, which would be necessary to guard us from France in our front . . . with hostile or suspected Ireland at our backs?'

There was, of course, little possibility of the stern Anglican being won over to the cause of Catholic emancipation once the question had been clouded by Irish violence and English party animosity. But although, as we have seen, it is unjust to say that he was inaccessible to persuasion, it is true that, in the physical sense, his mind was now to some extent closed. Wordsworth's optical disability has been fully discussed elsewhere,[1] but as an indication of what this disability, combined with the isolation of his situation, entailed, we need merely read an 1825 letter to Jacob Fletcher in which he wrote: '. . . very few modern publications find their way to me—we have no book-clubs in this neighbourhood—and when I am from home, in spring and summer, my eyes are so apt to be inflamed that I am able to profit little by anything that falls in my way'.

. . . . . .

The unexpected admission, referred to above, of the possibility of his being in error upon such a vital question as that of Catholic emancipation should prevent us from interpreting Wordsworth's usually forthright statements of his attitude to current questions as indications of dogmatism. He often felt the need of subsequent qualification to correct such a misapprehension, as when he hastily followed a gloomy political discourse to the journalist John Scott in 1816 with an explanatory letter in which he was at pains to correct any impression his correspondent might have gained 'that I think ill of mankind and feel dejectedly concerning human nature'.

In a series of letters to H. J. Rose in 1828 upon the question of national education, he had voiced his opposition to certain aspects of popular proposals with a vigour which we might be pardoned for interpreting as an indication of his general condemnation of the principle involved. But in a later letter to Christopher Wordsworth he is at pains to point out that he is but filling his accepted counterbalancing role, and we are not to be misled by the fervour of his anxiety 'to guard against too high expectations . . . to glance upon some grievous errors', into imagining that he is 'averse to the people being educated'.

Wordsworth's interest in the question of education has already been referred to, and his opinions upon the topic had changed remarkably little. Even in *The Excursion* he had pointed out the State's obligation in this sphere:

[1] See Dr Edith Batho, *The Later Wordsworth* (1933).

O for the coming of that glorious time
When, prizing knowledge as her noblest wealth
And best protection, this imperial Realm,
While she exacts allegiance, shall admit
An obligation, on her part, to *teach*
Them who are born to serve her and obey. . . .
                                   (IX, 293.)

He was still as dubious as he had been at the time of the *Lyrical Ballads* Preface, of the value of what the world calls 'education', still conscious of the difference between real education and the mere acquisition of knowledge, still convinced that 'positive instruction, even of a religious character, is much overrated'; and still certain that it was more needed at the head than at the base of society: 'We are on fire with zeal to educate the poor . . . (but) we stand more in need of an improved education of the middle and upper classes.'

He was therefore inevitably at war with Brougham and his 'steam-intellect societies', who thought that 'sharpening of intellect and attainment of knowledge (were) things good in themselves, without reference to the circumstances under which the intellect *is* sharpened, or to the quality of the knowledge acquired'. He could not acquiesce in an attack on the domestic relations, the separation of mother and child, for example, in the name of the superior virtues of formal tuition, and was only prepared to tolerate the infant schools, made necessary in industrial areas where the mother and older children were fully employed, as a temporarily unavoidable evil produced by 'a sad state of society'. Naturally, any educational proposals which expressly excluded religious instruction of any kind implied for him a contradiction in terms.

One of his letters on the topic to Rose in 1828 closes with a paragraph which is as complete a statement of his mature political philosophy as he ever made. His conviction of the necessity of balancing social and political forces, the sterner tone which experience had given his humanitarianism, his consciousness of the existence of real and remediable distress, and his essentially conservative approach to the social problems which it has created, these are its elements. 'The thirst of knowledge', he wrote, 'is spreading and will spread, whether virtue and duty go along with it or no. Grant it; but surely these observations may be of use if they tend to check unreasonable expectations. One of the most difficult tasks is to keep benevolence in alliance with beneficence. Of the former there is no want, but we do not see our way to the latter. Tenderness of heart is indispensable for a good man, but a certain sternness of heart is needful for a wise one. We are as impatient under the evils of society as under our own, and more so; for in the latter case necessity enforces submission. It is hard to look upon the condition in which so many of our fellow creatures are born, but they are not to be raised from it by partial and temporary expedients. . . . Circumstances have forced this nation to do, by its manufacturers, an undue proportion of the dirty and unwholesome work of the globe. The revolutions among which we have lived have unsettled the value of all kinds of property, and of labour, the most precious of all, to that degree that misery and privation are frightfully prevalent. We must bear the sight of this, and endure its pressure, till we have by reflection discovered the cause, and not till then can we hope even to palliate the evil. It is a thousand to one but that the means resorted to will aggravate it.'

In any consideration of Wordsworth's mature position, too much emphasis cannot be placed on this consciousness of the remediable suffering which modern society was producing, if we are to see his opposition to specific measures of reform in perspective. It must not be forgotten, for example, that the fierce opponent of Catholic emancipation was an ardent supporter of the principle of Poor Law relief: 'I am a zealous friend to the great principles of the Poor Laws as tending, if judiciously applied, much more to elevate than to depress the character of the labouring classes'; nor that, in 1829, the year before the culmination of the reform agitation and possibly about the time that he removed his tribute to Fox from *The Prelude*, the poet proclaimed his sympathies for the poor, and his condemnation of the brutal system which afflicted them:

> . . . from coast to coast,
> Though *fettered* slave be none, her [Britain's] floors and soil

Groan underneath a weight of slavish toil
For the poor Many, measured out by rules
Fetched with Cupidity from heartless schools,
That to an Idol, falsely called 'the Wealth
Of Nations', sacrifice a people's health,
Body and mind and soul . . .
                                    ('Humanity.')

Nor should we fail to compare these lines with the Whig
Macaulay's stout defence of the industrial system and of the theory
of necessary evil which such a defence demanded. It was Macaulay
who made such scornful play with the political *naïveté* of Southey,
the Utopian poet who condemned a whole system merely because
'the dwellings of cotton spinners are naked, and rectangular'. He
added, with rather ironic truth: 'It is not from bills of mortality
and statistical tables that Mr Southey has learned his political
creed.'[1] In an age of utilitarianism the humanitarianism of
Wordsworth and Southey was indeed outmoded.

The interpretation of Wordsworth's opposition to the Reform
Bill itself has suffered above all from the fatal tendency of critics
and historians towards oversimplification. Too often is the
political struggle which decided the issue seen merely as a contest
between right and wrong, between the champions of progress
and the forces of reaction, in which Wordsworth's loyalties
seem all too clear. But to Wordsworth, as to his contemporaries,
the position was far more complex. He connected the agitation,
for example, with Catholic emancipation, and saw it as a further
development of the same attack on the Constitution. Like many
of his contemporaries and most subsequent historians he recognized in the Bill itself a political manoeuvre, a Whig attempt to
'dish' their opponents, to cover up the deficiencies of other aspects
of their policy, and to ensure their position.

Any assumption that the merit lay all on one side must surely
be dissipated by a mere reference to the Parliamentary debates on
the topic; there we can see that as far as an accurate interpretation
of the effect of the Reform Bill was concerned, the Whigs were
wrong and the Tories right; for it was the Tories who more
accurately foresaw the future course of history, the succession

[1] *Edinburgh Review*, January, 1830.

of events which the first Reform Bill was to inaugurate. Their arguments against the Bill were based on principles of much greater logical and historical validity than those produced for it.

Some knowledge of the form which Parliamentary support of and opposition to the movement took is necessary if we wish to understand Wordsworth's reaction, for the arguments used in the Commons on both sides were of considerable importance in deciding his position.[1] The reformers had one trump card which they all played in the end—the fear of revolution. When all other arguments failed them, as they often did, they pointed meekly to the vociferous and arming mob, and said, in effect, that there was no alternative to concession. James Mackintosh's famous speech is typical: 'This is not solely a reformatory measure', he said; 'it is also conciliatory. If it were exclusively proposed for the amendment of institutions, I might join in the prevalent cry that it goes too far. . . . But as it is a means of regaining national confidence, it must be guided by other maxims.' Even Grey, although he did not indulge in the vague threats of his supporters, came too in the end to rest his case on 'the absolute necessity of satisfying' what he called 'the respectable and reasonable part of the community'.

On logical grounds the Tory case was palpably stronger. In reply to the demand for a radical alteration in the electoral system they demanded proof, first, of the actual suffering caused by the existing arrangements, and, secondly, of the solid benefits to be conferred upon the people by the new ones: both these proofs the Whigs were unable to supply. As Greville complained, 'as to this measure, the greatest evil of it is that it is a pure speculation, and may be productive of the best consequences, or the worst, or even of none at all, for all that its authors and abettors can explain to us or to themselves'.[2] Concession to popular clamour now, claimed the Tories, would but make all future resistance impossible. To this the Whigs, admitting that they were no more prepared for an era of endless political change than were

[1] Especially in view of his physical isolation at Rydal Mount, and his almost exclusive dependence upon newspaper reports of parliamentary debates for information about the contest.

[2] *Op. cit.*, II, p. 122-3.

N

their opponents, could not reply. Mackintosh's attempt to do so was hardly likely to reassure his hearers: 'Nothing human is . . . final. . . . But within the very limited horizon to which the view of politicians can reach, I . . . expect that a measure of concession, made in a spirit of unsuspecting confidence, may inspire the like sentiments, and believe that the majority of the people may acquiesce in a grant of privileges so extensive. . . .' Lord John Russell was less tactful, and Greville described his declaration of 11 August, 1831, that 'this Bill would not be final if it was not found to work as well as the people desired', as 'sufficiently impudent considering that hitherto they have always pretended that it was to be final, and that it was made so comprehensive only that it might be so'.[1]

But weak arguments in Parliament were made good by more forceful ones outside. The real battle was waged in the country itself by a populace organized behind the Bill as behind no earlier political measure; their weapons were armed force, violence and intimidation, and their threat was revolution. They convinced most people of the reality of the danger. Wordsworth was reminded of the early days of the French Revolution, and foreign influence was indeed at work, although of much more recent origin. The French revolt against Charles X's attempted re-establishment of absolutism and the risings in Belgium gave a new impetus to the English reform agitation, but also cast doubts on the spontaneity of the national movement. The comparatively bloodless outbreak in France somewhat re-habilitated the idea of revolution in the minds of reformers like Place,[2] and they began to face the possibility with some confidence. There can be no doubt that the followers of 'Captain Swing', who carried on in the south the traditions of the northern 'King Ludd', and the armed and drilled bands of reformers throughout the country, were anxious to imitate their colleagues in Brussels and Paris.

The extent of these disturbances and preparations was notorious. *The Times* spoke approvingly of the 'voluntary national

[1] *Op. cit.*, II, p. 180.
[2] Wallas, *Life of Place* (1918), p. 244. See *ibid.* Chap. XI for a full account of the state of the nation during the agitation.

armament' carried out by the National Political Union, but the
Tories were not alone in their fears. Even for Jeffrey of the
Edinburgh Review the apparent imminence of Revolution
overshadowed all other considerations. 'The real battle', he
wrote to Empson, 'is not between Whigs and Tories, Liberals and
Illiberals and such gentlemanlike denominations, but between
property and no property—Swing and the law'. The Duke of
Wellington thought that 1831 had seen 'a greater destruction of
life and property (in England) than in all the fifty years since
1780',[1] while Place feared that the country was 'within a moment
of general rebellion'. The Whig Sir William Napier was even
more positive, when the Reform Bill was thrown out, that there
was 'no chance of escaping a revolution'.[2] Even the seclusion of
the Lakes was not immune from the nationwide disturbances.
Southey was shocked to receive a hand-bill inviting 'a subscrip-
tion for arming the people against the police'. Wordsworth
reported that he had seen 'a hand-bill and placard circulated in
this neighbourhood calling upon the friends of the Bill to
massacre its opponents—the expression used is to give them "War
to the knife". Take this as an answer', he advised his correspondent,
'to your hopes that society has not been disturbed by Reform
among our mountains.' The 1831 election in Carlisle was reminiscent of those in the days of the 'bad Earl' of Lonsdale, with the
boot now upon the other foot. The 'blue' nominees (one of
whom, James, was an extreme radical, an advocate of annual
parliaments and universal suffrage, and subsequently an opponent
of the 'useless ceremony' of the Coronation) campaigned with all
the paraphernalia of tricolours, caps of liberty, and banners
proclaiming 'Liberty or Death', or 'He who would be free must
first strike the blow'.

It was his feeling that the fundamentals of the Constitution
were being changed by means of threats and violence that made
Wordsworth despair. He would not admit that the demands of
the mob could alter the justice or the morality of the measure,
though they might make it difficult for the correct course to be
followed. To accede to a major reform, whose positive defence

[1] Earl Stanhope, *Conversations with Wellington* (World's Classics, 1947), p. 28.
[2] See *Life and Correspondence*, ed. H. A. Bruce, 1864.

even its champions were apparently unprepared to undertake, merely out of a fear of the consequences of resistance, seemed to him not only to negate the whole logic of government, but to open the flood-gates, to establish a precedent for unimaginable demands and inevitable concessions in the future, 'opening a way for spoliation and subversion to any extent which the rash and iniquitous may be set upon'. Once again he was opposed not so much to this one measure considered in isolation, but to the first step in an inevitable succession. If the Bill resisted universal suffrage, he saw (with greater wisdom or honesty than most of the reformers) that it made that ultimate—or worse—inevitable. His mature view of the course of the French Revolution convinced him that he was witnessing his own country's first step along the same fatal road to despotism via anarchy, and therefore it must be 'fearlessly resisted, before the transfer of legislative power takes place'. At very best a reformed parliament would become what Burke feared, a mere concourse of delegates: 'Let but short parliaments follow, as they must, and there will be an end to all traces of a deliberative assembly, the nominal representatives will become mere delegates or tools of the narrow views of the most selfish, perhaps, and ignorant class of the community.'

Even so it is perhaps unfair to read too much into his gloomy prognostications or to see them as entirely due to his political apprehensions. As G. M. Harper has pointed out,[1] his personal life at the time of the Reform Bill agitation was clouded by his sister's ill-health and by the death of Scott. He was depressed too by a more general consequence of the political frenzy of the day, as he became aware of the growing influence of the measures of government upon the most private concerns and activities of the individual, and realized—

> that on public ends
> Domestic virtue vitally depends,
> That civic strife can turn the happiest hearth
> Into a grievous sore of self-tormenting earth.

'The time is hastening on', wrote Southey, 'when public concerns will affect the vital interests of every individual.

[1] *William Wordsworth*, 1929.

Wordsworth is made positively unhappy by this thought.'

He was depressed too by the bitterness which the conflict
incited, in others as in himself. He could not even offer his
whole-hearted congratulations to a friend who selected such an
unhappy moment to announce his conversion from radicalism:
'I wish . . . the change had taken place under less threatening
circumstances. The idle practice of recrimination is becoming
general. The Whigs upbraid the Tories as authors of the mischief
which all feel, by withstanding reform so obstinately; and the
Tories reproach the Whigs with having done all the harm by
incessant bawling for it.'

In any case, we should beware of taking too literally the
violence of his unpremeditated expressions of opinion. He knew
the dangers of his own strong emotions, and did not mean the
quotation from Bacon prefixed to the Cintra tract to be ignored:
'Bitter and earnest writing must not hastily be condemned: for
men cannot contend coldly, and without affection, about things
which they hold dear and precious. A politic man may write from
his brain, without touch and sense of his heart; as in a speculation
that appertaineth not to him—but a feeling Christian will express,
in his words, a character of hate or love.'

Moreover, to correct our rashness, we do have the testimony
of a most unbiassed visitor to the Lakes just at the height of
the agitation. John Stuart Mill was most impressed by the poet's
'extreme comprehensiveness and philosophic spirit . . . the direct
antithesis of . . . one-sidedness. Wordsworth', he wrote, 'seems
always to know the pros and cons of every question; and when
you think he strikes the balance wrong, it is only because you
think he estimates erroneously some matter of fact.' And another
contemporary, R. P. Graves, reported exactly the same political
tolerance: 'All who argued with him on politics had the satisfaction of seeing that the grounds of opinions opposite to his
own were not ignored. . . .' The sympathy for the poor expressed
in such a poem as 'The Highland Hut', composed in 1831, shows
that his humanitarianism was still strong. While alongside the
politician's gloomy interpretation of the 1831 cholera epidemic
as the affliction sent by an offended Deity should be placed his
sister's comment: 'One visible blessing seems already to be

coming upon us through the alarm of the cholera. Every rich man is now obliged to look into the miserable bye-lanes and corners inhabited by the poor; and many crying abuses are (even in our little town of Ambleside) about to be remedied.'

Evidence of this sort is obviously of more importance than the heated language of letters concerned with the denunciation, unmodified by 'cumbersome qualifying expressions', of a specific political measure, and a measure which, as we have seen, was usually proposed and defended on the worst possible principles.

So, when seen against its proper personal and political background, Wordsworth's opposition to the Reform Bill was not the expression of blind reaction. Its basis was his veneration for the British Constitution, a veneration, we might almost say, typical of the convert: 'The Constitution of England, which seems about to be destroyed, offers to my mind the sublimest contemplation which the history of society and government have ever presented to it; and for this cause especially, that its principles have the character of preconceived ideas, archetypes of the pure intellect, while in fact they are the results of a humble-minded experience.' Such a general attitude to the whole involved, especially in the face of current reforming proposals, a particular defence of the parts, and by this process (which had formerly led the benevolent pacifist to a defence of regicide and terror) the champion of the 'sublimest contemplation' became incidentally the defender of rotten boroughs and an exclusive franchise.

His preoccupation with the ideal of gradual modification had by now assumed the colour of a religious conviction: 'After all, the question is, fundamentally, one of piety and morals; of piety, as disposing men who are anxious for social improvement to wait patiently for God's good time; and of morals, as guarding them from doing evil that good may come, or thinking that any ends *can* be so good as to justify wrong means for attaining them.'

It was indeed the rash haste of the proposed change rather than the change itself that distressed him. 'I am averse', he wrote, '(with that wisest of the moderns, Mr Burke) to all *hot* reformations; that is, to every sudden change in political institutions upon a large scale. They who are forced to part with power are of course irritated, and they upon whom a large measure of it is at once conferred . . . know not how to use it.' He had arguments philosophical as well as psychological to put forward, although he borrowed his actual words from another opponent of reform, Sir J. B. Walsh: 'Extensive, sudden, and experimental innovation is diametrically opposed to the principle of progressiveness, which in every art, science, and path of human intellect is gradual.'

Nor was he alone in his surprise at the extensive nature of the reforms actually embodied in the final draft of the Bill. When Burdett received advance notice of the provisions his delight was tempered only by a fear that the measure might 'go too far'. The radical Hobhouse had the same misgivings, and voiced them in the House. When the Government announced its intention of creating peers sufficient to ensure the passage of the Bill through the Lords, Wordsworth was not surprisingly scandalized. This constituted a subversion of 'the principle for which the peers mainly exist', and, as he accurately foresaw, converted 'the House of Lords into the mere slave of any succeeding Ministry'. 'Cannot then Lord Grey', he pleaded, 'and his co-adjutors be brought—by a respect for reason or by a sense of shame from being involved in such a contradiction and absurdity —to desist from that course? . . . If this be done, the Constitution of England will be destroyed.'

So to Wordsworth the Whig Bill sacrificed principle to popular clamour by perpetrating a violence upon the Constitution which promised no solid benefit to the nation and only established a precedent for greater concessions in the future. 'The class that does the most harm', he wrote, 'consists of well-intentioned men who, being ignorant of human nature, think that they may help the thorough-paced reformers and revolutionists to a certain point, then stop, and that the machine will stop with them.' He was not opposed to the principle of moderate reform in keeping with traditional constitutional development, but he refused to give any countenance to a measure so extensive and immediate in operation.

Provided compensation was arranged, he was finally prepared to favour some disfranchisement, and, in certain cases, the enfranchisement of the new towns, if only to prove its futility:

'If it could have been shown of such or such a Borough that it claimed the right to send members to Parliament upon usurpation, or that it had made a grossly corrupt use of a legal privilege—in both these cases I would disfranchise and also with the consent of owners of burgage tenure, but beyond this I would not have gone a step. As to transferring the right of voting to large towns, my conviction is that they will be little the better for it—if at all—but e'en let them have their humour in certain cases, and try the result. In short the whole of my proceedings would have been tentative, and in no case would I have violated a principle of justice.'

So he did give way before circumstances sufficiently to admit that some reform along the lines actually proposed was inevitable, but he would not have the Whigs handle it: 'If a new reform bill cannot be brought forward and carried by a strong appeal to the sense, and not to the passions, of the country, I think there is no rational ground for hope. . . . Nevertheless I cannot but think that the country might still be preserved from revolution by a more sane ministry, which would undertake the question of reform with prudence and sincerity, combining with that measure wiser views on finance. . . .'[1]

He realized that Wellington's refusal to consider any measure of reform had played into the hands of the radicals: 'there is diffused through the country a large body of Whig partisans who, could their eyes be opened, would cease to support them, especially if they had hopes of a more moderate measure from other quarters.' He remained convinced of the practicability of a Tory reform bill, imagining, apparently, that his own views were typical of other supporters of the party: 'could a conservative ministry be established, the certain ruin that will follow upon the passing of this bill might be avoided. Thousands of respectable people have supported both bills, not as approving of a measure of this character or extent, but from fear that otherwise no reform at all would take place. Such men would be ready to support more moderate plans if they found the executive in hands that could be

---

[1] Letter 1009. Note that Wordsworth here hits on the real Whig weakness; the Reform Bill had the great—if not the major—attraction for the Government that it could direct public attention away from its financial ineptitude.

relied upon. Too true it is, no doubt . . . that opinions as to the extent and nature of advisable reform differ so widely as to throw great difficulties in the way of a new bill. But these . . . might be got over, so far as to place us upon ground allowing hope for the future.'

It is plain from these quotations that it is unjust to depreciate Wordsworth's assertion that, if he was against the Bill, he was not opposed to reform itself. The Bill was damned by the men who proposed it, and by the arguments which they used to support it. The pessimism which is so marked in the poet's letters during the years following the passing of the Bill needs of course no other explanation than the strength of his conviction that a grave political crime had been committed, and one which promised most dismally for the future. To an honest contemporary view there was no good reason for doubting the validity of his apprehensions. There was, after all, no effective guarantee that the newly endowed possessors of political power would not be seduced into misuse of it. When it became clear that this was not at least the immediate consequence, it is to Wordsworth's credit that his fears were allayed and his old hopes revived. His objection to sudden and sweeping reform remained strong, but it was still based on his fears of the damage inflicted upon the good cause by impatient rashness and premature action.

CHAPTER XI

Aftermath

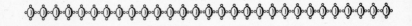

During the tour made in 1833 through Scotland and the North of England Wordsworth discovered that the beneficent influence of natural beauty had not lost its force, and that it was indeed peculiarly corrective of his current melancholy and exasperation. His misgivings for England's future seemed contradicted by the appearance of the land itself:

> . . . Can I ask (if)
> This face of rural beauty be a mask
> For discontent, and poverty, and crime;
> These spreading towns a cloak for lawless will?

There was no real need for 'the enthusiast, journeying through this Isle' to 'repine as if his hour were come too late'; for he found not signs of dismal subversion and decay, but proof 'if what is rightly reverenced may last', of a 'golden prospect for futurity'.

So he began to accept the political change which he had resisted. He was now prepared rather to leave judgment in the hands of posterity than to provoke his own anxiety by fruitless anticipation: 'the motives which led to this measure [the Reform Bill] and the good or evil which has attended or has risen from it, will be duly appreciated by future historians'. It was only in his darker moments[1] that his fears were revived of the inevitable sequence of events prophesied by Burke. 'My mind is calmly made up to the worst', he wrote to Crabb Robinson in 1834, 'it is simply a question of time. So no more about it, but let us be as cheerful as we can and each act guided by the best lights he can

[1] We should remember that the last fifteen years of his life were dominated by the mental illness of his sister.

procure.'[1] But it was still the tragedy of prematurity that he
lamented. He was sure that power would pass in time from the
'audacious and wicked to the more audacious and wicked . . . till
military despotism comes in as a quietus: and then . . . the struggle
for liberty will recommence'.

His opposition to the Reform Ministry and to the new parliament was not likely to be modified. The stout opposition to
Ashley's Ten Hours Bill maintained by the industrialists introduced into the Commons under the new dispensation, especially
when compared with the support given the measure by Tories like
Oastler, Sadler, Fielden and Wood, is, however, an indication of
the often surprising implications of party allegiance at the time.
In 1844 Crabb Robinson reported that 'on the Factory question'
Wordsworth was 'against the masters'. He goes on to make an
enlightening comparison between the Tory poet and an 'ultra-
radical' neighbour, who, being a factory master, was of quite
another mind; as he commented: 'it is a sad spectacle, how the
very best of men are unable to resist influences arising out of
interests'.

Once the Whigs had played their trump card they continued
in office only to prove their administrative debility and their
want both of policy and genius to cope with the economic distress
of the country. Wordsworth was at least convinced that the real
ills could not be cured by the Whig version of the 'dismal
science' but he did not see any political group prepared, as he was,
to seek a remedy in 'something deeper, purer, and higher'. 'A
world that deems itself most wise When most enslaved by gross
realities' needed spiritualization, the restoration of that moral
health and sanity which had been undermined by a growing
materialism. But the Tories gave as little hope in this direction as
did the Government, and in 1834 Crabb Robinson noted that
Wordsworth was not 'cheered by the prospect of a Wellington
ministry'. Wellington of course never completely redeemed
himself in Wordsworth's eyes after the Convention of Cintra,
but in 1838, in 1841 and 1845, his reaction to prospects of a Tory

[1] Cf. Croker to Peele, January, 1836: 'I look upon the Church and the
Peerage as doomed, but we ought to make a Parliamentary and literary fight
for them.' (*History of 'The Times'* (1935), I, p. 359.)

Government was the same. 'I learn from a pretty good quarter',
he wrote Robinson in 1838, 'that the Tories are building high
hopes upon the humiliation of the present ministry. I wish I
could share them, but I see no prospect of forming a government
at present in which any one party in the State can take the lead
without compromises and inconsistencies which are likely to
make common honesty a thing no longer to be looked for, in
public men.'

His main bone of contention with the Whig party had now
become its religious policy, which Wellington described as 'the
real question that now divides the country and which truly divides
the House of Commons'. Crabb Robinson reported in 1835 that
Wordsworth was 'interminable in his political tirades against the
ministry for their Church reforms', and ten years later he confessed to being 'more earnest in protecting the Church than the
land'. But he was opposed to Whig confiscation of Church
property not merely because he feared, as a devout Anglican, a
general attack on an institution to which he was so 'tenderly
attached'. For Wordsworth the only hope for the age rested in the
possibility of a moral and a spiritual regeneration which could be
most fittingly carried out in the religious sphere by that Church
whose establishment as a truly national institution fitted it ideally
for the task.

In the same way, the express exclusion of religious teaching
from any plan of education now seemed to him not only to be
cutting the age off from the most likely source of its salvation, but
to be contradicting the traditionally Christian basis of education
in England. For this reason he condemned the new University
College in London: 'Plague upon such liberality, and shame upon
a ministry who could consent that under the mask of old names
and honours, such a system should be smuggled into a country,
with whose laws and institutions Christianity is so intimately
blended, as with ours.' Orville Dewey reported that, in 1833,
'upon the value, and preciousness, and indispensableness of
religion . . . he talked very sagely, earnestly, and devoutly'.

But if the rest of the world was racing to ruin, the Lake
District was still the 'blessed spot' which, except perhaps for the
interludes of 1818 and 1831, it had always been. There at least

virtue and peace seemed to thrive. Not that everyone agreed
with the poet's view. Indeed, his persistent idealization of his
rustic neighbours tended to exasperate his friends. Harriet
Martineau, who was equally certain that the friend of Lowther
and Beaumont would revise his opinion of the virtues of the
ruling classes on a wider acquaintance, testified also to his biassed
affection for those lower on the social scale: 'While every Justice
of the Peace is filled with disgust and every clergyman with
almost despair at the drunkenness, quarrels, and extreme licen-
tiousness with women—here is dear good old Wordsworth for
ever talking of rural innocence and deprecating any intercourse
with the towns lest the purity of his neighbours should be
corrupted.'[1]

His conviction of the present unsuitability of the unfranchised
for government had not weakened his fundamental affection
for them, and he was still convinced that with education all things
would be possible. His great ambition for his own poetry was
that it might be a force in this educative process. As Justice
Coleridge reported, 'his hope was . . . that the sale of his poems
(should) increase among the classes below the middle'.[2]

It was to this reform by education, and to the political emancipation which would naturally follow it that he alluded in describing himself to Dewey in 1833 as a 'reformer', even though he told
Dewey that the people were 'not fit to govern themselves—
not yet certainly; public opinion, the foolish opinion of the
depraved, ignorant and concerted mass, ought not to be the law;
it ought not to be expressed in laws; it ought not to be represented in government; the true representative government should
represent the *mind* of a country, and that is not found in the mass,
nor is it to be expressed by universal suffrage'. Current demands
for immediate emancipation were to be resisted because they were
premature, and because any sudden transference of power must
be fatal: 'The tide is beating now against aristocracy and an
established religion, and if it prevails, anarchy and irreligion must
follow.' So while he admitted that 'hereditary rank and an

[1] *q.* W. L. Sperry, *Wordsworth's Anti-climax* (1935) , Chap. V.
[2] See 'Conversations and personal Reminiscences of Wordsworth', in *Prose
Works*, ed. Grosart, III, 426-7.

established priesthood are indefensible in the broadest views of human rights and interests', the argument for them was that they could not be removed 'without opening the door to greater evils —to the unrestrained licence of the multitude—to incessant change, disorder, uncertainty, and finally to oppression and tyranny'. As he put it in a note which he added to Barron Field's MS. biography: 'I am a lover of liberty, but know that liberty cannot exist apart from order; and the opinions in favour of aristocracy found in my works, the latter ones especially, all arise out of the consciousness I have that, in the present state of human knowledge, and its probable state for some ages, order cannot, and therefore liberty cannot be maintained, without degrees.'[1]

It is still clear that his recurrent forebodings of calamity sprang from his fears of the prematurity of the existing trend, and not from any positive condemnation of its principles. The danger he wished to avoid was the jeopardizing the triumph of liberty, or the purchasing it at too high a price of national turmoil and individual suffering, because of a want of patience among its misguided champions, because of their refusal to let political development take its natural course. So, with Dewey's defence of eventual democracy he calmly agreed, admitting 'that in other centuries some glorious results might be brought out', even though he saw nothing but 'darkness, disorder, and misery in the immediate prospect'. Some of his pessimism must, of course, be related to the often alarming complexion of the Chartist movement which culminated in the near-revolution of 1839. For if the composition of the reformed House of Commons did something to allay Wordsworth's earlier apprehensions, it proved to many of the supporters of the reform agitation that they had been duped. Disillusionment increased the influence of the champions of 'physical force' and this in turn seemed to justify the worst fears of the Tories.

A preoccupation with the dangerous possibilities of change, a concentration upon the risk rather than the goal, can of course lead to the most unattractive of political positions. For example, although there can be no doubt of Wordsworth's attitude to the

[1] q. Knight, *Life of William Wordsworth*, *Works* (1889), Vol. IX, 79.

principle of slavery, his concern with the perils involved in emancipation made him more than hesitant in expressing his convictions upon the subject. Here too his prejudice (hardened by successive defeats on Catholic emancipation and reform) against any proposals issuing from certain political quarters, made him all the more ready to see the weakness of the case for expediting emancipation. His suspicion of unreflecting liberalism, of the heart's predominance over the head, and that awareness of complexity which can be (and was so often in Wordsworth's case, however indicative of political maturity) such an effective restraint upon decisive action in any direction—all these traits of the mature outlook were at work to make him revise and modify his original position.[1]

A realization of the dangers involved in a too sudden emancipation was of course not confined to the Tories. Napoleon's experience and the outbreaks which followed the emancipation of Crown slaves in 1831, had sobered many enthusiasts. The *Edinburgh Review*, voicing general Whig uneasiness, deplored 'the extravagance of the anti-slavery party', and recognized the 'extraordinary difficulty of the question'. In the Commons even Hume was anxious lest rashness drive the country 'headlong into an abyss'. The eagerness which these critics reprobated was to Wordsworth but another example of that 'fanaticism' which he described as 'the disease of these times as much or more than of any other', and which was typified by a determination 'upon attainment of its ends with disregard of the means'. But in being even momentarily seduced by the plan of leaving the whole matter in the hands of the owners, he again betrayed excessive confidence in the influence of altruistic motives upon human action. 'It might be submitted', he wrote, 'to the consideration of the owner whether, in the present state of society, he can, as a matter of private conscience, retain his property in the slave, after he is convinced that it would be for the slave's benefit, civil, moral, and religious, that he should be emancipated.' If the owners were prepared to admit their moral obligation to emancipate, then 'whatever pecuniary loss might attend emancipation, it seems that a slave owner, taking a right view of the case, ought

[1] Apparently he had once taken part in anti-slavery petitions. See Letter 1355.

to be prepared to undergo it'. But in no circumstance would he countenance any legislative action which refused all compensation: 'by no means does it follow . . . that . . . the people of England, who through their legislature have sanctioned and even encouraged slavery, have a right to interfere for its destruction by a sweeping measure, of which an equivalent to the owner makes no part'.

In view of 'the excitement already existing in the public mind upon these, and so many other points of legislation and government', he was not prepared to take part in the anti-slavery agitation, however he admitted that 'no man can deplore more than I do the state of slavery in itself'.

Perhaps too much can be made of Wordsworth's doubts upon the advisability of a hasty emancipation: an even greater injustice has been done him by loose talk about his attitude to capital punishment. There is no evidence that he opposed the abolition of the death sentence for any crimes but those that are still capital offences to-day. His poems on the subject disclose a consistent humanitarianism, a desire to temper the violence of existing punishments as far as possible. The campaign waged by his friend Montagu against the death sentence for forgery and other crimes met with his entire approbation. In advocating the retention of a punishment which he could not regard as the most merciless retribution exacted by justice, he was, it should be remembered, voicing the opinion of a philosopher like Godwin, a revolutionary like Barrère, and that of the author of the Letter to Llandaff. At all times he sustained his argument upon the highest level of justice and charity, and he hopefully—too hopefully—looked forward to a time when the legal power of execution would 'drop for lack of use'.

.   .   .   .   .

Wordsworth was not unaware, in his later years, that hard arteries as well as hard experience were influencing his outlook. 'You are young', he pointed out to Henry Taylor of the Colonial Office in June, 1834, 'and therefore will naturally have more hope of public affairs than I can have.' With the same frankness of self-criticism, he told Gladstone that he was no longer qualified fairly to judge the merits of his literary contemporaries. According to Gladstone, he considered 'that old age in great measure disqualified him by its rigid fixity of habits from judging of the works of young poets', although, the statesman added, with more fairness than later commentators, 'I must say that he was here even over liberal in self-depreciation'.

It is clear, however, that he felt the need of clarifying his position in the eyes of the public, lest his notorious opposition to recent political measures be taken by it as a denial of his earlier and no less famous liberal humanitarianism. Aware too that 'expressions of regret for the past are seldom of much use as a preventive of future evils',[1] he included in the 1835 edition of his poems a Postscript which was to indicate the nature of his 'habitual feelings towards the poor and humbly employed', and to prove that, however the poet was convinced that 'so many of that class are seeking their happiness in ways which cannot lead to it ... he has not been an unthinking observer of their condition'.

Nowhere does Wordsworth better exemplify the nature and implications of that 'counterbalancing' political role which he latterly desired to fill. On measures such as the Reform Bill, Catholic emancipation and the abolition of slavery, he had pointed the dangers of an unreflecting benevolence, of a humanitarianism which refused to be modified by a consideration of circumstances: but in face of the heartless economic theory embodied in the new Whig Poor Law he appealed to that same benevolence, to that same human charity, to counter the dictates of the unfeeling intelligence. It is a tribute to his sincerity that his desire to recall legislators to their sentiments led him to as notable extremes in one direction as his previous anxiety to recall them to their senses had done in another. For that reason the Postscript makes refreshing reading.

The Reform Bill had, to Wordsworth, disclosed a criminal ignorance of the needs of the country on the part of Government: the Poor Law disclosed a criminal indifference to the rights of the poor, and he countered with a statement of these rights so extreme that even now we are hardly ready to accept it. 'All persons', he proclaimed, 'who cannot find employment, or

[1] See MS. of the Postscript, de Selincourt, IV, 426-7.

o

procure wages sufficient to support the body in health and strength, are entitled to a maintenance by law.' In his eagerness to balance the 'prudence of the head' by the 'wisdom of the heart' he even borrowed an argument from the Whig-radicals of the wartime opposition: 'as all rights in one party impose a correlative duty upon another, it follows that the right of the State to require the services of its members, even to the jeoparding their lives in the common defence, establishes a right in the people (not to be gainsaid by utilitarians and economists) to public support when . . . they may be unable to support themselves'.

It is plain too that his calm acceptance of the new political position was not alone the fruit of his certainty that eventual anarchy was inevitable. In the Postscript he admits that his original fears had proved too gloomy, and agrees to abandon his regrets for the past in favour of fresh hopes for the future. After a reference to the change wrought in the social system by the Reform Bill, and to his misgivings, he goes on: 'but let that pass; and let no opponent of the Bill be tempted to compliment his own foresight by exaggerating the mischiefs and dangers that have sprung from it: let not time be wasted in profitless regrets; and let those party distinctions vanish into their very names that have separated men who, whatever course they may have pursued, have ever had a bond of union in the wish to save the limited monarchy, and those other institutions that have, under Providence, rendered for so long a period of time this country the happiest and worthiest of which there is any record'.

In the first section of the Postscript Wordsworth is appealing sincerely and worthily for those who suffer from no fault of their own, for the innocent victims of circumstance; his faith in the fundamental virtue, honesty and independent spirit of the poor reveals itself as completely in 1835 as it had ever done in 1798, or in that early passage from *The Prelude* with which he closes the essay. His concern for the respect due to the individual was never as positively expressed as in his demand that, even in the dispensation of charity, 'lawgivers should take into account the various tempers and dispositions of mankind'; he will have no artisan used to 'some light and nice exercise of the fingers' forced to 'severe labour of the arms', and if he opposes the associations of the working class, he condemns with equal force 'the combinations of masters to keep down, unjustly, the price of labour'.

Discontent need not, he now sees, be answered by repression alone; by being encouraged to form joint-stock companies the working classes will be given an interest in the preservation of public tranquillity which will act with more strength than all the exhortations and devices of their employers. Although such an economic plan will, of course, stimulate a 'democratic and republican spirit', this 'would not . . . be dangerous in itself', provided that it is, in the true Wordsworthian style, 'counter-balanced, either by a landed proprietorship, or by a Church extending itself so as to embrace an evergrowing and evershifting population'.

As we should expect, Wordsworth's attitude to the current agitation for Church reform shows rather less compliant modification. The prevailing spirit of Erastian materialism plainly called for a countering support of the Established Church. He was aware of deficiencies, of faults to be remedied, of an ideal still to be attained, but 'in times when nothing . . . is generally acceptable but what we believe can be traced to preconceived intention, and specific acts and formal contrivances of human understanding', he was unwilling to expose the Church to the rationalizing schemes of the antipathetic.

He welcomed, as we know, the Oxford Movement. Although Crabb Robinson reported that he 'does not go all lengths with the Oxford School', the diarist recorded the poet's praise of the reformers 'for inspiring the age with deeper reverence for antiquity and a more cordial conformity with ritual observances, as well as a warmer piety'. But in the Postscript he did admit that more practical measures of reform, conducted by reverent hands, would not meet with his disapproval: 'a well-considered change in the distribution of some parts of the property at present possessed by the Church, a change scrupulously founded upon due respect to law and justice, will, we trust, bring about so much of what her friends desire, that the rest may be calmly waited for'.

The more charitable and acquiescent tone of the Postscript is typical of Wordsworth's political convictions for the remaining years of his life. Almost at once his friends start recording a notable moderation in his political temper. An 1835 note to a poem composed two years before voices his conviction that 'charity is, upon the whole, the safest guide that we can take, in judging our fellow men, whether of past ages, or of the present time . . .'; and it is apparent that he kept this rule fairly constantly before him. Writing to Crabb Robinson of the Whig who succeeded in the Cockermouth election of 1840, he pointed out that 'Horsman is a clever man, and to him personally I have no objection . . .'; he then goes on to admit that he was 'rather glad to see him in parliament, as some with his opinions will, and perhaps ought to be there'. He realized that his early fears of the disastrous effects of the Reform Bill upon the composition of the Commons were not borne out by the event; in the subsequent elections in Westmorland and Cumberland, for example, the Lowther interest did not lose much ground, and parliament was not flooded with Hunts and O'Connells. In 1837 a Radical proposal to increase the representation was defeated by 509 votes to 20.

Agitation for the secret ballot did revive his fears, but the condemnation which he voiced was after all the same as that made many years before by Godwin in *Political Justice*: secret voting was a contradiction of that frank and unashamed avowal of opinion which was endemic to his conception of political freedom and independence.

On his Christmas visit to Rydal in December, 1835, Crabb Robinson noted that Wordsworth was 'somewhat less intolerant than he used to be and we have had very little sparring yet on politics'. In 1836 the poet made an alteration to the apostrophe of freedom which concluded the 'Descriptive Sketches', but, as Dr Batho has pointed out, its significance resides mainly in the fact that it makes such a slight modification at so late a date, implying merely that tyrants may be reformed, and not necessarily destroyed. It is also significant that the revised lines are directly borrowed from a passage in Burke. Wordsworth wrote:

Great God! by whom the strifes of men are weighed
In an impartial balance, give thine aid
To the just cause; and oh! do Thou preside
Over the mighty stream now spreading wide:
So shall its waters, from the heavens supplied
In copious showers, from earth by wholesome springs,
Brood o'er the long-parched lands with Nile-like wings!
And grant that every sceptered child of clay
Who cries presumptuous, 'Here the flood shall stay,'
May in its progress see thy guiding hand,
And cease the acknowledged purpose to withstand.

And the link with the final paragraph of Burke's *Thoughts on French Affairs* is clear: 'if a great change is to be made in human affairs, the minds of men will be fitted to it, the general opinions and feelings will draw that way. Every fear, every hope will forward it; and then they, who persist in opposing this mighty current in human affairs, will appear rather to resist the decrees of Providence itself, than the mere designs of men. They will not be resolute and firm, but perverse and obstinate.'

In an interview with Gladstone in 1836 Wordsworth stressed again the need for a balance to the newly acquired democratic influence of the enfranchised towns, but sought it now in an entirely new quarter. As Gladstone reported the conversation, Wordsworth thought that 'the Reform Act had brought out too prominently a particular muscle of the national frame, the strength of the towns; that the cure was to be found in a large further enfranchisement, of the country chiefly: that you would thus extend the base of the pyramid and so give it strength. He wished the old institutions of the country preserved, and thought this the way to preserve them. He thought the political franchise upon the whole a good to the mass—regard being had to the state of human nature . . .'; and Gladstone added that this reasoning was 'against him'.

The restoration of the old social bonds was still the poet's ambition, but he had lost his confidence in the ability of the upper classes entirely to revive them. He was, in 1844, of the opinion that 'the upper classes had not virtue enough to prepare a remedy or material palliation' for the distress of their inferiors.

'It is melancholy', he wrote to an American correspondent in 1844, 'to think how little that portion of the community which is quite at ease in their circumstances, have to do in a social way with the humbler classes. . . . One would wish to see the rich mingle with the poor as much as may be upon a footing of fraternal equality. The old feudal relations and dependencies are almost gone from England, and nothing has yet come adequately to supply their place. . . . Why should not great landowners look for a substitute for what is lost of feudal paternity in the higher principles of christianized humanity, and humble-minded brotherhood?'

The Continental tour of 1837 revived his aspirations in the cause of national freedom, and prompted a series of poetic compositions often worthy to stand beside the sonnets of 1802. The Italian struggle for independence had long ago captured his imagination, and he had even been willing to have the unification and liberation of Italy effected by Napoleon. We can appreciate the passion which this concession represents, and so should not wonder at the later report from Mrs Fletcher, his neighbour at Lancrigg, that 'the poet, on Italian politics, is all we can desire . . . (he) spoke with strong and deep feeling of the present state of Italy, and the crushing despotism of Austria, supported as it is in secret by Russia and Prussia. . . . I cannot think that Milton himself could have talked more loftily against despotism, or more excellently on truth and justice. . . .'[1] The poems evoked by his actual inspection of the struggle bear similar witness to his interest and enthusiasm.

The last ten years of Wordsworth's life were fairly completely chronicled by a host of attentive and reverent neighbours, and they all speak of the growing strength of his liberal opinions. It is true that in 1839 Crabb Robinson thought he detected the beginnings of mental 'ossification' in the poet, but his fear that Wordsworth might lose his 'facility of . . . seeing things on all sides' was groundless. Two years later indeed he corrected himself by admitting that his friend's outlook was 'far more liberal than it used to be'.

His speaking 'with more liberality than we expected of the

[1] *Autobiography* (1875), 212.

Wordsworth in 1842 (*aet.* 72) from the painting by
Benjamin Robert Haydon

recent measures about the Corn Laws' was hailed by his neighbours in 1846 'as a sign that he was opening his mind to more
light on these subjects'.[1] In the same year Harriet Martineau
wrote: 'His mind must always have been essentially liberal, but
now it is more obviously and charmingly so than I understand it
used to appear. The mildness of age has succeeded to what used to
be thought a rather harsh particularity of opinion and manners.'

In 1846 he had an unlikely visitor in the shape of the Chartist,
Thomas Cooper. Their conversations, reported in Cooper's
autobiography[2] make rather extraordinary reading. Cooper
was certain that he made no errors in transcription; as he said:
'I think every word he uttered I can recollect.' Under the triumphant heading 'THE TORY IS A CHARTIST' he went on: 'nothing struck
me so much in Wordsworth's conversation as his remark concerning Chartism. . . . "You were right," he said. "I have always
said the people were right in what they asked, but you went the
wrong way to get it . . . there is nothing unreasonable in your
Charter: it is the foolish attempt at physical force for which many
of you have been blamable." '

These remarks would perhaps not have surprised Crabb Robinson, who in 1848 wrote to Mrs Wordsworth: 'I recollect once
hearing Mr Wordsworth say, half in joke, half in earnest—"I
have no respect whatever for Whigs, but I have a good deal of the
Chartist in me." To be sure he has. His early poems are full of
that intense love of the people, as such, which becomes Chartism
when the attempt is formally made to make their interests the
especial object of legislation as of deeper importance than the
positive rights hitherto accorded to the privileged orders.'

It is probable that just as Crabb Robinson under-estimated
the strength of Wordsworth's antipathy to the 'formal political
attempt' implied by the Chartist movement, so Cooper failed to
understand the full strength and implications of his condemnation
of any attempt to achieve reform by a threat of violence. The
same kind of agreement in principle, which we can well credit,
was probably the basis too for Cooper's report of the poet's
approbation of 'mechanics and similar institutions'.

There is certainly no need to doubt his statement that the

[1] Ossoli, *op. cit.*, II, 175.   [2] Pub. 1873, pp. 287 *et seq.*

poet believed that in Europe 'the different governments will have to give Constitutions to their people, for knowledge is spreading, and constitutional liberty is sure to follow'; and that in England 'he had the same views of the spread of freedom . . . in proportion to the increase of knowledge'. The account closes with a remark patently Wordsworthian: 'The people are sure to have the franchise . . . as knowledge increases; but you will not get all you seek at once—and you must never seek it again by physical force . . . it will only make you longer about it.'

These interviews to which the poet was subjected in his old age are often enlightening on other details. It is interesting, for example, to learn from Yarnall[1] that the part-author[2] of the 'Ode on the Installation of his Royal Highness Prince Albert as Chancellor of the University of Cambridge' in fact considered the Consort positively unsuited for the post, and, 'speaking strongly', regretted that 'the Heads of Houses . . . had allowed themselves to be influenced by a wish to please the Queen; which was not a worthy motive in a case like this'.

The same visitor records Wordsworth's condemnation of the forcing unwilling dons into Holy Orders under the terms of their fellowships, and his appreciation of the advantages of the celibacy of the Roman Catholic clergy—both of which opinions are valuable complements to those earlier expressed in the heat of religious controversy.

.   .   .   .   .

For reasons referred to in the Introduction, little attempt has been made to relate the later stages of Wordsworth's political development to the quality of his later poetry. Wordsworth frequently admitted, at times when the political scene was commanding all his attention, that poetry had been forced into the background, and there can be no doubt that he found his mature preoccupation with those political questions which affected him deeply, such as Catholic emancipation and the Reform Bill, inimical to poetic composition. The bitterness with which he waged the struggle, the animosity which it of necessity

[1] *Wordsworth and the Coleridges* (1899), 38-9.
[2] With his son-in-law.

stimulated, were themselves no fit accompaniments of an inspiration which drew its strength from far different emotional sources.

I believe it is also true to say that his conviction of the necessity of counterbalancing certain tendencies in the spirit of his age diverted his poetry into a didactic and moralizing vein which was disastrous to it.

It has been apparent that the move to conservatism was but one aspect, one expression of a gradual modification of outlook which showed itself in his religious development, by a move to orthodoxy, and in the artistic, by a closer attention to and respect for poetic tradition. Wordsworth's poetry suffered a change of emphasis from the spontaneity of his original inspiration to formalism, from the spirit of 'Expostulation and Reply' to that of the 'Ode to Duty'.

If we would seek a reason for the poetic decline other than the mere passage of time, we should turn our attention, not to the Addresses to the Freeholders of Westmorland, but rather to the 'Ode to Duty' and even to the *Ecclesiastical Sonnets*.

Before his death, Wordsworth's political apprehensions had been notably modified by a refreshing revival of that liberal sympathy and that intellectual independence so typical of his personality. After the shocks of the 'thirties, he found that there was a general concern among his contemporaries for those tendencies in modern life which perturbed him, and that his hopes of progress could not be nullified merely by the emancipation of the Catholics or the premature extension of the franchise.

The political faith which he had attained in his last years was not unattractive, not disfigured by intolerance, at no time indicative of that closed mind which Crabb Robinson feared. It was the result of his conviction of the superior advantages of order in the existing stage of political development and human enlightenment, but it looked hopefully forward, and was based essentially on a belief in inevitable progress towards an ideal state of human liberty and dignity. The story of Wordsworth's political development is one of growth, but not one of decline or apostasy; and through it all runs that theme of humanitarian sympathy which inspired some of the noblest of our poetry. The following lines continue that passage of the Fourteenth Book of *The Prelude* prefixed to this study; is to be hoped that their veracity has now to some extent been demonstrated:

> A meditative, oft a suffering, man—
> Do I declare . . .
> That, whatsoever falls my better mind,
> Revolving with the accidents of life,
> May have sustained, that, howsoe'er misled,
> Never did I, in quest of right and wrong,
> Tamper with conscience from a private aim;
> Nor was in any public hope the dupe
> Of selfish passions; nor did ever yield
> Wilfully to mean cares or low pursuits.
>
> (*Prel.*, XIV, 143-54.)

Wordsworth and Helen Maria Williams

[*An extract from an article published in* The Modern Language Review, *Vol. XLIII, No. 4, October, 1948*]

The first of Wordsworth's poems to be published was a sonnet, 'On Seeing Miss Helen Maria Williams weep at a Tale of Distress', which appeared in the *European Magazine* for March, 1787. The poem is a product typical of the young Wordsworth, imitative and conventional, written in that sentimental strain so profitably exploited by Miss Williams herself; indeed, it is indistinguishable from numerous contemporary poetic tributes to the same subject. But besides being a great poet's first appearance in public, this poem does mark the beginning of Wordsworth's interest in Helen Maria Williams (an interest rather more fruitful than has hitherto been suspected), and it does introduce us to a contemporary whose biography throws some light on the Wordsworth of the Revolutionary years.

Helen Maria Williams,[1] the daughter of an Army officer, was born in London in 1761. Eight years later, after the death of her father, the family moved to Berwick-on-Tweed, whence Helen returned to London in 1781 with the manuscript of her first poem, *Edwin and Eltruda*. Mainly through the assistance of Dr Kippis, then an important figure in the London literary world, this 'Legendary Tale' was published in the following year, and was well received. From then on his protégée maintained an output of poetry—sentimental, melancholic, and humanitarian—sufficient

[1] See Lionel D. Woodward, *Une Anglaise Amie de la Révolution Française; Hélène-Maria Williams et ses amis* (Paris, 1930); H. M. Williams, *Memoirs of the Reign of Robespierre*, with introduction by F. Funck-Brentano (London 1929).

to ensure her a considerable popularity. An 'Ode on the Peace' in 1783 was followed in the next year by 'Peru', a rather more ambitious complaint against the European exploitation of South America. The growing fame of the poetess then won her the patronage of the influential George Hardinge, who encouraged her literary efforts, assisted the 1786 publication of her *Poems*, and contributed materially to their success. In 1788 she returned to the theme of 'Peru' with 'A Poem on the Bill Lately Passed for Regulating the Slave Trade,' in which a glowing tribute to Pitt reminds us of his early popularity among liberals and humanitarians, and helps us to understand the bitterness of the subsequent attacks upon him.

As L. D. Woodward has pointed out in his biography, poetic tributes to Miss Williams, including a sonnet by Anna Seward in the *Gentleman's Magazine* for May, 1784, appeared frequently in periodicals after the publication of 'Peru', and Wordsworth's sonnet is only one of several that were published in the same year. The poem is, of course, a pure fiction, for Wordsworth and Miss Williams did not meet until 1820, and it appears that, as late as 1814, Miss Williams had not even heard of her more famous compatriot.[1] When the poem was written, the author was a schoolboy at Hawkshead, and the subject was living in Essex. Wordsworth evidently regarded the sonnet as too unimportant even for inclusion in his *Juvenilia*; in typical schoolboy fashion it was signed 'Axiologus',[2] a Greek 'translation' of his name, and never reprinted in his lifetime.

Then in 1790, by pure coincidence, both Wordsworth and Helen Maria Williams (whose first novel, *Julia*, appeared in that year) sailed for France at the same time. Since 1789, Helen and her sister Cecilia had been taking French lessons from their friend, the Baroness du Fossé; in 1790, the Baron, who had recently succeeded to an estate in France, invited the sisters to visit him. So, following Cecilia, Helen landed in France on 13 July, to be as thrilled by the spectacle of 'France standing on the top of golden

[1] Woodward, p. 179, and G. M. Harper, *William Wordsworth* (1916 ed.) Vol. I, p. 149n.

[2] See S. T. Coleridge's Hexameters. 'Ad Vilmum Axiologum' in *Poetical Works* (ed. E. H. Coleridge), Vol. I, p. 391.

hours' as were the two more famous pedestrians, who also chanced 'To land at Calais on the very eve Of that great federal day . . .'

It was in September, too, that Helen Maria Williams returned to England, anxious to proclaim her complete conversion to the principles of the Revolution. So she published at once *Letters Written in France in the Summer of 1790, to a Friend in England.* It was the 1795 edition of this volume that was in Wordsworth's possession at his death, but I shall defer for the moment any inquiry into the particular use he made of it.

In 1791 both poets were in France again. With her mother and sister, Miss Williams had arrived by 10 August, after publishing *A Farewell for Two Years to England*, in which she announced her intention of sojourning 'Where the slow Loire on borders ever gay, Delights to linger, in his sunny way'. At the same time Wordsworth, not unduly anxious about his future, conjured up an excuse for a continental journey, and left London on 22 November to await a boat at Brighton. His letter to Richard,[1] written at Orleans almost a fortnight after his arrival there, shows that he had not lost interest in Miss Williams, and that he had now been given the opportunity of meeting her.

'I was detained at Brighthelmstone,' he wrote, 'from Tuesday till Saturday evening, which time must have passed in a manner extremely disagreeable, if I had not bethought me of introducing myself to Mrs Charlotte Smith; she received me in the politest manner, and shewed me every possible civility. This with my best affection you will be so good as to mention to Captain and Mrs Wordsworth. . . . Mrs Smith, who was so good as to give me letters for Paris, furnished me with one for Miss Williams, an English lady, who resided here lately, but was gone before I arrived. This circumstance was a considerable disappointment to me.'

It appears from this that Wordsworth used the names of his cousin and his wife to introduce himself to Mrs Smith, and as

---

[1] *The Letters of William and Dorothy Wordsworth* (ed. de Selincourt), Vol. I, p. 66. Wordsworth was at Brighton from Tuesday, 22 November, not 6 December, as in de Selincourt; Wordsworth only reached Orleans 'a fortnight after quitting London'.

she was related to a Director of the East India Company in which Captain Wordsworth was serving, it is possible that they would have met. But she was already known to William as a literary figure. To-day Charlotte Smith is only remembered as the prolific author of sentimental novels, but the numerous editions of her *Elegiac Sonnets* and collected *Poems* testify to her equal fame as a poet. In a copy of the 1789 edition of her *Elegiac Sonnets*, preserved at the Wordsworth Museum in Grasmere, the names of W. Wordsworth and John Myers 'of St John's, Cambridge', have been added in writing to the list of subscribers, and, although the names are not printed in subsequent editions, this evidence would appear to be reliable.

Whatever Wordsworth's reaction to her politics, he was apparently delighted both to make her acquaintance, and to be given an introduction to Miss Williams—whose name would also be tainted with Jacobinism by this time. In this connection, it is perhaps significant that when, many years later, the Laureate was recalling the exciting days of the Revolution, the coupled names of Helen Maria Williams and Charlotte Smith at once came to his mind as prominent in the literary world of that time.[1]

As we have seen, the poet suffered 'a considerable disappointment' when he discovered that Miss Williams had left Orleans before his arrival and had settled in Paris. Yet he did have a later opportunity to contact her before he left France (for her two years' abroad lengthened into a lifetime). When the harassed poet returned to the capital in October, Miss Williams was still there, by that time a prominent figure in the circle of English supporters of the Revolution, and personally acquainted with most of the leaders of the Girondin party. Her political standing in Paris at the end of 1792 is important. During the two or three months that Wordsworth spent there, he must have known of her connections with the Girondin party; had his own relations with that group been as intimate as many of his biographers would have us believe (or even as *The Prelude* vaguely suggests), it is hardly credible that he would not have met the compatriot to whom he had been given a letter of introduction, for whose

[1] See Harper, Vol. I. p. 149, citing *Memoirs of William Wordsworth*, by Mrs John Davy.

poetry he had formed an early affection, and with whose politics he would feel so much sympathy. In accounts of the activities of the English colony in Paris contained in contemporary records[1] and in the reports prepared for the Foreign Office,[2] frequent mention is made of Miss Williams, of her acquaintance, Stone, and of numbers of other Jacobins: there is never any mention of Wordsworth, and, more significant, it is quite certain that he never met Helen Maria Williams before 1820. But before that date, evidently in 1804, Wordsworth wrote the tale of *Vaudracour and Julia*, originally intended for inclusion in *The Prelude*. This story has always been something of an enigma, and Wordsworth's own references to it do little to clarify the obscurity of its source and significance. Early versions of *The Prelude* (MSS. A, B and C, and possibly MS. D, in which the passage is not legible) announce the author's intention of drawing:

> ... from obscurity a tragic tale
> ... as I heard
> The events related by my patriot Friend
> And others who had borne a part therein.
> (IX, 549-53.)

But the published (1850) version ascribes the story to Beaupuy alone (see IX, 548); meanwhile, the episode had been published separately in 1820, and in the Fenwick note dictated for this poem in 1843, i.e. after the final MS. E of *The Prelude*—all previous explanations are cancelled by the statement that the poem is: 'Faithfully narrated, though with the omission of many pathetic circumstances, from the mouth of a French lady, who had been an eye and ear witness of all that was done and said. Many long years after I was told that Dupligne was then a monk in the Convent of La Trappe.' This note not only mentions the hero's name for the first time, and contradicts the author's earlier introductions of the story, but apparently overlooks the fact that Vaudracour, now evidently turned Trappist, was, when Wordsworth had left him in the poem, 'an imbecile mind'.

[1] See J. M. Thompson, *English Witnesses of the French Revolution* (1938); J. G. Algar, *Englishmen in the French Revolution* (1889).
[2] P.R.O.: F.O. 27/40

These varying and conflicting ascriptions lead us to suspect that Wordsworth was rather more anxious to disclaim originality than to give an exact account of his indebtedness, and the similarity between the story of William and Annette and that of Vaudracour and Julia can no doubt explain this. But allowing the 'omission of many pathetic circumstances', there is good reason to believe that Wordsworth had as much of the story as his own experience did not provide him with from Helen Maria Williams.

The full title of the volume published by Miss Williams in 1790 was: *Letters Written in France, in the Summer of 1790, to a Friend in England: Containing Various Anecdotes Relative to the French Revolution; and Memoirs of Mons. and Madame du F . . .* These memoirs occupy a third of the book, and quite obviously relate to the misfortunes of the author's friends, Monsieur and Madame du Fossé. She proposes to tell the story of their sufferings as an example of the deep-rooted nature of the tyranny of the *ancien régime*, just as Wordsworth told the story of Vaudracour and Julia in *The Prelude* (IX, 549) as a proof—

> . . . to what low depth had struck the roots,
> How widely spread the boughs of that old tree
> Which, as a deadly mischief, and a foul
> And black dishonour, France was weary of.

To anticipate other more definite indications of Wordsworth's indebtedness, the possibility that the name 'Dupligne' in the Fenwick note is a careless expansion of the 'du F . . .' of the *Letters* should not be ignored—a suspicion which the ascription of the story to a lady helps to strengthen. Nor should we forget that, by the time the Fenwick notes were composed, Wordsworth might well have had the story from the lips of Miss Williams as well as from her pen—and she had become a French citizen in 1817.

The earlier story concerns Antoine Augustin Thomas du F . . ., the son of proud Norman parents, who falls in love with Monique, the daughter of a respectable family which 'had great reason to believe' that it was of noble descent, but was unable to verify its nobility. Similarly, although the 1820 version of *Vaudracour and Julia* stresses the fact that '. . . the stock [was] Plebeian though

ingenuous', the earlier MSS. preserve a more exact account of
Julia's descent, and one much closer to that given by Miss
Williams. So in MS. A (IX, 563) Julia is

> . . . a bright maid, from Parents sprung
> Not mean in their condition; but with rights
> Unhonoured of Nobility. . . .

In the *Letters*, Monique becomes the 'companion' of du Fossé's
mother, so that 'he had constant opportunities of observing her
disposition and character; and the passion with which she at
length inspired him, was founded on the lasting basis of esteem'
(*Letters*, p. 128). Wordsworth describes a similar development of
affection by making his characters close neighbours, so that their
constant association supplied—

> . . . a basis . . . for deep and solid love,
> And endless constancy, and placid truth.

However, in both versions, the proud father of the noble lover
spurns '. . . the very thought Of such alliance.'

Du Fossé and Monique retaliate by being secretly married, and
this fact is only revealed to the mother of du Fossé when Monique's pregnancy renders it unavoidable. The variation made here
in *Vaudracour* only adds to the autobiographical significance of the
poem, for there Julia, like Annette,

> . . . wanting yet the name of wife,
> Carried about her for a secret grief
> The promise of a mother. . . .

But just as Madame du Fossé sends Monique to her brothers
as Caen, so Julia's parents 'Found means to hurry her away by
night.' It is interesting to note, however, that the motive for
concealing Monique's condition was fear of Baron du Fossé;
whereas Julia is moved in an attempt '. . . to conceal The
threatened shame,' and Vaudracour is not informed of the plan;
a variation which makes us wish that more were known of the
relations between Wordsworth and the Vallon family.

In both versions the tyrannical father replies with threats
of imprisonment; in the *Letters* du Fossé is warned of the imminence of a lettre de cachet, and he manages to escape with his

P

wife to Geneva, thence to England via Germany and Holland. When he is enticed back by the belief that his father has repented, he discovers that he is under surveillance, and is informed by his father that the marriage has been annulled. This flight is omitted by Wordsworth, but when Vaudracour returns from his visit to Julia he, too, is informed by his father that—

> You shall be baffled in your mad intent
> If there be justice in the court of France.

In the 1820 version only, the 'artful withdrawal' of his parents follows, and is the counterpart of the retirement (rather more logical) of du Fossé and his father to their house at Rouen, which takes place in the *Letters*. The 1820 version of *Vaudracour* also puts the time of the arrest at midnight, in exact agreement with Miss Williams. The attack is made in the son's own room in both accounts, and the 'three armed men' of *Vaudracour* correspond to the 'servant armed and two Cavaliers de Marechaussée' of the *Letters*. But du Fossé commits no murder, and he is imprisoned only because of his father's tyranny. The reason for this added complication in *Vaudracour* of the violence committed by 'the rash youth's ungovernable hand', as for his earlier 'perilous weakness', is probably to be found again in the author's recollection of the story of William and Annette, and in an exaggerated conception of his own guilty role therein.

Imprisonment follows in both cases, and in both the hero is given his liberty upon certain conditions which—'. . . liberty and love dispersed in air'. The lengthy account of du Fossé's sufferings and attempted escapes in the *Letters* is no doubt covered by the 'pathetic circumstances' of whose omission Wordsworth gave warning, but the final release in both cases is effected by 'private influence with the court'. In the earlier version of *The Prelude* (MS. A, I. 758), it is through the efforts of the magistrate who 'plac'd the Youth in custody' that Vaudracour is released; however, in the story as told by Helen Maria Williams, the magistrate who had confined the innocent du Fossé was determined to prevent his release, lest the injustice of the detention be exposed. It was probably reference to this fact that led Wordsworth to alter MS. A, so that the release is arranged merely by 'a magistrate', and then, in the 1820 version, to refer generally to 'private influence'.

Miss Williams reunites her lovers in England, until their perseverance is rewarded by the death of the domestic tyrant and their succession to his estate. But Wordsworth would find it hard to countenance a happy ending to a tale in which he saw so much to remind him of his own dismal experience. Significantly, he leaves Julia 'unwedded' (although for no adequate reason), and has recourse to a sudden determination by Julia's mother to dismiss her to a convent; so that at the conclusion of the tragedy Vaudracour and Julia, like William and Annette, are unmarried and separated for ever.

It is impossible to date *Vaudracour and Julia* accurately. We know of no earlier version than that in MS. A of *The Prelude*, but it is possible that the episode was written some time before 1804. Certainly, as the author realized, it forms no integral part of *The Prelude*, and its original inclusion was possibly an attempt to find a suitable setting for a poem already completed. The morbid tone of the conclusion, and the melancholy despair which pervades the whole story, are more typical of the Wordsworth who composed 'The Female Vagrant' and 'The Borderers', than of the essentially 'healthy' poet of 1804. It is also possible to detect other signs of immaturity in language (see, amongst others, lines 645-7, 687-8 and 701 in the early version), and in the lugubrious and ineffectual melancholy of lines 809-19 and 854-9.

In view of the high opinion which Wordsworth long held of the poetry of Miss Williams (see his letters to Dyce dated 10 May 1830, and spring of 1833), it is not surprising that we find, especially in his earlier work, a number of other examples of similarities too striking and frequent to be ignored. The late Professor de Selincourt pointed out the acquaintance with the popular sentimental verse of Charlotte Smith and Helen Maria Williams which is patent in the poetry of Wordsworth's school-days. The *Descriptive Sketches* is frequently reminiscent of Miss William's *Letters*, especially in those passages (ll. 726-39 and 762-9 of the 1793 version) which describe the transformation wrought by the advent of Liberty upon the appearance of the countryside;

for Miss Williams had also remarked that the French countryside seemed to possess a new beauty in 1790: 'the woods seemed to cast a more refreshing shade, and the lawns to wear a brighter verdure, while the carols of freedom burst from the cottage of the peasant, and the voice of joy resounded on the hill, and in the valley.' The bitter complaint against the savage despoliation of 'the Peruvian Vales' in the concluding stanzas of the first MS. of 'Guilt and Sorrow' also echoes the poem which Miss Williams devoted to the same subject. Similarly, the authoress of the *Letters* made use of the figure of Père Gérard to stress the virtues of the new régime in France, just as Wordsworth introduced him into the Letter to the Bishop of Llandaff for the same purpose; and, although we now move into the realm of pure hypothesis, it is noteworthy that Helen Maria Williams was a popular translator of Bernardin de Saint-Pierre, whose influence upon Wordsworth, especially in 'The Ruined Cottage' and 'Poems on the Naming of Places', has been suggested by both Hazlitt[1] and Legouis.[2]

Rather more flagrant was a poem composed by the mature Wordsworth in 1817, 'The Lament of Mary Queen of Scots', which is little more than a recasting of *Queen Mary's Lament*, first published in the 1786 edition of the poems of Helen Maria Williams. In both poems the Queen addresses her lament to the moon, whose beams, even in their beauty, can afford her no solace. So Helen Maria Williams:

> Pale moon! thy mild benignant light
> May glad some other captive's sight. . . .
> . . . What ray of thine
> Can soothe a misery like mine?

And Wordsworth:

> Smile of the moon!—for so I name
> That silent greeting from above . . .
> . . . Bright boon of pitying Heaven! Alas,
> I may not trust thy placid cheer!

[1] My First Acquaintance with Poets, *Works*, ed. Howe (1933), Vol. XVII, p. 116.

[2] *The Early Life of William Wordsworth* (1921), p. 355.

Although the earlier poem is not timed specifically, as is Wordsworth's, 'on the eve of a New Year', in the second stanza of both
poems the Queen is reminded of the passage of the years. In
both versions Mary sees her royal position as the main cause of
her misfortunes:

> Why did the regal garb array
> A breast that tender passions sway?
> (H.M.W.)

And

> It is my royal state that yields
> This bitterness of woe.
> (W.)

Regretful reminiscence takes the same form in both poems; in
Miss Williams:

> Where are the crowns that round my head
> A double glory vainly spread? . . .
> . . . Alas, had Fate designed to bless,
> Its equal hand had given me less.

And in Wordsworth:

> Born all too high, by wedlock raised
> Still higher—to be cast thus low!
> Would that mine eyes had never gazed
> On aught of more ambitious show
> Than the sweet flowerets of the fields!

The complaint against Elizabeth in Miss William's poem:

> Have not thy unrelenting hands
> Torn Nature's most endearing bands?
> Whate'er I hoped from woman's name,
> The ties of blood, the stranger's claim;
> A sister-queen's despairing breast
> On thee securely leaned for rest . . .

is neatly condensed in Wordsworth's:

> A woman rules my prison's key;
> A sister queen, against the bent

> Of law and holiest sympathy,
> Detains me, doubtful of the event. . . .

Finally, both poems conclude with the Queen seeing death as her only route to peace, and leave us with further proof that the mature Wordsworth found no reason to modify the judgment of the schoolboy 'Axiologus'.

Wordsworth and Helen Maria Williams were introduced by Henry Crabb Robinson during Wordsworth's visit to Paris in 1820. The two former revolutionaries discovered that once again they stood on common political ground; like so many of their generation, they had both lost faith, not in humanity, but in the power of political change to make men happier. With their different experiences of the Napoleonic dictatorship, they had both decided that the energies of their youth had been largely misdirected.

The Wordsworths were charmed with their new friend, and Helen's letter to Crabb Robinson after the meeting seems to indicate that Wordsworth had done something to repay the considerable debt he had accumulated; it also gives us an indication of the difference between the Wordsworth Miss Williams met in 1820, and the Wordsworth she almost met in 1792.

'I can hardly thank you enough', she wrote, '(for) your kindness in introducing me to the acquaintance of Mr Wordsworth and his fellow-travellers. . . . You will . . . easily believe with how much pleasure I left politics, the laws of election, and the charter —to take care of themselves while I was led by Mr Wordsworth's society to that world of poetical illusion, so full of charms, and from which I have been so long an exile.'[1]

[1] Woodward, p. 190.

The Stowey Spy

The relevant portions of the Home Office file which deals with the visit of the Government spy to Stowey in 1797 have already been published by A. G. Eagleston in *Coleridge*, edited by Griggs and Blunden (1934).

However, it is appropriate that the story should be retold here. The letters are in the Public Records Office, Home Office series, catalogue number 42.

On August 11, 1797, a Home Office agent called Walsh wrote to Whitehall from Hungerford in Berkshire to say that he had been informed of suspicious activities in Somerset by a recent arrival from Alfoxton, one Charles Mogg. Mogg had made the acquaintance in Alfoxton of Thomas Jones, who had told him that 'some French people had got possession of the mansion house . . . (and) they had taken the plan of all the places round that part of the Country'. The neighbours, according to Jones, were generally agreed that 'the French people were very suspicious persons and that they were doing no good there'. These 'French people' added Jones, were 'frequently out on the heights most part of the night'.

According to Walsh, Mogg had already transmitted his suspicions to the cook employed by a Dr Lysons of Bath. She in turn must have told her master, who had forwarded his information to the Home Secretary on 8 August. On the same day that Walsh reported, the patriotic Lysons dispatched a second letter to the Duke of Portland:

'MY LORD DUKE,—On the 8th instant I took the liberty to acquaint your Grace with a very suspicious business concerning an emigrant family who have contrived to get possession of a mansion house at Alfoxton. . . . I am since informed that the master of the House has no wife with him, but only a woman who passes for his sister.'

Mention is then made of the camp-stools in the possession of the pair, of their 'nocturnal or diurnal expeditions' and of 'a portfolio in which they enter their observations, which they have been heard to say were almost finished. They have been heard to say they should be rewarded for them, and were very attentive to the River near them. . . . These people may possibly be under Agents to some principal at Bristol.'

The reaction at the Home Office was immediate. Mr King wrote to Mr Walsh the following day: 'You will immediately proceed to Alfoxton. . . . If you are in want of further information or assistance, you will call on Sir P. Hale, Bart., of Boymore, nr Bridgewater . . . should they move, you must follow their tracks.'

Walsh obeyed promptly and three days later he was writing to Mr King from the Globe Inn, Stowey. His first item of news was of a conversation which he had overheard between the landlord of the Globe and one of his guests; his attention had first been attracted by the latter's asking, 'If Thelwall was gone?' From what ensued Walsh gathered that 'he (Thelwall) had been down some time, and that there was a nest of them at Alfoxton House, who were protected by a Mr Poole . . . and that he supposed Thelwall was there at this time.' It was no longer felt that the couple were French, 'but they are people that will do as much harm as all the French can do'.

'I think', proceeded Mr Walsh, 'this will turn out no French affair, but a mischievous gang of disaffected Englishmen. I have just procured the name of the person who took the House. His name is Wordsworth, a name I think known to Mr Ford.'

On August 16 a further budget of news was dispatched to Whitehall. 'The inhabitants of Alfoxton House', reported Walsh, 'are a set of violent Democrats'. Poole is described as 'a most violent member of the Corresponding Society, and a strenuous supporter of its friends', the more dangerous for 'having established in this town what he stiles The Poor Man's Club'.

He had now been able to contact Thomas Jones, the source of

Mogg's information. He confirmed Mogg's story with the following addition. On one occasion Jones had been asked to wait on a Sunday dinner at Alfoxton to which fourteen persons sat down. Thelwall was one of the guests on this occasion, reported Jones, and 'after dinner (he) got up and talked so loud and was in such a passion that Jones was frightened'. Jones further said that Wordsworth had gone back to the cottage he had formerly occupied in order to bring back a woman servant who had later informed Jones that her master was 'a Phylosopher'.

The timid Jones was not anxious to continue in his present position, but Walsh overcame his fears with a little cash and persuasion. 'It is reported', he concluded, 'that Thelwall is to return soon to this place and that he is to occupy a part of Alfoxton House.'

But there unfortunately the story ends; at least the official account of it is discontinued at that point, and only the account in Coleridge's *Biographia Literaria* can offer a conclusion.

Wordsworth and Annette Vallon

(*See p.* 41)

In view of his close friendship with Mathews, it is hardly credible that Wordsworth was deceiving him on a grand scale, i.e. by pretending that his plans were unchanged when he was aware they must be. Yet if he knew that a child had been conceived, and if he were planning, dutifully or not, to marry Annette and bring her to England as 'the curate's wife' after the birth of Caroline, it does seem strange that he should not have hinted at something of the sort to his friend in May, or even to his brother Richard in September, although it is true that the September note is almost exclusively taken up with business matters.

The first explanation would seem to be that in May Wordsworth had no intention of marrying Annette: yet there can be little doubt that she had already conceived his child. If Wordsworth did not know this, the fact that he had not changed his plans does suggest that he regarded the affair as an isolated lapse with a woman for whom he felt no deep affection, and with whom he did not imagine marriage would be either desirable or necessary.

If Wordsworth knew what had happened, and if his silence to Mathews indicates that he was still not changing his plans in any material particular, then the nature of his attitude to Annette is even more clearly brought out. This is equally true if we decide that the child had not yet been conceived. Conception must have occurred immediately after the May letter, and the intimacy between the two 'lovers' could hardly have been the climax of a long and passionate attachment; again we have the suggestion of a chance encounter inaugurating rather than climaxing an acquaintance.

Select Bibliography

[Generally excluding those books to which direct reference is made in the text or notes]

EDITH BATHO: *The Later Wordsworth.* 1933.

C. BRINTON: *The Political Ideas of the English Romanticists.* 1926.

C. CESTRE: *La Révolution française et les poètes anglais.* 1906. *John Thelwall.* 1906.

E. K. CHAMBERS: *Samuel Taylor Coleridge.* 1938.

A. COBBAN: *Edmund Burke and the Revolt against the Eighteenth Century.* 1929.

S. T. COLERIDGE:*The Poetical Works,* ed. E. H. Coleridge. Oxford. 1912.

Letters, Conversations and Recollections, ed. Thos. Allsop. 1884.

Letters, ed. E. H. Coleridge. 1895.

Unpublished Letters, ed. E. L. Griggs. 1932.

Anima Poetae, ed. E. H. Coleridge. 1895.

Biographia Literaria. 1817.

Essays on His Own Times, ed. Sara Coleridge. 1850.

See Chambers.

W. J. COURTHOPE: *The Liberal Movement in English Literature.* 1885.

T. DE QUINCEY: *Reminiscences of the English Lake Poets.* (Everyman ed.). 1929.

E. DE SELINCOURT: *Dorothy Wordsworth.* 1933. *The Early Wordsworth.* 1936.

E. DOWDEN: *The French Revolution and English Literature.* 1897.

H. W. GARROD: *Wordsworth.* 1927. (2nd ed.).

W. HALLER: *The Early Life of Robert Southey.* 1917.

G. M. HARPER: *William Wordsworth.* 1929.

E. LEGOUIS: *The Early Life of Wordsworth.* 1921. (trans. J. Matthews).

HARRIET MARTINEAU: *Autobiography.* 1877.

J. S. MILL: *Autobiography.* (World's Classics ed.) 1940.
Letters, ed. H. Elliot. 1910.

T. POOLE: See Sandford.

W. RALEIGH: Wordsworth. 1912.

J. F. RICHARDSON: *A Neglected Aspect of the English Romantic Revolt.* 1915.

H. C. ROBINSON: *The Correspondence of H.C.R. with the Wordsworth Circle,* ed. E. J. Morley. 1927.
Blake, Coleridge, Wordsworth, Lamb, etc.: Being selections from the Remains of H.C.R., ed. Morley. 1932.
Diary, Reminiscences and Correspondence, ed. Sadler. 1869.
H.C.R. on Books and Their Writers, ed. Morley. 1938.

MARGARET SANDFORD: *Thomas Poole and His Friends.* 1888.

J. SIMMONS: *Robert Southey.* 1945.

R. SOUTHEY: *Life and Correspondence of Robert Southey,* ed. C. C. Southey. 1849.
Selections from the Letters of Robert Southey, ed. J. W. Warter. 1856.
See Haller. Simmons.

D. STUART: *Letters from the Lake Poets to D. Stuart,* comp. M. Stuart, ed. E. H. Coleridge. 1889.

J. THELWALL: See Cestre.

W. H. WHITE: *An Examination of the Charge of Apostasy against Wordsworth.* 1898.

C. WORDSWORTH: *Memoirs of William Wordsworth.* 1851.

D. WORDSWORTH: *The Journals,* ed. de Selincourt. 1952. See de Selincourt.

W. WORDSWORTH: *The Poetical Works of William Wordsworth* ed. de Selincourt and Darbishire, Oxford, 1940-49, (five vols).
The Prelude, ed. de Selincourt, Oxford, 1928 (2nd Imp.).
The Letters of William and Dorothy Wordsworth, ed. de Selincourt, Oxford, 1935-39 (six vols.).
Some Letters of the Wordsworth Family, ed. L. N. Broughton. 1943.
The Prose Works of William Wordsworth, ed. A. B. Grosart. 1875.
The Prose Works of William Wordsworth, ed. W. Knight. 1896.
See Batho; de Selincourt; Garrod; Harper; Legouis; Raleigh; White; C. Wordsworth.

INDEX

A